A Political and Social History
of Guyana, 1945–1983

Westview Replica Editions

The concept of Westview Replica Editions is a response to the continuing crisis in academic and informational publishing. Library budgets for books have been severely curtailed. Ever larger portions of general library budgets are being diverted from the purchase of books and used for data banks, computers, micromedia, and other methods of information retrieval. Interlibrary loan structures further reduce the edition sizes required to satisfy the needs of the scholarly community. Economic pressures on the university presses and the few private scholarly publishing companies have severely limited the capacity of the industry to properly serve the academic and research communities. As a result, many manuscripts dealing with important subjects, often representing the highest level of scholarship, are no longer economically viable publishing projects--or, if accepted for publication, are typically subject to lead times ranging from one to three years.

Westview Replica Editions are our practical solution to the problem. We accept a manuscript in camera-ready form, typed according to our specifications, and move it immediately into the production process. As always, the selection criteria include the importance of the subject, the work's contribution to scholarship, and its insight, originality of thought, and excellence of exposition. The responsibility for editing and proofreading lies with the author or sponsoring institution. We prepare chapter headings and display pages, file for copyright, and obtain Library of Congress Cataloging in Publication Data. A detailed manual contains simple instructions for preparing the final typescript, and our editorial staff is always available to answer questions.

The end result is a book printed on acid-free paper and bound in sturdy library-quality soft covers. We manufacture these books ourselves using equipment that does not require a lengthy make-ready process and that allows us to publish first editions of 300 to 600 copies and to reprint even smaller quantities as needed. Thus, we can produce Replica Editions quickly and can keep even very specialized books in print as long as there is a demand for them.

About the Book and Author

A Political and Social History of Guyana, 1945–1983
Thomas J. Spinner, Jr.

The Jonestown catastrophe of 1978 turned the attention of the world to Guyana, a small state on the northern coast of South America. Many people were surprised to discover an extraordinary ethnic mosaic dominated by the descendants of Black slaves and indentured East Indian laborers--an ethnic mix that has been troubled by racial strife. Two charismatic leaders, the Soviet-influenced East Indian, Cheddi Jagan, and the Black moderate socialist, Forbes Burnham, have towered over Guyana's political life. U.S. assistance pushed Burnham to power in 1964 as Washington feared Jagan might become another Castro. Yet, shortly after his rise to power, Burnham turned to the left. Twenty years later, he remains in control even though he has lost support from his Black followers; there have been well-substantiated accusations of electoral fraud and his political base has so narrowed that he now relies for support on the police and the Guyana Defense Force.

Concentrating on the period since 1945, Dr. Spinner investigates the historical origins of the political, economic, and social problems that confront the Guyanese people. He analyzes the options available to them, assesses the possible role of the new multiracial party, the Working People's Alliance, and considers whether it was inevitable that a pluralistic society should break apart when the British departed, or whether it was ambitious political leaders, cold-war machinations, and foreign intervention that led to violence between East Indians and Blacks.

Dr. Thomas J. Spinner, Jr., professor of history, University of Vermont, is a former Visiting Fulbright Lecturer at the University of Guyana.

A Political and Social History of Guyana, 1945–1983

Thomas J. Spinner, Jr.

Westview Press / Boulder and London

Copyright © 1984 by Westview Press, Inc.

Published in 1984 in the United States of America by
   Westview Press, Inc.
   5500 Central Avenue
   Boulder, Colorado 80301
   Frederick A. Praeger, Publisher

Library of Congress Catalog Card Number: 84-40377
ISBN 0-86531-852-2

Printed and bound in the United States of America
10 9 8 7 6 5 4 3 2 1

To Nicole, Carolyn, and Tommy

Contents

Foreword

It is easy to forget that Guyana's history is about the Guyanese people. Reference is made so constantly to the racial parts constituting the whole that one may neglect the valiant efforts being made by so many Guyanese to fulfill the national motto: "One People, One Nation, One Destiny."

But the harsh reality of racial tension and violence cannot be avoided. The descendants of Africans, East Indians, Portuguese, English, Chinese, and Amerindians have not yet constructed an integrated society. Central to an understanding of Guyana today is the brutal bitterness and hostility that came to divide, in particular, the East Indian and African peoples.

Unlike many Caribbean communities, Guyanese of African descent seem to prefer the term "African" to either "black" or "negro." "Colored" or "mixed" are the words employed for the mulatto or for any blacks who are partially white. While the colored people aspired to be a part of white society during the slave era, they now identify themselves with the black or African community in the confrontation with the East Indians. One element of confusion--among many others--is that the East Indian, while caucasian or white, may be quite brown. For that matter, as A. J. P. Taylor noted, there is no "white" race; "white" people are really rather "pinkish."

Although the East Indians have, in general, married within their own community, some have not. It becomes almost impossible--perhaps a good sign--to classify the permutations and combinations that can occur when you mix African, East Indian, Chinese, English, Portuguese, and Amerindian. While many valid generalizations can be made with regard to racial attitudes, some exceptions are inevitable.

Ultimately, what matters most is the search for one's own identity. This search too seldomly concludes with a recognition of the common humanity uniting us all. Herder, Mazzini, and other great liberal and cultural nationalists conceived of nationalism as a step toward

the full realization of one's human qualities. Unfortunately, the generous nationalism of an earlier age has
too often degenerated into the fierce, barbarous cries
of national superiority that have poisoned the twentieth
century. Nationalism may turn cruel and vicious, but it
can also be kind and generous. Patriotism may be the
last refuge of a scoundrel; it can also be the means by
which unity and a sense of purpose are achieved, especially in an artificially created state in a hostile
geographic region to which were transported thousands of
slaves and indentured laborers.

Surrounded as we are with racial, ethnic, religious,
and political conflict, it may seem pointless to investigate the problems of a tiny, English-speaking state in
the northern part of South America. Yet, this country
contains such a variety of ethnic groups, religious
bodies, and political factions that it is possible to
enlarge our understanding of both ourselves and the
world by a careful observation of Guyanese history in
the twentieth century. There is tragedy and grandeur in
the story of this small nation called British Guiana
prior to independence in 1966.

Until the Jonestown catastrophe of 1978, few Americans had given much thought to Guyana. As large as
Great Britain in area, most of Guyana's population of
800,000 is wedged into a narrow coastal strip. One of
the world's more cosmopolitan, smaller nations, East Indians comprise 51 percent of the population; blacks and
mulattoes, 43 percent; the original Amerindian inhabitants, about 4 percent; while a final 2 percent is made
up mostly of Portuguese, English, and Chinese. About 55
percent of the population is Christian, 36 percent Hindu,
and 9 percent Moslem. Few nations could boast, during
the 1970s, a Chinese president, Arthur Chung, a black
prime minister, Forbes Burnham, and an East Indian,
Cheddi Jagan, leading the major opposition party.

Unfortunately, the superficial press coverage of
the setting in which the Reverend Jim Jones and his
flock destroyed themselves failed to discuss the role of
the United States in bringing Forbes Burnham to power.
Without the direct intervention of United States intelligence agencies, he would never have become first, Guyana's prime minister, and now, her executive president.

Obsessed by the specter of British Guiana as another Cuba if it achieved independence under the leadership of the romantic Stalinist, Cheddi Jagan, the Kennedy
and Johnson administrations, assisted by the British,
sabotaged the elected government of the colony between
1961 and 1964. Jagan was finally ejected from office in
December 1964; Burnham became prime minister and led
Guyana to independence two years later. After sixteen
years, three rigged elections, and a bogus plebiscite,
he still retains power--but the crown no longer sits
easily on his head.

This study is based upon original research with governmental records and parliamentary debates and reports. Many published books and articles have also been consulted. I am especially indebted to the many individuals who agreed to talk with me about Guyana and the Guyanese during a sabbatical leave spent in Guyana and London in 1977-1978. Three newspapers have been especially helpful: the daily and Sunday issues of the Guyana Graphic before it was taken over by the government in the mid-1970s, the weekly Catholic Standard of Guyana, and the monthly publication of the Caribbean Conference of Churches, Caribbean Contact. Many librarians and their staffs must be thanked for their gracious assistance.

It is a pleasure to express appreciation to my colleagues and students at the University of Guyana, where I was Visiting Fulbright Lecturer in 1972-1973 and where I was first introduced to the intricacies and fascination of Guyanese history. Having travelled there a specialist in Victorian England, I came away with an abiding interest in the Caribbean region. Since that visit, my family and I have journeyed to many countries in the area; we returned to Guyana during the summer of 1977 to assess the deterioration in the political and economic life of the nation. The University of Vermont provided me with helpful Summer Research Grants in 1975 and 1979. My thanks to Caribbean Review and Florida International University for permitting me to include short sections of two articles (Fall 1980 and Fall 1982) which first appeared in that publication. I also wish to thank Random House, Inc., for permitting me to quote from Eugene O'Neill's The Emperor Jones which it published in Three Plays in 1937.

My children, Carolyn and Tommy, are delighted the Guyana manuscript has finally been completed, but they will, I suspect, soon miss the many happy hours spent in the Caribbean sun. The assistance of my wife has been indispensable; she typed draft after draft as well as assisting with the research and writing. What the four of us will always retain are the sweet memories of the kindly, generous Guyanese people struggling to build a better society. Thanks also to Jane McGraw for editorial assistance and for typing the final manuscript.

Benedetto Croce observed that all history is contemporary history. He was correct; history does not write itself. It is written by the historian and, at its best, is a blend of art, science, and poetry which creates a perception of truth as seen through the eyes of one observer. The charge that contemporary history is little more than current events is both inaccurate and unreflective if one accepts Croce's dictum. It has been especially rewarding for one who previously worked in the musty papers of nineteenth-century statesmen to interview some of the individuals who made the decisions contributing so much--for both good and bad--to the development of Guyana's history. Karl Marx once wrote that, "History is made behind men's backs." An attempt is made in the pages which follow to discover behind some of those backs why Guyana has descended to a point where a government subverts its own constitution and to where talk of violence, partition, and racial war fill the air.

Thomas J. Spinner, Jr.
University of Vermont

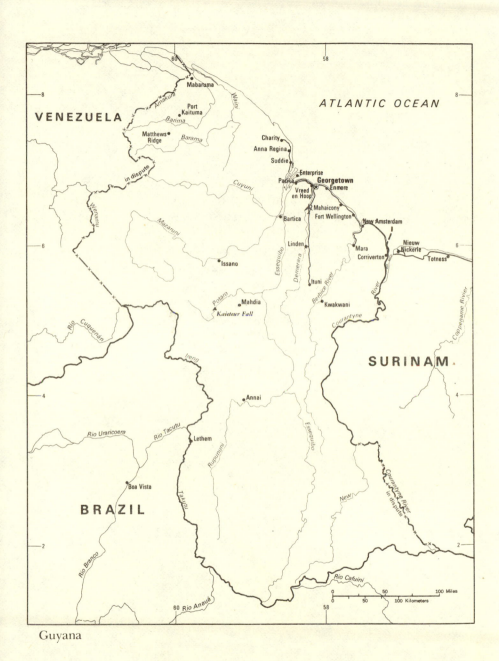

Guyana

What happens to a dream deferred?

Does it dry up
like a raisin in the sun?
Or fester like a sore—
and then run?
Does it stink like rotten meat?
Or crust and sugar over—
like a syrupy sweet?

Maybe it just sags
like a heavy load.

Or does it explode?

Langston Hughes

1
The People and the Land

Many travellers are astonished to discover that in
the northern part of South America there is a nation as
large as Great Britain in area which had--in the 1970s--
a Chinese president (Arthur Chung), a black African
prime minister (Forbes Burnham), and an East Indian
leader of the opposition (Cheddi Jagan). All three men
were born in British Guiana, now the Cooperative Republic of Guyana; they represent the three non-Western cultures which have shaped this fascinating, though bitterly divided, country.[1]
British Guiana, Dutch Guiana, and French Guiana
were never more than tiny enclaves in the massive em-
pires carved out by the Spanish and Portuguese on the
South American mainland. Christopher Columbus sailed
along the Guiana coast, but no serious attempt at trade
and colonization occurred until the region was penetrated
by seamen and adventurers a century later. Sir Walter
Raleigh was convinced that the area between the mouths
of the Orinoco and Amazon rivers contained the fabled
golden city, El Dorado. His book, describing the wealth
and beauty of the region, aroused considerable interest;
Sir John Falstaff referred to Mistress Page as "a region
in Guyana, all gold and bounty." The Pilgrim Fathers
contemplated a move to the Guiana coast, but prudently
decided in favor of New England.
Actually, there was little gold and less bounty in
what was to become British Guiana. Raleigh's failure to
find any wealth helped bring him to the executioner's
block in 1618. Writing some three hundred years later,
James Rodway conceded that a "narrow line of sugar estates seems but a very poor showing for such a long
struggle with nature, but when all the circumstances are
taken into consideration, it is almost a wonder that the
colony has not been abandoned altogether." A certain
fascination with the area has continued as readers of
W. H. Hudson's Green Mansions and Sir Arthur Conan
Doyle's Lost World can testify.
When the first British, Dutch, and French traders

entered the region, they encountered an Amerindian population of hostile Caribs and friendly Arawaks. Finding only small amounts of gold and not much of value to barter for, the Europeans turned to the cultivation of cotton, tobacco, and, most important, sugar.

The Dutch initially constructed and developed the trading posts, plantations, villages, and towns that would become British Guiana. Incorporated in 1621, the Dutch West India Company's men and ships were soon moving along the Essequibo, Demerara, and Berbice rivers. The soil on the river banks was not particularly fertile and, as the planters turned more and more to sugar, they moved back down the rivers into the coastal plain. As might be expected, the Dutch excelled at establishing and maintaining a complex system of dams and dykes, needed to reclaim a coastal plain that consisted mostly of mangrove swamps and was usually below sea level at high tide. During the two rainy seasons, both a hostile sea and the surging interior rivers needed to be confronted.

The word "Guiana" is of Amerindian origin and means "land of waters." It is an appropriate designation, for the region not only contains many streams and bodies of water but is bounded by the Orinoco, Negro, and Amazon rivers. Nature can never be ignored in this area; the dry season is very hot while torrential rain can cause rapid flooding in the rainy season. Fortunately, in the evening a refreshing breeze almost always blows in from the Caribbean. But during the day newcomers must adjust to the debilitating effects of a hot, steamy climate.

Eventually the sugar planters carved out a coastal strip running from the Corentyne River boundary with Surinam--formerly Dutch Guiana--to the Venezuelan frontier. The properly drained part of the fertile coastal strip is often not more than three or four miles in width, and cultivation almost never extends beyond ten miles from the sea. While the coastal belt makes up only about 4 percent of the total land area of Guyana, it contains more than 90 percent of the population. Forbidding to the Dutch, the lush tropical forest comprising more than 80 percent of the land remains inhospitable more than three hundred years after colonization. Hopes for mineral wealth in the forest region have never been fully realized. Some gold and diamonds have been found and, most important, bauxite was discovered in the twentieth century. The forest zone ends in mountains which reach a height of 10,000 feet and in the savannah grasslands where a small cattle industry has been established.

The Dutch planters and traders attempted to enslave the Amerindians, who either retreated to the safety of the interior or succumbed to European diseases. Today the Amerindians constitute about 4 percent of the population and are a negligible political factor. Roman

Catholic missionaries have been quite successful in winning converts and building schools. Some attempts have
been made to protect their cultural heritage, but a debate rages as to whether they should be fully integrated
into Guyanese society or allowed to retain their ancient
ways.[2]

Unsuccessful with the Amerindians, the Dutch turned
to the importation of African slaves. Soon there were
far more slaves than free whites in the region, a constant source of worry for the Dutch plantocracy. Slave
revolts occurred frequently, but were repressed with
barbarous efficiency. No settlement of runaway slaves,
similar to the Bush Negroes of Surinam or the Maroons of
Jamaica, managed to survive. The most significant of
the slave rebellions was led by Guyana's national hero,
Cuffy, in 1763. Triumphant for almost a year in the
Berbice region, the movement failed to spread into Demerara and Essequibo and was finally crushed by the
Dutch.

The horrors of the slave trade and slavery have
been well documented. Doctor George Pinckard recorded
the tragedy of a slave auction in British Guiana in 1796.
He witnessed "numbers of our fellow beings regularly
bartered for gold, and transferred, like cattle, or any
common merchandise, from one possessor to another." The
Africans were forced to remove their clothes so that
they might be "minutely inspected" by the prospective
purchasers. Even more dreadful scenes were to follow:

> In one part of the building was seen a wife clinging to
> her husband, and beseeching, in the strongest eloquence
> of nature, not to be left behind him. Here was a sister
> hanging upon the neck of her brother, and, with tears,
> entreating to be led to the same home of captivity.
> There stood two brothers, enfolded in each other's arms,
> mutually bewailing their threatened separation. In oth-
> er parts were friends, relatives and companions, praying
> to be sold to the same master, using signs to signify
> that they would be content with slavery, might they but
> toil together.[3]

Although conditions varied from plantation to plantation, the evidence demonstrates that the life of the
slave was wretched and degrading. Consciously and un-
consciously the memories of slavery remain a major element in shaping the Guyanese outlook in the twentieth
century.

Dutch activity centered on the Essequibo portion of
the area that was to become British Guiana; the entire
region was transformed by the appointment of Laurens
Storm van's Gravesande as commander in 1742. A man of
intelligence and imagination, Storm had arrived in the
colony four years before as a secretary to the West India Company. He served as commander for thirty years,

before retiring to his plantation where he died in 1775. During these years, Demerara was finally opened to development; British planters rushed in, fleeing from the ruined soil of Barbados and the other West Indian islands. Storm reorganized the government of the colony, pushed into the interior of Essequibo, and encouraged the hard-working British planters in Demerara while objecting to their attempts to avoid taxation.

By 1770, there were about 10,000 slaves in Essequibo and Demerara, and some 4,000 slaves and 350 whites in Berbice. Berbice, only very loosely regulated by the West India Company, had developed a governmental structure independent of the one controlling Essequibo and Demerara. The wishes of the Estates-General in the Netherlands and the influence of the local plantocracy remained the dominating elements in both regions.

The eighteenth century was characterized by a massive struggle among the European states for trade and empire. Spain and Portugal, the sixteenth-century victors, were elbowed aside in the seventeenth century; Britain, France, and the Dutch Republic emerged as the principal contestants. The Dutch were weakened by three gruelling wars with the British between 1652 and 1674, and by being forced to counter the aggressive blows of Louis XIV. Between 1689 and 1815, Britain and France fought a second Hundred Years' War. This time, Britain's aristocratic and merchant elite did not covet France herself; instead, they fancied the French Empire in Canada, India, Africa, and the West Indies. The final, titanic conflict would be a part of the American and French revolutionary wars. Nothing would be the same again after the dramatic political, economic, and social events which occurred between 1775 and 1815.

While the British momentarily lost control of the seas--and the American colonies along with it--British seapower ultimately proved decisive. During the forty years of war and revolution between 1775 and 1815, possession of Essequibo, Demerara, and Berbice changed hands a number of times. Essequibo and Demerara were taken by Admiral Rodney in 1781 after the Dutch joined the Armed Neutrality against Britain. But France, allied to the Dutch, chased out the British the following year. The short occupations by the British and French had profound consequences; they gave Demerara a new capital. The colony had been administered from an island in the Demerara River, but the British and the French quickly recognized the strategic importance of the point at which the river flowed into the Caribbean Sea.

While the British only built a fort at the site of the present capital, Georgetown, the French commander, the Comte de Kersaint, planned the construction of a proper town. He grandiosely proclaimed that the capital of the colony must,

> . . . become the business centre, where Religion will
> have a temple, Justice a palace, War its arsenals, Com-
> merce its counting-houses, Industry its factories, and
> where the inhabitants may enjoy the advantages of so-
> cial intercourse. (Smith 1962:20)

It was extraordinary, the Count concluded, that the colony had "arrived at some magnificence without the establishment of either town or village." Two years later,
the Dutch returned and baptized Kersaint's new town,
Stabroek. Within a few years, there were almost one
thousand inhabitants, whites numbering about one-third,
with the remainder mostly slaves plus a small number of
freed blacks and mulattoes. By 1810, the population had
soared to almost ten thousand.

The British seized Essequibo, Demerara, and Berbice,
once again, in 1796. Briefly returned to the Dutch after the Treaty of Amiens in 1802, the colonies were
snatched by the British permanently in 1803, and their
control was ratified by the Congress of Vienna in 1815.
Eager to win the loyalty of the residents, the British
retained the main features of Dutch government; but, the
administrative structure of the less progressive Berbice
proved too cumbersome and British Guiana was finally
created in 1831 when Berbice was united with Essequibo
and Demerara.[4]

Having pledged in 1803 that "the laws and usages of
the colony shall remain in force and be respected," the
British were unable to rule British Guiana as a Crown
Colony in which the governor and the Colonial Office monopolized political power. Instead, they saddled themselves with a system in which the governor shared authority and influence with several elected bodies dominated by the wealthy planters. For instance, a Court of
Policy was partially chosen by the sugar barons and,
even more important, six financial representatives were
also elected by the plantocracy to meet with the Court
of Policy as a Combined Court when new taxes were required.

After 1831, the governor's nominees outnumbered the
elected members of the Court of Policy, but the Combined
Court contained a majority of elected representatives.
While the governor and the Court of Policy exercised the
legislative and executive powers of the colony, the Combined Court retained the authority to check the public
accounts and to raise taxes. Planter domination of the
country's political life was assured by high property
qualifications for both voting and holding office. This
arrangement remained in effect until a significant liberalization of the property requirements was introduced
in 1891.[5] Sugar reigned throughout the nineteenth century; the needs of this industry affected every aspect
of Guyanese life and ultimately brought about the fascinating ethnic mix that has become modern Guyana.[6]

During the first third of the nineteenth century,
British Guiana's small white population lived in fear of
a slave majority. The great house on the plantation was
the center both of sugar production and of society itself. Mulattoes were an important intermediary group.
Normally freed by their white fathers, they tried desperately to identify with white society. Interesting
distinctions also developed among the slaves. Those
toiling in the great house were regarded as superior to
the cane cutters, and the locally born slave was assigned a higher rung in the social hierarchy than the
one imported in chains from Africa.

Economic necessity and humanitarianism combined to
bring about the British decisions to end the slave trade
in 1807 and slavery in 1833. Britain's emerging market
economy coupled with the profound transformation of the
world's first industrial revolution compelled both free
trade and free labor. There was no room for slavery and
the special preferences awarded to the West Indian sugar
barons. Missionaries and other humanitarians denounced
the horrors of slavery, and the martyred Congregational
minister, John Smith, went to an early grave in 1823 as
a consequence of his struggle to aid the slaves.

The abolition of slavery brought the planters of
British Guiana more than four million pounds in compensation for the almost eighty-five thousand emancipated
slaves. A period of semislavery and adjustment followed
until complete liberation in 1838. Emancipation was a
traumatic event for both planters and slaves; the freed
blacks tried valiantly to run abandoned sugar plantations or to establish cooperative ventures on the land;
but, by the 1850s their heroic efforts had failed. Without capital to fully develop their small plots, they often needed to seek seasonal labor on the hated, white-
owned plantations. Rather than do this, many blacks
moved to the villages and towns where they became a new
urban proletariat.

The high hopes of the freed slaves were really defeated by the determination of the plantocracy to retain
its political, economic, and social supremacy. The sugar industry requires large supplies of additional field
workers during the two cutting seasons. Freed slaves
anticipated being able to negotiate high wages when
their labor was needed. But the planters refused to
lose either power or profits, and rapidly evolved a response to emancipation--indenture.

Indentured labor--usually for a five-year term--was
introduced immediately after emancipation. Conditions
were slightly better than under slavery; at the end of
the indenture term, one was free to remain in British
Guiana or to collect one's savings and return home.
Small numbers of English, Irish, and Germans tried the
difficult climate and the demanding work; they rapidly
succumbed to disease or drink. The survivors deserted

the plantations for other work as quickly as possible.
But three groups of indentured laborers assumed an im-
portant role in the history of the colony: Portuguese,
Chinese, and East Indians.

Most of the thirty thousand indentured Portuguese
workers arrived from the Madeira Islands prior to 1860.
They loathed plantation work, and the moment their indenture was completed they moved into the retail trades--
as small shopkeepers, peddlers, pawnbrokers--which they
promptly dominated. By the 1850s, 173 of the 296 li-
censed shops in Georgetown were owned by Portuguese;
they were also predominant in the colony's second largest town, New Amsterdam, and in the rural districts.
Because of this dominance, the Portuguese shopkeeper was
a target for all those unable to pay their bills. Anti-
Portuguese riots took place in 1856, 1889, and 1905.
Their Roman Catholicism in a Protestant-ruled society
also gave reason for suspicion.[7]

Some fourteen thousand Chinese came to British
Guiana as indentured laborers, mostly in the 1850s and
1860s. They also left the plantations as quickly as
possible for the towns, villages, and the retail trades.
The Chinese gave up their language and most of their
traditional customs, intermarried, and became among the
most assimilated of the ethnic groups.[8]

Having failed with Europeans, Portuguese, and Chinese, the planters finally found a source for a large,
underemployed, rural proletariat in that rich jewel of
the British Empire--India. Beginning in 1838 and continuing until 1917, almost 240,000 East Indians were imported into British Guiana as indentured laborers. Contrary to popular belief, only about one-third of the
Hindu majority of immigrants were from low-caste or out-
caste groups. About 16 percent were Moslems. Considering the caste hostility which continues in India and the
communal strife which has often characterized Hindu-
Moslem relations, it is remarkable that caste distinctions and Hindu-Moslem antagonism have never been serious issues in Guyana. The enormity of the problems to
be confronted on the plantations and by life in a strange
land created an East Indian unity, partially shaped in
response to the creole society being hammered out by the
English, Portuguese, Africans, and Chinese. Like the
Amerindians, the East Indians viewed this creole society
with mixed feelings.[9]

Creole life was dominated by the values of those
two odd companions: Christianity and materialism. The
East Indian was regarded as an ignorant "coolie" who
performed the harsh tasks no longer acceptable to the
blacks. The "coolie," however, had one great comfort--
his cultural heritage, whether it be Hindu or Moslem.
To the East Indian, the black and mulatto majority of
creole society were people without traditions or heritage; they sought only to impersonate white people. And

so the two largest ethnic groups in British Guiana--
black African and East Indian--developed, initially at
any rate, as two separate societies. They had little
contact with one another and no respect for each other
when they did. One was essentially an urban proletariat,
the other a rural proletariat. The planters were not
unhappy to make cultural concessions to the East Indians
as it intensified their isolation and made them easier
to subjugate.[10]
    Unlike the slave, an indentured worker could not be
owned as property, and, in theory, retained certain
rights. But he was usually worked very hard and found
it extremely difficult to obtain justice in the courts.
During a twenty-year period at the end of the nineteenth
century, about two hundred employers were punished for
violating the indenture laws while almost seventy thousand indentured workers were found guilty of crimes
against the plantocracy. Just under fourteen thousand
of these convictions were related to desertion from the
estates. Long hours, low pay, cruel work conditions,
and insufficient numbers of indentured women created
acute physical and psychological distress. In 1863, the
chief justice of British Guiana called indentured labor
a "monstrous rotten system." One contemporary concluded:

> Take a large factory in Manchester or Birmingham or Bel-
> fast, build a wall around it, shut in its work-people
> from all intercourse, save, at rare intervals, with the
> outside world, keep them in absolute ignorance and get
> all the work you can get out of them, treat them not un-
> kindly, leave their social habits in relation to them-
> selves as matters not concerning you who make the money
> from their labour and you would have constituted a lit-
> tle community, resembling in no small degree a sugar es-
> tate village in British Guiana.[11]

    The East Indian indentured worker did receive as-
sistance from the office of the Agent-General for Immigrants. James Crosby, a graduate of Trinity College,
Cambridge, and a lawyer, assumed this position in 1858
and served until 1880. A legend to the East Indian community, he fought vigorously for their rights, willing
to battle governors, planters, and the Colonial Office
in London.
    George William Des Voeux was another champion of
the indentured laborers. Descendant of a Huguenot family which had moved to Ireland in the eighteenth century,
he was sent to British Guiana as a stipendiary magistrate in 1863. Dismayed by the lack of respect for common law procedures when indentured workers were improperly arrested for minor violations of the labor laws,
Des Voeux acted:

> On the mere sight of it, I of course discharged them as

> being in illegal custody, and continuing this practice,
> I at once aroused the indignation of several influential
> managers, who severally and at one time or another in no
> very courteous language, threatened legal proceedings
> and other means of intimidation. (Nath 1970:58-59)

Eventually he complained at length to the Colonial Office, denouncing the wickedness of the indenture system
and specifying the culpability of the planters and their
acolytes. His howl of outrage induced considerable discussion in the London newspapers and the establishment
of a commission to investigate. Unfortunately, some of
Des Voeux's accusations had been too sweeping; documentary proof was not available. Medical officers and magistrates, influenced by the planters, failed to substantiate a number of Des Voeux's charges. While criticized
by the commission, Des Voeux still claimed victory since
many of the reform recommendations in the final report
paralleled his own.[12]   Thirty years later he reflected
that the commission "had brought to light more than I
had expected and almost as much as I desired."

By 1900, significant changes had occurred in British Guiana. East Indians had discovered the possibilities in rice cultivation; it could liberate them from
the sugar plantations and provide an opportunity for acquiring land of their own. In the first years of the
twentieth century, British Guiana became an exporter of
rice. The cultivation of sugar needed heavy capitaliza-
tion; one square mile of arable land could require forty-
nine miles of drainage canals and sixteen miles of high-
level irrigation canals. In contrast, rice required
only a small initial investment, could be grown in modest plots, and could be refined in a locally owned mill;
therefore, many East Indians became rice cultivators. A
few East Indians even entered the retail trades and the
professions, bringing them into contact with the English,
Portuguese, and Chinese who made up the bulk of the tiny
middle class and with the small number of blacks, especially mulattoes, also in these occupations.

Consolidation transformed the sugar industry in the
twentieth century. The more than two hundred estates
existing at the start of the nineteenth century had been
combined and recombined. By the 1950s, only one independent plantation would remain out of nineteen. Even
more significant, the giant corporation, Booker Brothers,
McConnell & Company, Ltd., owned fifteen of these nineteen estates. Some even referred to British Guiana as
Booker's Guiana. What is now a huge, multinational corporation began with the arrival of twenty-two-year-old
Josias Booker in 1815. A young merchant from Lancashire,
he and his brothers decided to try sugar planting in
British Guiana. Planting led to a number of related industries and, before long, they were involved with rum,
shopkeeping, coastal shipping, timber, balata, and

cattle.[13]

The dawn of the twentieth century found the sugar industry in distress as a consequence of British free trade policies and the expansion of the European beet sugar industry. A new Guyanese middle class, with interests other than sugar, challenged the sugar barons and argued that the future of the country lay in developing the interior. Only minor constitutional changes occurred after 1831 until, in 1891, a major reform enlarged the electorate and lowered property requirements for membership in the Court of Policy and the Combined Court.[14]

This reform allowed the new middle class, primarily Portuguese, Chinese, and mulattoes, to more effectively fight the sugar interest and, if they cooperated, to control the financial system through their power on the Combined Court. The electorate now contained a majority of mulattoes and blacks. The Africans made up the largest portion of the only major city, Georgetown, and of the one town of importance, New Amsterdam. East Indians still took little part in the political life of the nation.[15]

By 1915, about 4300 people were entitled to vote. Of this eligible electorate, more than 60 percent were of African descent, just under 20 percent were of British parentage, about 11 percent were of Portuguese descent, and only 6 percent were of East Indian ancestry, although the latter group was estimated to comprise about 50 percent of the adult male population. The British represented less than 2 percent of the adult males, yet 46 percent of them managed to qualify as electors. Less than 1 percent of East Indian adult males and only about 7 percent of Africans were able to exercise the franchise. The Portuguese, with 3 percent of the adult males, had placed almost 20 percent of them on the electoral registers.[16]

The First World War led to an increase in the price of both sugar and rice, and, in 1914, the Demerara Bauxite Company was established. Diamonds and gold had lured men into Guyana's interior but were never found in significant quantities. The "pork-knocker"--Guyana's name for the prospector--remains a symbol of the free-minded soul, usually black, who rejects the inhibitions of civilization and searches for gold and glory. The discovery of bauxite in the vicinity of Mackenzie (now Linden), about seventy miles up the Demerara River from Georgetown, provided a great boost for British Guiana's economy. American and Canadian companies moved to develop the bauxite areas. Aluminium of Canada controlled the Demerara Bauxite Company while the American organization, Reynolds Metals Company, began to exploit the Kwakwani region on the Berbice River during the 1950s. Guyana's bauxite is high grade, and estimated reserves place her among the top bauxite regions of the world.

Unfortunately, Guyana, lacking the funds to develop her
hydroelectric potential, has not been able to construct
a bauxite smelting refinery of her own. This deficiency
necessitates exporting the unrefined ore, greatly de-
creasing the possible profits for the Guyanese.

Sugar prices slumped badly in the 1920s; the planters denounced the Combined Court for refusing to appropriate funds for new drainage and irrigation schemes required to modernize the industry. The British government sided with the planters in 1928 and, over the objections of the elected members of the Combined Court
and the Court of Policy, imposed a more traditional,
Crown Colony form of government. A Legislative Council
with a majority of nominated members replaced the Combined Court and the Court of Policy. The governor's
powers were strengthened by these changes, enabling the
sugar interests to more easily control the colony.[17]

The Great Depression of the 1930s further weakened
the Guyanese economy. Low prices for rice, sugar, and
bauxite led to high unemployment and violent demonstrations throughout Britain's West Indian possessions in
1937 and 1938. In 1938-1939 a Royal Commission under
Lord Moyne was sent to investigate the social and economic conditions which had caused the riots and disturbances in the British Caribbean. In the past, other
Royal Commissions had investigated particular problems,
probed in a comparatively superficial fashion, and then
usually denounced local agitators while applauding the
wisdom of the colonial officials. The Moyne Commission,
in stark contrast to its predecessors, embarked upon a
comprehensive study lasting more than a year; almost
four hundred witnesses testified and some eight hundred
memoranda of various lengths were submitted.[18] Presenting evidence to the commission, the League of Coloured
Peoples, an organization dominated by West Indian blacks
with a global view of problems confronted by black people, concluded: "Today when the rape of Ethiopia has
given a great stimulus to growing negro-consciousness,
it is not a question of rebellions if, but rebellions
unless, democratic government is granted."

British Guiana's problems were different from those
faced by the solidly black islands of Jamaica and Barbados, but somewhat similar to those of Trinidad. Trinidad also contains a sizable East Indian community (about
40 percent of the population in 1980), but Trinidad's
East Indians were rather more assimilated than those in
British Guiana in the 1930s.[19] There was not quite the
same sharp contrast between rural proletariat (East Indian) and urban proletariat (black). The Moyne Commission heard testimony from many Guyanese individuals and
groups; most were professionals, intellectuals, and
business leaders, but there were also representatives
from British Guiana's small, but growing, trade union
movement. While some commercial groups had reservations

about extending the franchise too rapidly, majority
opinion favored expanding the electorate, removing the
nominated members from the Legislative Council, and
placing additional elected members on the governor's
Executive Council. Representatives of various black
groups advocated the establishment of industrial and
agricultural schools so their people could master the
techniques required to raise them from the ranks of the
unskilled proletariat to talented craftsmen or independent small farmers.

A worrying note, however, was sounded by some members of the East Indian intelligentsia. They acknowledged that the blacks had successfully advanced into a
variety of civil service and governmental jobs, in contrast to the East Indians, and they recognized the reason for this success: the intelligent black had attended
English schools and become Europeanized.

The clever East Indian also aspired to move forward
into governmental and professional posts, but he was appalled at the concessions and compromises required.
Must he repudiate his identity and his heritage? East
Indians conceded that the British government had allowed
them "to live according to their national customs and
usages." But they were fearful that their children
would accept what the parents rejected. They worried
that, "cut off from India for want of direct communication, East Indians of the younger generation are fast
losing their best national traits and characteristics,
and are adopting the not very best customs of West Indians cum Americanism, which disintegrate their morals
and manners." Applauding their own good sense for having rejected the "grosser caste idiosyncrasies of India,"
they still wished "to avoid the tragic fate of the negro
community of the Americas, which, having been cut off
from the homeland and language, have lost their identity
as a race." And they trembled before the "not distant
possibility" of East Indians marrying "negro and other
races without fear of social consequences."

A hasty reading of these views provides much ammunition for the cultural pluralists, who have stressed the
inevitability of a clash between blacks and East Indians.
This particular testimony, however, shows a distaste for
intermarrying not only with blacks, but also with "other
races." More importantly, however, the expression of
concern by parents provides proof that second- and third-
generation East Indian Guyanese were moving into creole
society, prepared to accept its values and standards.
This movement would make the next two decades extremely
crucial in determining if Guyana was to become a melting
pot or a mixed salad, an integrated society or two seg-
regated communities.

Although the start of the Second World War impeded
the implementation of its recommendations, the Moyne
Commission proposed increased democratization of govern-

ment plus profound economic and social reforms. Elections had been conducted in British Guiana in 1935; the choice of four East Indian professionals among the elected members demonstrated the continuing process of assimilation. A higher birth rate coupled with the control of malaria meant that East Indians could look forward to becoming a majority of the Guyanese population. Most leaders of the black community had never considered the implications of this fact, especially if the lowly "coolie" acquired a proper education and began demanding equality and justice in the search for housing and jobs.

The appointment of the progressive-minded Sir Gordon Lethem as governor in 1941 brought further change to British Guiana. While vast sums of money were not to be found during the Second World War, Lethem made very effective use of all available funds. Under the Great Britain-United States "bases for destroyers" agreement of 1940, the Americans built a modern air base, Atkinson Field--now Timehri Airport--thirty miles up the Demerara River from Georgetown. In 1943, the constitution was liberalized; property qualifications for both office and the franchise were reduced, and the elected members became a majority on the Legislative Council. But the war and immediate postwar problems delayed new elections until November 1947.

One of the more remarkable aspects of the period between the World Wars was the ability of the imperial powers to retain control of their colonies, despite the Bolshevik Revolution and Wilsonian idealism about self-determination. World War II heralded the end of that brief moment of Western political domination of the world. The struggle against German and Japanese aggression and the promulgation of the Atlantic Charter in 1941 pointed the way to colonial emancipation.

The winds of change roared through the British Empire as the war moved to its turbulent conclusion. But British Guiana, like so many territories whose frontiers were drawn arbitrarily by European adventurers and traders, had to confront severe boundary problems before thinking of independence and the departure of British troops. A comparatively minor dispute with Dutch Guiana (since 1975 the independent nation of Surinam--another fascinating mix of ethnic groups) is not too important.[20] Of much greater significance is the boundary controversy between British Guiana and Venezuela. In 1895, a blustering United States contemplated war with Great Britain. President Grover Cleveland, eager to twist the lion's tail and to gain public support for a Democratic administration in disarray, jumped in to support Venezuela's long-standing claim to the entire Essequibo area, about one-half of British Guiana's territory.

Fortunately, the conciliatory British prime minister, Lord Salisbury, realistically concluded that President Cleveland and Secretary of State Richard Olney were

playing to the galleries while looking for an escape
hatch. Eventually, an Arbitration Commission was established with two American and two British judges, presided over by a Russian. Their award, in 1899, was a great
victory for Britain and British Guiana. Venezuela did
receive secure control of the mouth of the Orinoco River,
but most of the Essequibo region was granted to British
Guiana. All argument seemed settled until one of the
minor participants in the arbitration events, Severo
Mallet-Prevost, a United States citizen who had acted as
one of Venezuela's lawyers, intervened. In a document
published in 1949, the year after his death, Mallet-
Prevost argued that justice had been denied in 1899; a
deal had been arranged between the Russian president of
the tribunal and the two British judges at the expense
of Venezuela. This statement led to the reopening of
the Venezuelan claim, since it is believed that the
sparsely populated Essequibo River basin may be rich in
minerals and oil.[21]

The 1940s were decisive years for many reasons; the
Second World War ended with atomic explosions at Hiro-
shima and Nagasaki; the war-time alliance collapsed as
the United States and the Soviet Union jousted for control of Eastern and Western Europe; and Great Britain,
unable to compete with the two superpowers, sought a new
role without being certain if the empire should be transformed into a genuine multiracial commonwealth, if Great
Britain should become a part of a unified Western Europe,
if she should build a close "special relationship" with
the United States, or if the country should become a socialist Jerusalem pointing the way to a future free from
the inequalities of the United States and the political
repression of the Soviet Union. In the midst of these
heroic, Wagnerian events, the failure of the world's
statesmen to notice the return of an obscure young dentist to British Guiana in 1943 after seven years of
study in the United States was not unexpected. Ten
years later, however, Dr. Cheddi Jagan was page one news
throughout the world.

NOTES

1. The best general treatment of Guyana's history is Raymond
T. Smith's British Guiana (Oxford, 1962). This introductory chap-
ter also draws upon Harold A. Lutchman, From Colonialism to Co-
operative Republic (Rio Piedras, Puerto Rico, 1974); Vere T. Daly,
A Short History of the Guyanese People (London, 1975); James Rodway,
History of British Guiana from 1668, 3 vols. (Georgetown, 1891-94);
Dwarka Nath, A History of Guyana, 3 vols. (London, 1974-76); and
Leo A. Despres, Cultural Pluralism and Nationalist Politics in
British Guiana (Chicago, 1967).

2. See Mary Noel Menezes, British Policy Towards the Amerindians in British Guiana, 1803-1873 (Oxford, 1977).

3. See David B. Davis, The Problem of Slavery in Western Culture (Ithaca, 1966); and idem, The Problem of Slavery in the Age of Revolution (Ithaca, 1975).

4. The standard work is Sir Cecil Clementi's, A Constitutional History of British Guiana (London, 1937).

5. Lutchman, From Colonialism to Co-operative Republic, pp. 11-35.

6. Along with the books already mentioned, see Roy A. Glasgow, Guyana: Race and Politics among Africans and East Indians (The Hague, 1970); Peter Newman, British Guiana: Problems of Cohesion in an Immigrant Society (Oxford, 1964); and William Mitchell et al., Area Handbook for Guyana (Washington, 1969). The latter book was prepared under the auspices of the Foreign Area Studies of the American University to assist United States military and other personnel requiring an "objective description" of Guyana.

7. Smith, British Guiana, pp. 42-46.

8. Ibid., pp. 104-5.

9. See Dwarka Nath, A History of Indians in Guyana (London, 1970); and Chandra Jayawardena, "Religious Belief and Social Change: Aspects of the Development of Hinduism in British Guiana," Comparative Studies in Society and History, 8 (1966), pp. 211-40.

10. A vast literature exists on cultural pluralism and its significance. For an introduction to the problem, see Michael G. Smith, The Plural Society in the British West Indies (Berkeley, 1965). Smith's theoretical concepts about the divisive characteristics of culturally plural societies are applied in Despres, Cultural Pluralism. For the opposite view, which stresses the essential unity of the Guyanese people despite their ethnic and cultural differences, see Smith, British Guiana, pp. 198-206. See also Lloyd Braithwaite's article, "Social Stratification and Cultural Pluralism," in Michael M. Horowitz, ed., Peoples and Cultures of the Caribbean (Garden City, New York, 1971), pp. 95-116.

11. Despres, Cultural Pluralism, pp. 54-62.

12. Alan H. Adamson, Sugar Without Slaves: The Political Economy of British Guiana, 1838-1904 (New Haven, Connecticut, 1972), pp. 109-32.

13. Smith, British Guiana, pp. 59-67 and 82-87. See Sir Jock Campbell (then chairman of Booker Brothers, McConnell & Co., Ltd.), "The Development and Organisation of Bookers" (Paper delivered to a seminar at the London School of Economics on Problems in Industrial Administration, London, November 1959).

14. Lutchman, From Colonialism to Co-operative Republic, pp. 30-35.

15. See Walter Rodney, A History of the Guyanese Working People, 1881-1905 (Baltimore, 1981).

16. Despres, Cultural Pluralism, p. 40.

17. Lutchman, From Colonialism to Co-operative Republic, pp. 158-80. Evelyn Waugh, the British novelist, visited the colony in the early 1930s. See his Ninety-Two Days (London, 1934).

18. Report of the West India Royal Commission 1938-39, (Cmnd. 6607, 1945). The conclusions reached by Lord Moyne's group were so critical of British policy that its publication was delayed

until the end of World War II. See also John La Guerre, "The Moyne
Commission and the West Indian Intelligentsia, 1938-39," Journal
of Commonwealth Political Studies, 9 (July 1971), pp. 134-57.

19. For Trinidad see Selwyn D. Ryan, Race and Nationalism in
Trinidad and Tobago: A Study of Decolonization in a Multiracial
Society (Toronto, 1972); and the fine essays in John La Guerre,
ed., Calcutta to Caroni: The East Indians of Trinidad (London,
1974).

20. See Edward Dew, The Difficult Flowering of Surinam: Eth-
nicity and Politics in a Plural Society (The Hague, 1979). For a
Surinam view of the border dispute see F. E. M. Mitrasing, The
Border-Conflict between Surinam and Guiana (Paramaribo, 1975).

21. Leslie B. Rout, Jr., Which Way Out? A Study of the Guyana-
Venezuela Boundary Dispute (Lansing, Michigan, 1971).

2
Cheddi Jagan, Forbes Burnham, and the People's Progressive Party

Without Janet Rosenberg, Cheddi Jagan might very well have become a prosperous, contented Georgetown dentist. The Chicago girl molded and reshaped the vague sense of injustice only partially formed by the impressionable student's experiences on the sugar plantations of British Guiana and in the racial and social atmosphere of America in the 1930s.

Cheddi Jagan was born deep in the heart of East Indian territory, the land between the Corentyne and Berbice rivers, at the sugar estate of Port Mourant. His parents, while still infants, had been carried to British Guiana in 1901 as part of a small group of indentured laborers from the Uttar Pradesh district of India. Within a few years the young children were in the cane fields themselves, Jagan's father at Albion and his mother at Port Mourant. In the East Indian tradition, a marriage was arranged in 1909 when his father was ten years old and his mother slightly younger. Not until they were sixteen did the two young people establish a marital relationship when, as was the custom, his mother moved to the home of her in-laws. Both Hindus, Cheddi's mother was far more religious than his father.[1]

Cheddi, the eldest surviving son, was born on 22 March 1918; five brothers and five sisters would also grow to maturity. Both parents toiled long hours in the cane fields for very little pay, but his father, a good cutter and hard worker, climbed upward to become a driver, or headman. The estate manager dominated the small, all-embracing world of the self-sufficient plantation. Under the manager were the overseers, white, but usually very rough in contrast to the manager and his lady in the great house.

At the broad base of the social pyramid were the cane cutters, living in their miserable huts and barracks. A small, middle group of religious leaders, teachers, clerks, and drivers linked the top and bottom of the social ladder; the ambitious field worker could claw his way into these occupations. Drivers were

17

selected from the most competent and toughest of the
cane cutters. Their reward was to supervise their less
fortunate brethren and to enforce the demands of the
overseers. His father's position brought an element of
ambiguity into Cheddi Jagan's life. Although sympathiz-
ing with the exploited cutters, his father, a driver, at
the bottom of the middle ranks, was an agent of the op-
pressors--the manager and the overseers.

While possibly not true of Cheddi Jagan's father,
many drivers obtained promotion by bribing the overseer.
To pay the overseer and retain the job, it was often
necessary to extort money from the ill-paid cutters. To
have been a part of this repressive structure and to
have had a portion of his higher education paid for by
money derived from a hated system must have provided
some difficult moments in the conscious and unconscious
mind of Cheddi Jagan. He argues that his father loathed
the exploitation and secretly encouraged the cutters to
improve their conditions; but, Cheddi Jagan had no doubt
that his father "was at the lowest level of the middle
stratum" and that this position posed a "real dilemma."

Despite the harsh conditions of the sugar industry,
Cheddi Jagan retained fond memories of growing to maturity on a plantation. His parents had always insisted
their eldest son must not limit his horizon to sugar.
With great strength of character and much hard work,
they set out to furnish the opportunities for Cheddi and
their other children that were denied them. While the
father was a good provider, he also enjoyed pleasant
times and good rum. His will and character were strong
to the end, preferring to die from a gangrenous foot
rather than have it amputated. It was Cheddi's mother,
however, who really controlled the family and kept its
sights on what might be achieved. Cheddi remembered his
father as a good leader who was "bold and flamboyant,"
while his mother "tackled the more mundane and difficult
task of balancing the family budget."

Most schools in British Guiana were managed by various Christian denominations, another East Indian grievance since the vast majority of teachers were Christians. The government provided many of the buildings
and teacher salaries. A bright young boy, Cheddi Jagan
attended the Anglican-controlled Port Mourant Primary
School. There were few secondary schools in the colony,
however, and most had high tuition fees. In 1933, at
age fifteen, Cheddi's parents gambled on his intelligence; he was enrolled in the outstanding secondary
school, Queen's College in Georgetown. Here, indeed,
was the beginning of a great adventure not yet over.

At Port Mourant, shoes had not been necessary until
Cheddi was twelve, and he, occasionally, skipped school
to help on the family's five acres of rice fields. Day
after day the family methodically devoured rice, split
peas, bread, and fish, except for an occasional Saturday

treat of sardines or cheese. In Georgetown, Cheddi
found a more cosmopolitan world. Containing a charming
central area with wide streets, Georgetown is one of the
Caribbean's more attractive cities.[2] Dominated by the
world's largest wooden cathedral, St. George's, and by
the Stabroek Market, it also includes the governor's
home, the Legislative Assembly, and the law courts.
Compared to Europe, the city was small and provincial;
by Port Mourant standards, it was huge, fascinating,
exotic, a brave new world. With its many wooden buildings built on high stilts, Georgetown does, however,
suffer from a chronic fire problem and, in 1945, much of
the central part of the city was destroyed. Young Jagan
did well in his studies and by 1935 had passed the required examinations and had graduated from Queen's College. He was even prouder of his achievements at cricket.

     Seventeen years of age and well educated by Guyan-
ese standards, Cheddi Jagan was unable to find a job.
His parents objected to employment on the sugar estates;
a teaching post was ruled out when there were suggestions that it might be wise to become a Christian. No
vacancies existed in the civil service. Two of his
classmates, sons of dentists, intended to study dentistry at Howard University in the United States. Both father and son were curious about the expenses and the
amount of time required. The father leaned to the law
and legal training, but Cheddi, not yet aware of his
considerable oratorical skills, preferred to try dentistry. Law school meant England, and both felt it would
be easier for Cheddi to work his way through school in
the United States. The elder Jagan managed to come up
with five hundred dollars for his son. About one hundred would be spent immediately for his passage, while
the remainder was to see Cheddi through two years at
Howard's pre-dental school. In September 1936, travelling with his black classmate, Orrin Dummett, Cheddi departed for the United States where he would spend the
next seven years, two in Washington, D.C., with the summers spent in New York City, and five in Chicago, Illi-
nois. This move was a far more fantastic change than the
move to Georgetown; these years were immensely significant in Jagan's intellectual and political development.

     Howard University was one of the finest black uni-
versities in the United States. Segregation in education would not be branded unconstitutional by the Supreme Court until 1954. Washington, D.C., contained a
large number of blacks and was very southern in its racial attitudes; Jagan found he was occasionally discrim-
inated against because of his brownish skin. While he
could pass for white and attend white-only theaters, he
soon decided he preferred to identify with the black
community. He had tasted discrimination in British Guiana from the small white community, but now he found it

blunter and more pervasive.

Shortly after arriving in Washington, he obtained a job as a tailor in a combination pawnshop-retail store near the black ghetto. He also peddled Christmas cards and, during his summers in the black New York City ghetto of Harlem, delivered newspapers, sold ice cream bars, and worked as a salesman for both a restaurant supplier and a patent medicine firm. The crowded conditions of Harlem's black community were shocking and made a profound impression on Jagan.

The long hours spent earning money did not hurt Jagan's academic performance. He earned a free tuition scholarship for his second year at Howard University, and was accepted at the prestigious Northwestern University Dental School in Chicago. Expenses were high and he continued to work during his four years at Northwestern. He washed dishes and then, luckily, obtained work as an elevator operator in a hotel. As only whites were supposed to work in this position, Cheddi Jagan was placed on the midnight shift, where, it was hoped, few would see him.

Recognizing his too narrow specialization in the exact sciences and influenced by Mahatma Ghandi and the Indian struggle for freedom, Jagan set out to acquire a greater knowledge of the political, economic, and social problems of the world. How could these problems be avoided? In 1936, when Jagan arrived in the United States, Franklin Delano Roosevelt was reelected to the presidency by a massive margin, but the new Deal ran out of ideas as "balance-the-budget" replaced a slap-dash Keynesianism. Unemployment remained high, and Western capitalism continued in crisis until the Second World War brought unemployment to an end with conscription and a massive armament program. Jagan was now living through the Munich Agreement of September 1938, the Nazi-Soviet Non-Aggression Pact of August 1939, the start of World War II a few days later, the fall of France in June 1940, the Battle of Britain, Hitler's attack on the Soviet Union in 1941, and the Japanese bombing of Pearl Harbor in December of that year. These were dangerous, exciting years. Roosevelt and Churchill captured the imagination of the free world in August 1941 when they enunciated the "four freedoms." Now, not only was there a commitment to the traditional freedoms of worship and speech, but there was a recognition of the broader needs of humanity in a world grown much smaller but with many more people. Freedom from want and freedom from fear were stunning reminders of prewar deficiencies and postwar hopes.

To learn more about the world, Cheddi Jagan enrolled in summer and evening classes in history and political science at the Young Men's Christian Association in Chicago. He was impressed by Charles Beard's economic interpretation of the Constitution of the United States,

and read sharp criticism of capitalism by Matthew Joseph-
son and George Seldes. It was at this time that he met
the quiet, introspective Janet Rosenberg. She was dis-
tinctly left-wing in her politics and may, or may not,
have been a formal member of official Communist groups.
Though much has been made of whether she had actual membership cards in Communist bodies, the matter is really
of little significance. What does matter is that both
individuals were active politically, and, given the war-
time attitudes of 1941-1943, it was not strange that
their opinions reflected radical, socialist, Marxist,
and Stalinist ideas.

The writings of Marx, Lenin, and Stalin were a re-
velation for Cheddi Jagan. There is much validity in
Karl Marx's analysis of the achievements of capitalism
and of the contradictions in the mode of production that
would cause the system to collapse prior to the triumph
of the proletariat and the creation of a socialist society. Unfortunately, Cheddi Jagan failed to regard Marxism as simply one way, among others, of viewing the
problems of British Guiana. Instead, he adopted the Soviet version of Marxism and eventually concluded the
Russians could do little wrong.

In 1942, Cheddi Jagan received his dentistry degree
from Northwestern. The years of work and study, though,
had taken their toll; a routine x-ray examination revealed a small spot on one lung. Diagnosed as tubercu-
lous, he was sent to a sanatorium about thirty miles
from Chicago. Rest, reading, and relaxation provided a
quick cure, and by the spring of 1943 he was released
with an admonition to be careful. Interestingly, he remained in the United States at this time, although he
had been away from home since 1936 and had completed his
studies. He even gave thought to staying permanently in
the United States but, though not from India, the immigration authorities had classified him as an oriental.
This classification placed restrictions on his becoming
a United States citizen. Unfortunately, dentistry could
not be practiced without certification by a state board,
and state boards were not then examining noncitizens.
Cheddi Jagan was trapped in a Kafkaesque situation,
which became even more grotesque when he received his
draft notice in the summer of 1943. Although delighted
with the improvement in health which enabled him to pass
the physical examination for military service, he complained that the officials of the United States, "unwilling to let me become a citizen, were quite ready to
draft me as a private."

Jagan protested to the Selective Service Board that
it was unfair to draft him as a private; he was entitled
to a commission on the basis of his dentistry degree.
The Draft Board relented when he said he would go to
prison rather than become a private. They gave him six
months to obtain a state board examination certificate,

but did not explain how this was to be accomplished without his United States citizenship. Disgusted, he resolved to return home.

He married Janet Rosenberg during the summer, over the objections of both sets of parents; Janet's father "threatened to shoot" his daughter's suitor. Jagan left for British Guiana in October, while Janet remained behind in her job as a proofreader for the American Medical Association. Cheddi's task was "to woo my parents into accepting her and finding the money to pay for her passage." Just before Christmas, Janet arrived in her strange new home. Much has been written about the relationship between Cheddi and Janet Jagan. She is surely not a gray eminence controlling a puppet; her husband might even have become a socialist without her, though perhaps not such an ardent advocate for the Soviet Union. She lacks his charisma, charm, and oratorical skills, but his thinking tends to the superficial while she is more analytical and more practical. She has fine organizational skills and became an effective administrator. While their commitment to the Soviet version of international communism has provided them strength by joining them to a worldwide movement, it has also seriously limited their effectiveness.

Janet Jagan captivated her in-laws by initially playing the role of a submissive East Indian wife. Once accepted, she set out to build a more equal society for all Guyanese. Eventually, Jagan's parents came to love and admire the "blue-eyed sister-in-law." She accepted Cheddi Jagan's responsibility to aid his brothers and sisters; three of his five brothers studied abroad—one became a dentist, another a medical doctor, and one a lawyer. Four of his five sisters were trained in the United Kingdom—two nurses, one beautician, and one optician.

Shortly after the arrival of Janet and his dental equipment, Jagan established an office on Main Street, in the heart of Georgetown. Having had training as a nurse, Janet became his dental hygienist. Reestablished in British Guiana after his lengthy absence, Cheddi Jagan and his wife began an intense scrutiny of Guyanese society to ascertain how they could ameliorate the lives of the Guyanese people and further the momentum for self-government and independence. There had never been a really successful political party in British Guiana. Groups of individuals might support a particular issue at election time, but the organization required to keep a party in existence had failed to develop. Usually, colored and black middle class personalities from Georgetown would organize around the issue of enlarging the size of the electorate and increasing the power of the Legislative Council. All elected members in the Legislative Council chosen in 1935 served as individuals, not as representatives of parties with specific programs.[3]

More significant, and with far greater continuity than the nebulous political parties, were the League of Coloured People (LCP) and the British Guiana East Indian Association (BGEIA). Both groups primarily represented the interests of the small middle class of professionals, civil servants, and businessmen, the first for the blacks and mulattoes, the second for the East Indians.[4] The Jagans, however, had no sympathy for middle class ethnic groups.

But the small trade union movement looked much more promising.[5] Strikes and labor disturbances occurred in British Guiana prior to World War I, but the first labor union, the British Guiana Labour Union (BGLU), was organized by Hubert Nathaniel Critchlow only in 1919. Critchlow (1884-1958), a black waterfront worker in Georgetown, remains a national hero because of his struggle to aid the working class. The BGLU, powerful among the black proletariat of Georgetown, included numerous other workers along with those toiling on the waterfront until more specialized unions came into existence. An unfortunate early development which has continued was the decision to award key union offices to professionals and businessmen, nonworking members of the union.

Ayube Edun, the East Indian counterpart to Critchlow, organized the plantation cutters; but, while Critchlow was a down-to-earth, bread-and-butter trade unionist, Edun had visions of a transformed British Empire based on rational-practical idealism. In 1937, he established the grandiosely named Man-Power Citizens Association (MPCA) which embarked upon the rather more prosaic task of improving the life of the sugar worker. Two years later, the association won recognition from the Sugar Producers Association. Some began to feel, however, that Edun and his supporters were growing too close to the sugar barons and were no longer representing the interests of the cane cutters. Cheddi Jagan became treasurer of the MPCA in 1945 but left, or was discharged, after one year. He argued that the union officials were collaborating with the bosses.

By 1941, the trade unions had established a Trades Union Council (TUC) "to promote the interest of all its affiliated organizations and generally to improve the economic and social conditions of the workers and to secure united action on questions affecting or likely to affect their interests." The TUC became affiliated to the Fabian Colonial Bureau in 1944, and a year later sent representatives to the first conference of the World Federation of Trade Unions (WFTU). By 1947, there were some twenty unions in British Guiana, but only the MPCA had more than one thousand members.

World War II ended in 1945 and the Caribbean reverberated with excitement. Men who had served in the British army returned with the belief that a war for

democracy had been won abroad and must now be brought
home. A West Indian conference in Georgetown brought
together Norman Manley and Richard Hart from Jamaica,
Grantley Adams of Barbados, and Albert Gomes of Trinidad. The conference established a Caribbean Labour Congress, designed to improve the appalling conditions of
the Caribbean people so clearly revealed in the now fully published report of Lord Moyne's commission.

The Jagans had become prominent members of a discussion group at the Carnegie Library in Georgetown.
Letters to the editor flowed from their pens. Janet attracted much criticism due to her vigorous endorsement
of birth control. Both Jagans were convinced a formal
political group was needed with a theoretical organ of
its own. Along with the white Marxist, H. J. M. Hubbard,
and the black trade unionist, Ashton Chase, they organized the Political Affairs Committee (PAC) in 1946, borrowing the name from the Political Affairs Committee of
the then left-leaning Congress of Industrial Organizations in the United States. That same year, Janet Jagan
and Winifred Gaskin formed the Women's Political and
Economic Organization.[6] While the women's group was designed to fight for improvement in such matters as housing and health, the PAC was committed "to assist the
growth and development of Labour and Progressive Movements of British Guiana to the end of establishing a
strong, disciplined and enlightened Party, equipped with
the theory of Scientific Socialism." The committee,
though dominated by Marxists, soon attracted almost
everyone committed to self-government. No attempt was
made to impose discipline; all points of view were heard
and discussed.[7]

The appeal of the PAC crossed ethnic lines by bas-
ing itself upon a class analysis aimed at unifying the
largest body of people in British Guiana, the working
class of urban blacks and rural East Indians. Self-
government and adult suffrage were the immediate political aims and, once achieved, would provide the means
through which economic and social justice could be obtained. Effective use was made of Lord Moyne's report
which had laid bare so precisely the deplorable conditions in which the vast majority of Guyanese were living.

Sir Gordon Lethem, a popular and progressive governor, had hoped for a second term of five years. But
second terms were not customary and Lethem had bruised
some Colonial Office officials with his criticism of the
status quo. Fortunately for British Guiana, an equally
generous and conciliatory governor was dispatched in
early 1947. Sir Charles Woolley had served with distinction as governor of Cyprus during World War II. Before that, he had fought with great bravery during World
War I and served for many years in Ceylon, then going to
Jamaica and Nigeria.[8] He was familiar with ethnic rivalries: Tamil and Sinhalese in Ceylon, Hausa and Ibo in

Nigeria, and Greek and Turk in Cyprus. When he arrived in Georgetown, the PAC realized that elections were imminent. Here was the moment to bring their ideas to the entire community. It would be a time of testing, and of opportunity. India had just been granted independence and this event sent a surge of elation through the hearts of colonial people throughout the world, especially of British Guiana's East Indian population. The British Labour party, in power in Britain since July 1945 and for the first time with a proper majority, had no intention of reneging on its past promises. Unlike the Conservatives, they were prepared to preside over the dissolution of the British Empire, though they hoped to transform the empire into a voluntarily cooperating commonwealth. After India, Pakistan, and Burma, there could be no turning back.

The British Guiana census of 1940 had revealed a population of 347,000. By 1959, it would reach just over 425,000: 191,000 East Indians, 156,000 Africans, 45,000 mixed or colored, 17,000 Amerindians, 8,800 Portuguese, 3,800 other Europeans, and 3,500 Chinese. The first elections in British Guiana since 1935 finally occurred in late 1947. Fourteen constituencies were fought over by a swarm of candidates. Numerous independents stepped forward, along with candidates sponsored by the LCP, BGEIA, and MPCA. A so-called Labour party was hastily patched together by some of Georgetown's trade union leaders. But no properly organized political party existed. As a consequence of lowering the requirements for voting, the electorate had increased more than fivefold, to almost 60,000. Three members of the Political Affairs Committee, Cheddi Jagan, Janet Jagan, and H. J. M. Hubbard, ran for office. Cheddi Jagan was the only victor, taking Central Demerara, just next to Georgetown, where there were many East Indians. He also received considerable African support as a result of help from the capable black school teacher, Sydney King. Janet lost a Georgetown seat to John Fernandes, a wealthy Portuguese businessman, and Hubbard also lost a Georgetown seat.

It was a great moment for Cheddi Jagan when he entered the Legislative Council on 18 December 1947 at age twenty-nine, the youngest member. The governor, Sir Charles Woolley, also president of the Council, congratulated the citizenry on the 70 percent turnout at the polls, but expressed regret "that during the elections a good deal of racial feeling was engendered in some quarters." This racism could only "be a major hindrance to progress constitutionally and otherwise in this colony." But the governor was convinced that racial animosity was not "deep-seated or widespread among the people themselves." Most Guyanese lived "in amity and concord together and as good neighbours." They must make their "different characteristics . . . a source of our strength not weakness, and all for the common good."

In words not unlike those uttered yearly by Guyana's present leader, Sir Charles reminded the people that it was "imperative for us by our own efforts to raise the level of our national output and income." Agricultural and industrial production must be increased, and the vast interior of the country finally opened to development. Confident that the Ten-Year Plan for social and economic transformation, prepared by the last Council, would point the way forward, he expressed pleasure that working people had elected their own representatives to the present Council. Trade unionism must also be applauded

> as a part of our social system. . . . The Government's policy has been, and will continue to be, not only to recognise Trades Unions but to foster their healthy growth and to provide by law the machinery to facilitate the settlement of disputes, and in a manner securing to both parties a square deal.[9]

A relatively liberal speech, it failed to satisfy Cheddi Jagan. Naive and with little knowledge of parliamentary rules, he was eager to learn; his criticism could be slashing and offensive, but he was always good natured and sociable. He endured a good number of blows, for after a short period of cooperation with the loosely formed Labour party, that body collapsed and he was left on his own. Hammering away at the sugar interests and the foreign-owned bauxite mines, Cheddi Jagan became an immensely appealing figure to a large number of dispossessed Guyanese. He demanded adequate taxation of sugar and bauxite, better housing for the worker, improved health standards, redistribution of the excess land owned by the sugar plantations, government-sponsored drainage and irrigation schemes to help small farmers and rice growers, and universal adult suffrage.[10]

What brought the Jagans even further into the limelight was the killing of five cane cutters at the Enmore Sugar Estate in 1948. Labor relations on the sugar estates had always been characterized by strikes and work stoppages due to the primitive conditions in which the cutters lived and toiled. When the Man-Power Citizens Association received recognition as their bargaining agent in 1939, hopes were high for a better day. As the MPCA developed cozy relations with the Sugar Producers Association, bitter disillusionment set in among the cutters. Responding to this sorry state of affairs in 1946, Dr. J. P. Lachhmansingh and A. A. Rangela organized the Guiana Industrial Workers Union (GIWU), aimed at replacing the MPCA as the representative of the sugar workers. Dissatisfaction in the fields was particularly intense due to the recently adopted system of "cut and load" in place of "cut and drop." Previously, the cutters allowed the cane to drop, later to be picked up and loaded in small boats (punts) to be carried to the factory. Management now insisted that the cutter load the cane on the punt after it had been cut. The leadership of the MPCA capitulated, but the workers rebelled. Their cause was taken up by GIWU and promptly endorsed by the Political Affairs Committee.[11]

In April 1948, the sugar workers along the east coast of Demerara began to lay down their cutlasses. The strike continued into June without agreement; a meeting between the MPCA and SPA failed to bring settlement on 14 June. The workers preferred GIWU but were stuck with the MPCA. A large demonstration at Enmore estate grew to some six hundred people by 10:00 A.M. on the morning of 16 June. Fearing the strikers might destroy the sugar factory, a small number of beleaguered policemen, worrying about their own safety and not quite sure what to do, opened fire. Five workers were killed, now known as the Enmore Martyrs. Yearly pilgrimages are made to their graves and to the monument commemorating the event. The strike and the shooting incident were brilliantly exploited by the Political Affairs Committee. The colonial administration was denounced for protecting private property at the expense of striking workers, whose wages were low and whose conditions of life were deplorable. Cheddi and Janet Jagan led a great funeral march from Enmore to Georgetown, sixteen miles away.

Sir Charles Woolley set up a commission to investigate the incident; arguing the investigation would be a whitewash, the Jagans refused to testify. The commission justified the police decision to shoot, but conceded that too many bullets had been fired since several of the dead men had been shot in the back while running away. A Royal Commission was then established under the chairmanship of J. A. Venn, president of Queen's College, Cambridge, to investigate conditions in the sugar industry. During two months in Georgetown, the members of the commission heard testimony from about two hundred people; a final report appeared in 1949. Paying special attention to the fact that 30 percent of the employees on the estates were women, the report insisted on some immediate improvements. Women drivers should replace men where gangs of women were working in the fields. At specified times, they must be allowed to return home to care for their children.

The Venn commission further recommended the Medical Department inspect and report on housing, water supply, and sanitation. Proper plots of land should be given to all regular workers for farming and growing rice. It was imperative that there "be a clearance of all 'ranges' and re-housing of sugar workers by the end of 1953." The commission had been appalled by the housing problem.

In quite a number the corrugated iron roofs were leaking

and the fabric of the buildings was in a general state
of decay. In numerous instances temporary sheets of
awnings have been fixed over the beds to keep off the
rain. They had mud floors and, consequently, with the
rain dripping from the roofs, these were made slippery
and dangerous; in many cases we found bags laid over
the floor to prevent slipping. They are built without
any plan on low-lying, uneven ground. There are few,
if any, proper footpaths, and in rainy weather communication is difficult. The common latrines often built
over drainage trenches are frequently in a bad state
of repair, with little privacy. (Jagan 1972: 81-82)

While praising the Estate Joint Committees, established in 1945 to allow presentation of the workers'
complaints, the commission rejected recognition for GIWU.
This union would duplicate the tasks already being adequately carried out by the MPCA. The commission did advocate a Wages Board to set pay scales for the entire
sugar industry and a contributory pension scheme. Both
proposals were successfully opposed by the owners.[12]
   Cheddi Jagan's activities in the Legislative Council plus the publicity garnered during the Enmore shooting crisis convinced the PAC leadership that the moment
had arrived to organize a mass political party. Rumors
were rampant that a Royal Commission would shortly be
appointed to investigate conditions throughout British
Guiana. The commission was expected to recommend the
establishment of self-government in the colony as a step
toward Dominion status within the Commonwealth, either
as an independent state or as part of a West Indies Federation.
   Although Ashton Chase, a respected African trade
unionist, was a founding member of the PAC, the top
leaders believed an even more prestigious black was required to show the multiracial quality of the new political party. The perfect choice was just packing his
bags for Georgetown after having completed legal studies
in London.
   Forbes Burnham's background in a middle class,
black family, comfortably established in Georgetown, was
very dissimilar to that of Cheddi Jagan.[13] Born Linden
Forbes Sampson Burnham in the village of Kitty, a Georgetown suburb, on 20 February 1923, he was the second son
in a family of five children. His father, headmaster of
a Methodist Primary School in Kitty, did not receive a
large wage, but the home provided an intellectual atmosphere for a bright, perceptive boy. Educated at his
father's school, then briefly at Central High School, he
followed Cheddi Jagan's path to Queen's College. After
a year, his parents despaired of finding sufficient
funds to keep him there. Fortunately, his keen mind had
been discovered by the teachers and he won a scholarship
to pay his tuition. One of his school reports noted he

was "a natural leader . . . diligent and studious but
not aloof . . . a great favorite with others in his
class."

The British government provided one scholarship for
the outstanding Guyanese student of the year to complete
a university education in the United Kingdom. Burnham
earned the award in 1942 but the war delayed his journey
to London until 1945. In the intervening years, he completed an external Bachelor's Degree and taught in a
private secondary school and later as an assistant master at Queen's College.

Deciding upon legal studies at London University,
he quickly exhibited his oratorical skills by winning
the Best Speaker's Cup at the Law Faculty. In 1947, he
received a law degree with honors and was called to the
bar at Gray's Inn the following year. Active politically, especially in the cause of colonial people of the
world, he was president of the West Indies Student Union
in 1947, vice-president of the London Branch of the Caribbean Labour Congress, and led the West Indian Students' Delegation to the World Youth Festival in Czech-
oslovakia. He established close ties with left-wingers
in the British Labour party and also with a variety of
groups sponsored by the British Communist party. He acquired a commitment to socialism, but it was to be a
more pragmatic, flexible--perhaps opportunistic--social-
ism than the more doctrinaire approach of Cheddi Jagan.

Scarred by the racial discrimination he experienced
in London, Burnham could be quite arrogant when negotiating with whites. Involved also with the League of
Coloured Peoples, he helped organize mass demonstrations
in the streets of London. In 1949, he returned to British Guiana to discover a colony seething with political
ferment. How nice indeed to have skipped the tedious
preparatory work done by the Jagans and others and still
to be rewarded with the chairmanship of the new party.
Jagan later wrote, "Actually Ashton Chase should have
been chairman, but he gave way to Burnham who had an impressive scholastic record."[14]

Borrowing from Henry Wallace's Progressive party in
the United States (which had participated in the 1948
presidential election as an alternative to what were
perceived as the cold war policies of both Democratic
and Republican parties), and from Norman Manley's People's National party in Jamaica, the Political Affairs
Committee opted to call its mass party, the People's
Progressive party (PPP). Burnham was to be chairman,
Jagan the leader, and Janet Jagan the general secretary.
Sydney King, an Afro-Guyanese, became assistant secretary, and Clinton Wong, of Chinese background, was senior vice-chairman. Cheddi Jagan was also designated
second vice-chairman, while Rory Westmaas, an Afro-
Guyanese, was made junior vice-chairman. Ram Karran, an
East Indian, became the treasurer. The Executive

Committee included prominent East Indian leaders like
Dr. J. P. Lachhmansingh of GIWU and Jai Narine Singh.
Jagan's position as leader of the parliamentary section
of the party meant that, at the time, he led himself.
There could be a quarrel, however, if Burnham, the chairman of the party, entered Parliament and both claimed
the top position. [15]
     Officially launched in 1950, the PPP leaders adopt-
ed a highly centralized party structure at its first
Congress in April 1951. The Party Executive, charged
with responsibility for day-to-day activities, was composed of the party's officers. Required to meet with
delegates from the General Council at least once each
month, it then became the party's Executive Committee
and could do anything not prohibited by the constitution.
The smallest unit, the local cell, needed a minimum of
twelve members, a chairman, treasurer, and secretary.
Local cells and constituency committees sent delegates
to the party Congress, at which the General Council,
Executive Committee, and party officers were elected.
The system seemed quite democratic but, as with most organizations, the "iron law of oligarchy" gave tremendous
power and prestige to the party officers.
     Even before the first Congress, the party's new
monthly magazine, Thunder, boldly affirmed the aims of
the PPP.

> The People's Progressive Party, recognizing that the fi-
> nal abolition of exploitation and oppression, of economic
> crises and unemployment and war will be achieved only by
> the Socialist reorganization of society, pledges itself
> to the task of winning a free and independent Guiana, of
> building a just socialist society, in which the industries
> of the country shall be socially and democratically owned
> and managed for the common good, a society in which se-
> curity, plenty, peace, and freedom shall be the heritage
> of all.

The PPP demanded universal suffrage, independence as
quickly as possible, and economic and social justice for
all. While most Guyanese had no knowledge of scientific
socialism, they could easily comprehend the simple program brought from village to village by the PPP activists. The proponents were young and idealistic; their
cause was a good one. Vested interests mobilized against
the PPP through radio and the newspapers, and excitement
pervaded British Guiana throughout 1950 and 1951.
     Unfortunately, events in British Guiana could not
be separated from international politics. Between 1944
and 1947, suspicions between the United States and the
Soviet Union might have been smoothed out, but the Tru-
man Doctrine of March 1947, the Prague coup of February
1948, the Berlin Airlift of 1948-1949, the establishment
of the North Atlantic Treaty Organization in 1949, and

the explosion of the Soviet Union's first atomic bomb in 1949 indicated that the cold war was very frigid. In June 1950, international tensions peaked when North Korea marched south.

Cheddi and Janet Jagan had already been vilified as communist subversives by the more conservative elements in British Guiana. During the sugar strikes of 1948, Cheddi had been banned from some Booker estates even though they were located within his constituency. Attempts were made to restrict public meetings, and, while visiting St. Vincent in 1949, the Jagans's passports were seized. In 1952, Trinidad and Grenada designated the Jagans prohibited immigrants.

Conservative members of the Legislative Council denounced the PAC for meaning "Push All Communism." The PAC and then the PPP had imported vast quantities of socialist and communist material from London. Arguing that he had failed to obtain an import license, the government seized and burned nine crates of literature addressed to Cheddi Jagan. This act was followed in 1952 by the passage of an Undesirable Publications Act prohibiting the importation of "literature, publications, propaganda or films which are subversive or contrary to public interest." Only Cheddi Jagan spoke against this foolish attempt at censorship. For some conservatives, any demand for reform, no matter how badly needed, smelt of radicalism and communism. [16]

Working class groups grew more appreciative of the new political party. If the local aristocracy were opposed to the PPP, then there might be excellent grounds for industrial workers and agricultural laborers to rally behind its banners. Contesting three of nine wards in Georgetown's municipal elections of 1950, Cheddi Jagan and Forbes Burnham suffered defeat but Janet Jagan was victorious. [17]

By the fall of 1950, Sir E. J. Waddington, Professor V. T. Harlow, and Dr. Rita Hinden had been appointed to a Royal Commission to investigate the political structure and economic capabilities of the colony. They were to make recommendations aimed at bringing British Guiana along the road to self-government. The members of the PPP looked forward to testifying before the commission when it arrived. New elections were imminent, and the party planned to bring its message of independence and social reform to the people. [18]

NOTES

1. Cheddi Jagan, The West on Trial (East Berlin, 1972), pp. 11-68. The following assessment of Jagan's early life is derived primarily from this book.

2. There is much of interest in the strongly pro-British books of Michael Swan: British Guiana: The Land of Six Peoples (London, 1957); and The Marches of El Dorado: British Guiana, Brazil, Venezuela (Boston, 1958).

3. See Harold A. Lutchman, Constitutional Developments in Guyana During the Second World War, Occasional Paper Number One, Department of Political Science, University of Guyana, Georgetown, Guyana, 1972.

4. Despres, Cultural Pluralism, pp. 121-76.

5. Ashton Chase, A History of Trade Unionism in Guyana, 1900 to 1961 (Georgetown, Guyana, 1964).

6. Public Record Office, Kew Gardens, C.O. 111/787/60542, British Guiana Correspondence. There are some interesting letters written by Janet Jagan to various administrative officials complaining about the quality of low-cost housing in the colony.

7. Ralph R. Premdas, "The Rise of the First Mass-Based Multi-Racial Party in Guyana," Caribbean Quarterly, 20 (1974), pp. 6-20.

8. Personal interview with Sir Charles Woolley, Royal Commonwealth Society, 8 December 1977.

9. Address by the governor, Sir Charles Woolley, to the First Session of the Fourth Legislative Council of British Guiana, 18 December 1947.

10. Jagan, The West on Trial, pp. 69-106.

11. Chase, Trade Unionism in Guyana, pp. 140-51. See also Paul G. Singh, Landmarks in Working-Class Revolt in Guyana: Enmore, 1948 (Georgetown, Guyana, 1973).

12. Report of a Commission of Inquiry into the Sugar Industry of British Guiana, Colonial Office, No. 249, 1949. See also Jay R. Mandle, The Plantation Economy: Population and Economic Change in Guyana 1838-1960 (Philadelphia, 1973).

13. C. A. Nascimento and R. A. Burrowes, eds., A Destiny to Mould: Selected Discourses by the Prime Minister of Guyana (London, 1970). This collection of Forbes Burnham's speeches also contains a biographical sketch by the editors.

14. Jagan, The West on Trial, p. 98.

15. Despres, Cultural Pluralism, pp. 184-94.

16. Smith, British Guiana, pp. 167-70.

17. Jagan, The West on Trial, pp. 99-100.

18. Sociologists and anthropologists have found the Guyanese people a fertile field for study. See Raymond T. Smith, The Negro Family in British Guiana: Family Structure and Social Status in the Villages (London, 1956); Chandra Jayawardena, Conflict and Solidarity in a Guianese Plantation (London, 1963); Mohammad A. Rauf, Indian Village in Guyana: A Study of Cultural Change and Ethnic Identity (Leiden, 1974); and Marilyn Silverman, Rich People and Rice (Leiden, 1980).

3
Elections and Gunboats

The Waddington Commission arrived in British Guiana in December 1950. Sir E. J. Waddington, a former colonial official, served as acting governor of British Guiana in the 1930s, while Dr. Rita Hinden was active with the colonial bureau of the Fabian Society. The Waddington Commission remained in British Guiana for two months, hearing testimony, usually in public but sometimes in private, from many groups and individuals. Not content to stay in Georgetown, the commission travelled throughout the country. Their findings were published before the end of 1951.[1] Rejecting the pessimism of the cultural pluralists, the commission did concede that some racial discontent existed in British Guiana. They concluded, however, that the source of the present tension would have beneficial results, for it originated in the ambition of younger East Indians to become part of an integrated society. "Indian aloofness has now given place to a realization of their permanent place in Guianese life and to a demand for equal participation in it." Fortunately, there were "many heartening signs of the development of a genuine Guianese outlook." Especially impressive to commission members was "the amity with which peoples of all races live side by side in the villages, where mutual dependence is, of necessity, recognized."[2]

While some witnesses urged the retention of literacy or property qualifications for the vote, the commission demurred and endorsed universal adult suffrage for men and women. They disagreed on whether a unicameral or a bicameral legislature should be established; Waddington preferred the former. Ministers would be individually responsible for their offices since, despite the agitation of the PPP, the commission did not foresee the development of disciplined political parties in British Guiana. The governor would retain specified reserve powers for emergencies, but it was not anticipated that he would be forced to invoke them.

The Colonial Office carefully considered the report

of the Waddington Commission, discussed it with Sir
Charles Woolley, and then issued a final decision on 6
October 1951.[3] Universal adult suffrage was accepted;
elected members must be literate in English, but the
property and income qualifications were eliminated. There
would be a bicameral legislature: a House of Assembly,
or Legislative Assembly, composed of twenty-four elected
members from single-member constituencies, plus three
ex-officio members (the chief secretary, financial secretary, and attorney-general); and an upper house, the
State Council, consisting of nine members, six selected
by the governor, two from the majority group in the Assembly, and one from the minority group. The Executive
Council would include the governor, the chief secretary,
the financial secretary, and the attorney-general, plus
six ministers from the Assembly and one from the State
Council. Ministers were to be individually responsible
to the governor, who retained considerable power and influence. His three close associates, the chief secretary, financial secretary, and attorney-general, belonged to both the Legislative Assembly and the Executive Council. Dominated by his appointees, the State
Council could be relied upon not to repudiate his wishes,
and, ultimately, the governor retained the authority to
veto legislation.

These new constitutional proposals were a massive
stride forward, even though they failed to enchant the
leaders of the People's Progressive party. The latter
argued that the will of the Guyanese people could only
be ascertained by electing a Guyanese constituent assembly by universal suffrage. Such a body should then proceed to write a constitution providing British Guiana
with full, internal self-government immediately. The
governor would be transformed into a constitutional mon-
arch carrying out the wishes of his ministers. Unwilling to be stampeded, the British responded that excessive haste could be harmful rather than beneficial.
British Guiana must move through prescribed, preparatory
stages before following the path of Nehru's India. Despite his objections, even Cheddi Jagan acknowledged
that it was "one of the most advanced colonial constitutions for that period."[4]

The Waddington Commission had conducted its investigation during Britain's Labour regime of Clement
Attlee. Battered in the 1950 general election, the Labour party was swept from power in the fall of the following year. A shudder of alarm swept through the colonial regions of the British Empire. Winston Churchill,
the arch-imperialist, was back in office; would this
mean a change in Labour's enlightened policies toward
the Commonwealth-empire?

Though the PPP fulminated against the Waddington
proposals for not advocating complete self-government,
it still prepared to fight in the elections scheduled

for April 1953. Political discussion saturated the colony as politicians roamed the countryside in search of
voters. The long years of PAC and PPP organizational
work paid handsome dividends. Activists did not carry a
complicated Marxist-Leninist gospel to the villages and
sugar estates. Their message was a simple one: self-
government and economic and social reforms, all leading
to a socialist society.[5]

But a "socialist society" can mean many things. Although most of the PPP leadership urged some form of
"socialism," no consensus existed as to what this term
meant or how this form of society was to be achieved.
Many of these differences, especially those between doctrinaire Marxists and pragmatic socialists, were disre-
garded so long as the emphasis remained on the struggle
against British imperialism and the conservative local
elite.

The small Guyanese middle class was horrified at
the growing strength of the PPP. Controlling all the
newspapers of the colony, they began a campaign of vili-
fication, accusing the PPP of being under the thumb of
Moscow. In 1951, Cheddi Jagan had visited the United
Kingdom for the first time and strengthened his ties
with the Communist party of Great Britain, which was
supplying some funds and plenty of literature. Journey-
ing on to the World Youth Festival in Berlin, he was impressed by developments in East Germany.[6] Jagan's trip
to Europe further dismayed the local elite, which also
began preparations for the upcoming election.

One of Cheddi Jagan's most persistent opponents
through the years has been his fellow East Indian, Lionel
Luckhoo.[7] Luckhoo's grandfather, an indentured laborer,
arrived in British Guiana in the 1850s. Hard work and a
good marriage transformed him into a very wealthy merchant. His sons and grandsons became prominent merchants
and professionals, especially active in the legal field.
Lionel Luckhoo, a nominated member of the Legislative
Council, authored the Undesirable Publications Act of
1952, but soon discovered that the "forbidden fruit" became even more popular once placed on the banned list.

The year before, Luckhoo had joined with John Carter, a prominent lawyer of African descent and an elected member of the Legislative Council, to form the National Democratic party (NDP). A multiracial organization, it was controlled by the African, East Indian, and
Portuguese bourgeoisie. It thundered, ad infinitum: the
PPP is dominated by Soviet-line communists.[8]

Sir Charles Woolley's term as governor expired in
late 1952 and a new governor, Sir Alfred Savage, arrived
in early 1953. Savage had just completed four successful years in Barbados, but it left him unprepared for
the hectic, frantic political life of British Guiana.
Calm, tranquil, and more like Kent or Sussex than the
usually turbulent Caribbean, Barbados is a solidly black

island with few ethnic problems. A nationalist movement
led by the moderate Grantley Adams was pushing for self-
government, and Frank Walcott was prodding the trade
union movement into action, but the whole environment
was totally different from the one Savage would encounter in British Guiana.[9]

By the time the new governor arrived, the election
campaign was in full swing with the PPP far and away the
best organized party in the field. The NDP endorsed a
number of candidates, and several insignificant minor
parties also participated; but 80 of the 130 candidates
contesting the twenty-four seats called themselves "independents."[10]

Comprehensive and easy to understand, the PPP program advocated the construction of low-rental houses,
the reduction of indirect taxes and an increase in direct taxation, a start toward a free health service,
workmen's compensation, removal of denominational control of schools while retaining religious education,
more nursery schools, and additional secondary school
scholarships. The PPP also wanted many more independent
small farmers to securely own their plot of land. This
ownership could be achieved by taking away unused land
from the great sugar estates and enabling landless agricultural laborers and small farmers to purchase it with
the assistance of government loans. The PPP advocated a
comprehensive drainage and irrigation system for the un-
cultivated land hoarded by the great sugar companies.
This land could then be confiscated and redistributed to
the working people. Finally, the PPP urged the encouragement of new industries and the strengthening of trade
unions by passing legislation similar to the Wagner Labor Relations Act in the United States.[11]

The PPP ran for twenty-two of the twenty-four seats,
not bothering with the remote Amerindian areas too ex-
pensive to fight. Janet Jagan supervised Essequibo and
West Demerara, Cheddi Jagan led the assault on the east
coast of Demerara and Berbice, while Forbes Burnham conducted the campaign in Georgetown. Although sensing
that the people were responding to their appeal, most
PPP leaders could still not visualize winning more than
five to seven seats. This result, however, would leave
them a well-organized, disciplined opposition in the
Legislative Assembly, capable of sniping away at those
aspects of the Waddington constitution they disliked.

As the votes were tallied, the PPP were as surprised
as its opponents were horrified. With almost 75 percent
of registered voters participating, the PPP garnered 51
percent of the popular vote and won eighteen of the
twenty-four seats. The people of British Guiana had
voted decisively for change and transformation. Out of
some 210,000 names on the electoral registers, more than
150,000 had cast valid votes. The NDP, winning 13 percent of the total votes cast, acquired only two seats,

and independents, usually popular local community leaders, obtained four. The participation of so many independents meant that the victorious PPP candidates lacked an absolute majority in seven of the eighteen constituencies. In one constituency, the triumphant PPP nominee won just over 29 percent of the vote, while, in another constituency, one independent winner squeezed by with 27 percent of the total vote cast.

Despite its slim popular majority, it was still an astonishing victory for the PPP. Significant racial cooperation characterized the PPP campaign. In one predominantly East Indian constituency, the PPP ran the Afro-Guyanese, Fred Bowman. To the delight of the leadership, Bowman defeated Dr. J. B. Singh, who had been supported by the East Indian Association. Though Bowman ran against three other East Indian opponents and their total vote exceeded his, his election still proved that a significant number of East Indians were willing to vote for a black nominee. Janet Jagan was victorious in an East Indian district of Western Essequibo. Black Georgetown awarded all five seats to the PPP, which also won all eight seats in the East Indian sugar belt. It was a triumph for the Guyanese working class.

Signs of stress and strain were not absent at the moment of exaltation, and they focussed upon Burnham's ambitions to be parliamentary leader of the party as well as chairman.[12] By challenging Jagan on no issue of significance, except the desire to be number one, the conflict, for some, acquired a racial tone. Jagan, however, retained the overwhelming support of the party, including such black militants as Sydney King, Ashton Chase, Martin Carter, and Rory Westmaas. At the PPP Congress in March, just before the election, one of Burnham's allies moved that the leader not be elected at the annual Congress, but be chosen by the General Council after the general election. Burnham anticipated a majority in the latter body. The Congress, however, rejected the motion and Jagan remained leader with Burnham as chairman.

Deeply distressed, Burnham prepared to challenge Jagan again after the remarkable electoral victory. Although each government minister would be individually responsible for his post, the leader of the Legislative Assembly would resemble a prime minister, even if his powers were limited. Forgetting the joy of their multiracial triumph, a struggle for the spoils began. The ambitious Burnham distrusted the extreme Marxism of his associates; they, in turn, suspected him because he kept the Marxists at a distance. Burnham demanded the leadership and tried to rouse his black supporters in Georgetown. By the middle of the week, however, he recognized failure and agreed to discuss the selection of ministers.

The original plan was to nominate Cheddi and Janet Jagan, Sydney King, Dr. J. P. Lachhmansingh, Ashton

Chase, and Burnham as the six ministers. Burnham disagreed; he favored Jai Narine Singh and Dr. Hanoman-
Singh. Eventually, Janet Jagan accepted the deputy
speakership so that Jai Narine Singh, a very erratic
politician, might be included. Burnham also managed to
alter the PPP's two designees for the State Council.

After reaching agreement, the PPP members of the
Legislative Assembly marched off from party headquarters
in white sharkskin suits for the opening of the Legislative Assembly. Responsible now for governing British
Guiana, the youthful politicians ignored a fundamental
fact; they did not really accept the constitution under
which they were to administer the country. Although familiar with colonial agitators who, once elected to office, moderated their views as they accepted the responsibilities of administration, the British, however, also
had an ancient tradition of gunboats and incarceration
for colonial troublemakers.

Many of the proposals advanced by the PPP leaders
during the next few months were wise and needed, but
they were trying to storm heaven in a very short period
of time. By moving so rapidly the PPP alienated a not-
unsympathetic governor and the Churchill government in
London; it also attracted the attention of a Washington
still under the sway of the fierce communist-hunter from
Wisconsin, Senator Joseph McCarthy. Though Stalin died
in March 1953 and the Korean War ended in stalemate in
July, the cold war between the United States and the Soviet Union still dominated the international scene. The
workers' rising in East Berlin was brutally smashed by
the Russians, who also detonated their first hydrogen
bomb that year. A Republican was in the White House for
the first time in twenty years; President Dwight David
Eisenhower and his secretary of state, John Foster
Dulles, were determined to show that twenty years of,
what they called, "treason and Yalta giveaways to international communism," were at an end. Newspapers and
magazines had already sounded the alarm over the communist leanings of the PPP in British Guiana. Why battle
communism in Korea if it became established in your own
sphere of influence, especially when the Monroe Doctrine
could always justify various forms of intervention. The
Eisenhower administration was already appalled at the
sharp leftward swing of President Jacobo Arbenz Guzman
in Guatemala.

No sinister figure in Moscow seems to have manipu-
lated strings controlling communist sympathizers in
British Guiana. The men in the Kremlin were engaged in
a ruthless struggle to determine Stalin's successor;
this was no time to provoke the United States. Given
the nature of international relations, both countries
are always prepared to score off the other if a good opportunity, with little risk, presents itself. The Russian leaders, however, were unlikely to provide substan-

tial support for the Marxist leadership of the PPP if
trouble developed, for British Guiana was far from the
major security interests of the Soviet Union.

The PPP leadership failed to carefully evaluate the
strength of both their internal and external opponents.
Fundamental reform, they insisted, would commence immediately. One may admire their enthusiasm and dedication,
but they must also be assessed by the consequences of
their acts which, ultimately, brought catastrophe to
their cause. They moved quickly to implement the planks
in the party platform upon which they had stood during
the election.[13] Prompt opposition emerged in the con-
servative-dominated State Council. While the Georgetown
newspapers were hysterical, the Booker Corporation had
begun to ride with the tide, appointing the socialist-
minded Jock Campbell (now Lord Campbell of Eskan) as its
chairman in 1952. The Legislative Assembly rescinded
the ban on the entry of West Indians judged politically
subversive. But the attempt to annul the Undesirable
Publications Act stalled briefly in the State Council,
even though the Archbishop of the West Indies, Alan J.
Knight, a member of that body, concluded that the act
had been "ineffective, ill-timed, undesirable and entirely mischievous. . . . If absolute freedom is license,
then this is absolute tyranny."[14]

Even though half the Guyanese population was non-
Christian, 95 percent of the schools were run by Christian denominations. The PPP was determined to institute
governmental supervision, coupled with direct administration by local education committees; time would be
provided for religious education. Local government was
to be transformed by removing ownership and rental qualifications, introducing universal adult suffrage, and
abolishing nominated seats. Until then, three of Georgetown's twelve councillors had been nominated. In village districts, one-third of the councillors had been
nominated, while in country districts all members were
nominated.

The excise, sugar, and acreage taxes, repealed in
January 1953 to the joy of the sugar industry, were to
be restored. Higher taxes on the mining industries were
proposed. Committees were established to scrutinize the
problems of domestic workers, to revise the workmen's
compensation laws, and to plan for the establishment of
a machine pool for farmers. More scholarships were to
be provided for university study.

So far as the PPP was concerned, this was the platform on which they had been elected. There was nothing
Russian about it; it was simply an attempt to provide
justice for the people of British Guiana. While the
conservative forces in society had been indignant at the
PPP's refusal to appropriate funds to send representatives to meet with the Queen when she visited Jamaica
(the PPP argued that too much had already been spent on

the coronation), they were even more profoundly disturbed
by an amendment to the Rice Farmers (Security of Tenure)
Act of 1945. That act provided penalties for both landlords and tenants who did not practice good estate management. The tenant could be evicted for his deficiencies. If the landlord neglected his responsibilities,
however, the tenant could do little. There was no effective penalty for the landlord who failed to provide
proper drainage facilities for his tenants. The PPP
rushed a measure through the Legislative Assembly enabling the government-appointed district commissioner to
inform landlords that itemized repairs must be completed
in a specified period of time. If they were not, the
district commissioner could authorize the repairs and
send the bill to the landlord. If the bill was not hon-
ored, the land would be sold.

Unfortunately, the PPP used its majority in the
Legislative Assembly to suspend the rules and to push
the bill through all its readings in one day. This hasty action occurred just as a Select Committee prepared
to present a report on the subject.[15] The move seemed
to be a massive attack upon property rights, and Lionel
Luckhoo, member of the State Council, denounced it as an
"invasion and infringment of the personal rights of the
subject" when it arrived before that body for its second
reading. Defeated by a vote of six to two, only the two
PPP-sponsored members voted affirmatively.[16]

This proposed law was linked to a PPP plan to set
up a Land Authority that would investigate land utiliza-
tion throughout British Guiana. Already refusing to
grant leases of Crown lands to landlords with large
holdings, the PPP leadership wanted to expropriate the
unused lands maintained by the great sugar estates.

As might have been expected, it was over the sugar
industry that the confrontation between the governor and
the PPP first began to heat up. Dr. Lachhmansingh,
GIWU's president, was also one of the six PPP ministers.
Determined to replace the MPCA with GIWU, the PPP leaders
were sure of winning a representation election, since
the MPCA had little support. The entire trade union
movement of British Guiana was suddenly immersed in cold
war politics. The approximately thirty trade unions
were characterized by considerable overlap, insufficient
dues-paying members, and too few rank-and-file leaders.
The British Guiana Trades Union Council (BGTUC) had
joined the World Federation of Trade Unions (WFTU) when
it was established in 1945. In 1949, the noncommunist
and anticommunist trade unions departed to form the International Confederation of Free Trade Unions (ICFTU),
and the BGTUC left the WFTU but failed to join the ICFTU.
The MPCA objected to the support the BGTUC gave to GIWU,
and in 1952 it resigned from the BGTUC and joined the
ICFTU. By late 1952, the BGTUC also tried to affiliate
with the ICFTU, but a visit to Guyana from the strongly

anticommunist Serafino Romualdi, director of the Inter-
American Regional Workers Organization and close friend
of the United States trade union chief, George Meany,
led to the rejection of the application. Romualdi met
with Lionel Luckhoo, then president of the MPCA, and
Luckhoo convinced Romualdi the BGTUC was dominated by
Jagan-style communists.[17] The MPCA became a key element
in subverting the PPP.

The PPP knew the sugar workers preferred GIWU to
the MPCA; a Labour Relations Bill allowing a free and
fair vote to the sugar workers was all that was needed.
At the end of August, a strike swept across almost all
the sugar estates. Ostensibly, the strikers wanted
higher wages and better working conditions; in reality,
it was a battle to the death between GIWU, supported by
the PPP, and the company union, the MPCA. The conflict
lasted for twenty-five days and eventually brought out
sympathetic strikers from other unions. Dr. Lachhmansingh's position was ambiguous; a member of the PPP government, he was also president of GIWU. A moderate, he
had reservations about the strike and was prepared to
accept a major measure of appeasement from the Sugar
Producers Association when it offered to recognize GIWU
as the representative of the field workers, with the
MPCA continuing to speak for the factory workers. This
proposal was a major concession which Dr. Lachhmansingh
was inclined to accept. But the militants urged resistance, and the cane cutters did not resume work until 24
September when the PPP ministers produced their Labour
Relations Bill.[18]

The strike intensified the atmosphere of crisis and
hysteria throughout the colony. Conservative groups in
British Guiana were outraged that Dr. Lachhmansingh was
leading the strike as GIWU's chieftain while remaining
minister of health and housing in the governor's Executive Council. Uncertainty about the government's future
policies led some people to ship their money abroad. On
10 September, Cheddi Jagan promised not to freeze depos-
its in Post Office Savings Banks. Rumors began to spread
about the imminent suspension of the constitution.
Speaking on the same day as Jagan, Forbes Burnham thundered: "I hear the pratings in certain places about the
possibility of our present Constitution being taken from
us. Perhaps, who knows, that may be in their minds but
I believe I am speaking for the Majority Party when I
say that any such attempt will be met with as much force
as is necessary in the circumstances." The gallery
roared its approval.[19]

Meeting on 24 September 1953, moderate members of
the Legislative Assembly received Dr. Lachhmansingh's
happy news that the sugar strike was over and that the
annual sugar quota could still be achieved. Then came
an unexpected disclosure: Ashton Chase, minister of labour, announced that the sugar workers only returned to

work when the government promised them an opportunity to
choose a new union bargaining agent. Chase demanded the
suspension of standing orders so that this urgent measure could pass the Legislative Assembly, like the Rice
Tenants Bill, in one day. The Speaker, Sir Eustace
Woolford, rejected the motion, arguing that the bill was
controversial and required lengthy discussion rather
than a hasty push. He opined that it was "the most important piece of domestic legislation in my time." An
irritated Burnham remonstrated that the original passage
of the Undesirable Publications Bill had been rammed
through under the old constitution. Speaker Woolford
was adamant; whereupon, the PPP members, including the
ministers, promptly marched from the Assembly. Bedlam
enveloped the gallery. W. O. R. (Rudy) Kendall, a member of the New Democratic party was minority leader in
the Assembly. An immensely popular black leader from
New Amsterdam, Kendall denounced the PPP withdrawal,
shuddered at the noise and commotion, and shouted, "I
say now on behalf of all right-thinking responsible persons in this country, that the quicker this Constitution
is taken away from us the better it will be."[20]

A few days before (21 September) in the State Council, Archbishop Knight, disturbed over the violence on
the estates, had moved that the participation of government ministers "in promoting and sustaining this strike"
was a "grave danger to the Constitution . . . a direct
threat to the peace and security of the citizens of the
Colony." The archbishop requested the colonial secretary "after due enquiry to take such action as he may
see fit to ensure confidence in the Government." Knight
argued that he had never seen a situation "in which certain Ministers of the Crown not only act in a political
manner as between the disputants in an industrial dispute but themselves have been actively engaged in permitting and fostering the strike."

Approved by a vote of six to two, the archbishop's
motion was supported by several who still hoped the constitution would not be suspended. Noting the immaturity
of the PPP ministers, R. B. Gajraj still believed that
"youth must have its chance." Some "splendid ideas" had
been advanced; "the fault lies in their methods of approach." Only the two PPP members of the State Council,
U. A. Fingall and G. L. Robertson, voted against the
archbishop's motion, which they felt was based upon
false rumors; the working people of British Guiana were
only struggling for their just rights.[21]

When the Legislative Assembly met again on 29 September, the Speaker regretted the walkout by ministers
of the Crown. It was a dreadful precedent; only Burnham
had bowed properly to the Chair at the moment of departure. Before packed public galleries and with demonstrations taking place outside, debate began on the Labour
Relations Bill. The PPP argued the bill was patterned

after the Wagner Labor Relations Act in the United
States. While slightly more advanced than the Wagner
Act, it was certainly not as radical as its enemies contended. The latter denounced it as "vicious, wicked"
slave legislation that would destroy individual rights;
"no capitalists would come in if you have a law like
this."[22]

Although giving considerable authority to the minister of labour, the primary purpose of the bill was to
establish machinery for fair collective bargaining elections. It also established penalties for employers
guilty of unfair practices or who refused to recognize
certified unions. A union needed only 51 percent of the
vote to be recognized as a bargaining agent, but a new
union could only replace an old one by receiving 65 percent of the vote.

The heart of the matter was not a theoretical dispute about trade unionism, but whether the MPCA would be
ejected by GIWU. Absolutely convinced that GIWU would
win, the PPP was prepared to accept the 65 percent figure rather than a mere 51 percent. The MPCA and SPA denounced the bill because they also knew GIWU would win.

By this time, domestic and international pressures
were building to the boiling point. Oliver Lyttelton
(later Viscount Chandos) had been appointed colonial
secretary by Winston Churchill in 1951. A great indus-
trialist who had entered political life during World War
II, Lyttelton would have preferred the chancellorship of
the Exchequer. His problems were many: Mau Mau in Kenya,
Communists in Malaya, the Central African Federation,
Nkrumah in the Gold Coast, and now, on top of the major
crises, came British Guiana and the alarm expressed by
the United States.

The crucial figure, Governor Alfred Savage, felt
overwhelmed by the hostile demonstrations and the deterioration of parliamentary life; apparently the situation was beyond redemption. He convinced Churchill and
Lyttelton that action was required immediately and, on
the eve of the annual conference of the Conservative
party, the British Lion judged that, at least in one
part of the world, Palmerstonian-style gunboats could
still do the job. Lyttelton reports in the three pages
alloted to British Guiana in his memoirs--while chapters
are spent on Malaya, the Central African Federation, and
Kenya--that he received "grave reports" in September
that the PPP was "trying to use the machinery of democracy to destroy democracy and substitute rule by one
party on the Communist model." The intelligence services had reported that "riots and bloodshed would soon
break out" and that there was a "plot to burn down the
wooden capital."[23]

On Sunday morning, 4 October 1953, Cheddi Jagan was
awakened on a typically bright and sunny day in Georgetown by a friend informing him that British troops were

on the way to suspend the constitution. He found this
rumor absurd, since the sugar strike had ended and there
was no reason for intervention. Cheddi Jagan's infor-
mant, however, was correct; on that very day Oliver Lyttelton, Sir David Maxwell Fyfe, the home secretary, and
Sir Sydney Abrahams, senior legal assistant to the Colonial Office, journeyed to see the queen at Balmoral
Castle. When they returned, the home secretary reported
it was only a normal visit from some members of the
Privy Council. It may have been "normal" for the British politicians and civil servants, but it was abnormal
for the people of British Guiana since the queen signed
the Order-in-Council suspending the constitution of
British Guiana and dispatching the necessary troops.

It is not difficult to understand why, considering
the temper of the time, the British government took this
action. British troops were fighting communists in Malaya, Governor Savage feared for the safety of the entire English community in Georgetown, the United States
government was agitated over the deteriorating situation,
and the violence in British Guiana might affect the entire British Caribbean and impede the planning for a
federation of the British West Indies.

Despite the rumors flying through Georgetown, the
Legislative Assembly met on Monday, 5 October, and the
second reading of the Labour Relations Bill was passed by
a vote of sixteen to six. Cheddi Jagan requested, unsuccessfully, an evening session to continue the committee stage of the bill since Ashton Chase, the minister
of labour, was scheduled to visit Brazil.[24]

On Tuesday, the BBC announced that communist activities in British Guiana necessitated sending military
and naval units. Troops were being sent from Jamaica on
the cruiser Superb, the frigates Bigbury Bay and Burg-
head Bay were steaming from Bermuda to British Guiana,
and the aircraft carrier Implacable was due from Great
Britain at the end of the week. But no one was absolutely certain how far the British government would go.
John Gutch, the chief secretary and principal adviser to
Governor Savage, had responded by telephone to a London
reporter on Sunday. While conceding that there was
"still unrest on some sugar estates," Gutch concluded
that "we have not asked for a cruiser to be sent"; and,
the Daily Mail reported on 7 October that it had spoken
by radio-telephone to the deputy police commissioner,
who had sounded "calm and unperturbed" when he stated,
"There are no demonstrations, there is no general strike,
there is nothing abnormal happening here whatsoever."[25]

When the Legislative Assembly met again on Wednesday, 7 October, Cheddi Jagan attempted to raise the matter of troop movements. He acknowledged a "constitutional crisis," but this crisis existed only because the
PPP wished to change the constitution through peaceful
means. Intimidation and violence were excluded; British

troops would only provoke trouble and make matters worse. The Speaker refused to entertain Jagan's motion since insufficient notice had been given and there was no proof of Jagan's assertions about British troops and ships. Debate then resumed on the Labour Relations Bill. On the following day, Cheddi Jagan, in great distress, demanded once again that the rules be suspended so that his motion against British intervention could be debated. The Speaker admitted seeing troops, but assumed they were present for reasons of "peace and security." He could not himself say why they had been sent, but was sure that the governor would soon inform them. Jagan's motion could be debated on the following day.[26]

The Legislative Assembly never met again; on Friday, 9 October, John Gutch, the chief secretary, announced that the constitution "must be suspended to prevent Communist subversion of the Government and a dangerous crisis both in public order and in economic affairs." Gutch accused the PPP leaders of being willing to "go to any lengths, including violence, to turn British Guiana into a Communist state." The governor, therefore, assumed emergency powers and fired the six PPP ministers. "Armed forces have landed to support the police and to prevent any public disorders, which might be fomented by Communist supporters."[27] All political meetings were cancelled, and police descended upon the house of a pajama-clad Jagan and confiscated his papers. For the Guyanese, this day would be remembered as "Black Friday." Try though he may, however, the correspondent for the Daily Herald could find only one crisis really worrying the local people--a cricket match with Trinidad.[28]

Though some of the sensational tabloids wrote with gusto of an attempted communist seizure of power in British Guiana, the more respectable newspapers and journals waited to see what evidence would be produced.[29] The Conservative government in Great Britain had additional time to prepare a White Paper explaining its action, since Parliament was in recess due to the annual party congresses. Moderate leaders of the British Labour party cautiously criticized Churchill's action, arguing that other measures could have been tried before suspending the constitution. A debate was finally arranged for 22 October, and Jagan and Burnham prepared to embark for London to present their case to the British public. Numerous roadblocks made departure from British Guiana very difficult; Trinidad, Barbados, Jamaica, and the United States would not allow them entry. As a result, United States, French, and British airlines refused to sell them tickets. Surinam, however, permitted them to pass through the country, but not to stay overnight. This restriction forced them to charter a privately owned airplane at great expense in order to make connections with a KLM flight to London. Bad weather caused further complications and they arrived in London just as the debate was due to begin.[30]

Jagan and Burnham presented their case: British Guiana was quiet, Georgetown was not in flames, and the PPP, despite all the bombastic rhetoric, had counselled the people of British Guiana to be calm as the British troops disembarked. No resistance had developed, and an attempt to organize a general strike had failed. How indeed could the colonial secretary justify the extreme step of suspending the constitution? Did the decision to suspend the constitution really avert a communist seizure of power and a reign of terror? How, Jagan and Burnham argued, could a few communists in British Guiana ever accomplish such a feat?

The eyes of the world turned in the direction of Westminster. A legally elected Legislative Assembly had been ousted by a government which represented the Mother of Parliaments. Britain claimed to be a part of the "free" world, locked in a titanic conflict with the "undemocratic" Soviet Union. But now Britain had arbitrarily overruled the wishes of the people of British Guiana. Were two different standards being applied, or could the Conservative government prove both the wisdom and the morality of the action it had taken?

NOTES

1. _Report of the British Guiana Constitutional Commission_, Colonial Office, No. 280, 1951.

2. See Raymond T. Smith, "Social Stratification, Cultural Pluralism and Integration in West Indian Societies," in S. Lewis and T. G. Mathews, eds., _Caribbean Integration_ (Rio Piedras, Puerto Rico, 1967), pp. 226-58. This book is composed of papers delivered at the Third Caribbean Scholars' Conference held in Guyana in 1966.

3. Address by the governor, Sir Charles Woolley, to the Fourth Session of the Fourth Legislative Council of British Guiana, 19 October 1951.

4. Jagan, _The West on Trial_, p. 100.

5. See Colin A. Hughes, "The British Guiana General Elections, 1953," _Parliamentary Affairs_, 7 (Spring 1954), pp. 213-20.

6. Jagan, _The West on Trial_, p. 106.

7. Nath, _Indians in Guyana_, pp. 201-3, 209-10.

8. Smith, _British Guiana_, pp. 169-71; and Despres, _Cultural Pluralism_, pp. 201-2.

9. See Gordon Lewis, _The Growth of the Modern West Indies_ (New York, 1968), pp. 226-56.

10. Jagan, _The West on Trial_, pp. 107-21.

11. Smith, _British Guiana_, pp. 173-75; and Premdas, "First Mass-Based Multi-Racial Party," p. 15.

12. The following account is based upon Jagan, _The West on Trial_, pp. 116-18; and Peter Simms, _Trouble in Guyana_ (London, 1966), pp. 105-10.

13. For a defense of the PPP's activities while in office in 1953 see Cheddi Jagan, Forbidden Freedom: The Story of British Guiana (London, 1954); and Ashton Chase, 133 Days Towards Freedom in Guyana (Georgetown, 1954).

14. As quoted in Jagan, The West on Trial, pp. 120-21.

15. Debates of the British Guiana House of Assembly, 4 September 1953.

16. Debates of the British Guiana State Council, 23 September 1953.

17. Serafino Romualdi, Presidents and Peons (New York, 1967), pp. 345-48.

18. Chase, Trade Unionism in Guyana, pp. 202-11.

19. Debates of the British Guiana House of Assembly, 10 September 1953.

20. Ibid., 24 September 1953.

21. Debates of the British Guiana State Council, 21 September 1953.

22. Debates of the British Guiana House of Assembly, 29 September 1953.

23. Viscount Chandos (Oliver Lyttelton), The Memoirs of Lord Chandos (London, 1962), pp. 427-30.

24. Debates of the British Guiana House of Assembly, 5 October 1953.

25. Jagan, The West on Trial, pp. 124-27; and Simms, Trouble in Guyana, pp. 111-25. The author wishes to acknowledge an illuminating interview with Sir John Gutch at the Royal Commonwealth Society on 13 December 1977.

26. Debates of the British Guiana House of Assembly, 7 October 1953 and 8 October 1953.

27. See the Colonial Report, British Guiana, 1953 (London, 1955).

28. For local coverage in a paper hostile to the PPP see the reports in The Daily Argosy. See also Ronald V. Sires, "British Guiana: Suspension of the Constitution," Western Political Quarterly, 7 (December, 1954), pp. 554-69.

29. See The Economist, 10 October 1953, pp. 87-88; idem, 17 October 1953, pp. 155-56; idem, 24 October 1953, p. 228; The New Statesman, 17 October 1953, pp. 449-54; and Sam Pope Brewer, "Bitterness in Guyana's Sugar Bowl," The New York Times Magazine, 1 November 1953, pp. 1-6.

30. Jagan, The West on Trial, pp. 127-28.

4
Strife and Division

Stung by criticism that it had overreacted to events in British Guiana, the Colonial Office issued a defensive White Paper just prior to the arrival of Jagan and Burnham and the opening of debate in the House of Commons.[1] The White Paper contended that the PPP ministers had neglected "the true welfare of the Colony and threatened its progress as an orderly state." British Guiana had been hurtling to a "collapse" that could have "seriously endangered the economic life of the country."

The White Paper stated that, neglecting their constitutional obligations, the PPP ministers had fomented strikes for political ends, attempted to oust established trade unions by legislative action, removed the ban on the entry of West Indian communists, and flooded the territory with communist literature. The PPP was also accused of misusing appointments to boards and committees, spreading racial hatred, planning to secularize Church schools and to rewrite textbooks with a political bias, ignoring their administrative duties, undermining the loyalty of the police, trying to gain control of the civil service, and making threats of violence to achieve their goals. "Each one of these acts judged separately was serious enough, and the cumulative effect was disastrous. Viewed in the light of the communist connexions of Ministers, their aim was unmistakable." The White Paper concluded that the PPP ministers had

> . . . shown by their speeches and writings that they are
> zealots in the cause of communism and have demonstrated
> by their actions that their objective is to impose a to-
> talitarian control on the PPP, the Trade Unions, the po-
> lice force, the youth organizations and the State itself.
> All the Ministers have supported the extremists, have
> shown that they were prepared to be guided by them and
> cannot, therefore, evade responsibility for what has oc-
> curred.[2]

Starting the debate in the House of Commons on 22

October 1953, Oliver Lyttelton, the colonial secretary, skillfully reminded his audience that many prominent West Indian leaders, Grantley Adams of Barbados and both Alexander Bustamante and Norman Manley of Jamaica, had supported the British government's action. Grantley Adams regretted the suspension of the constitution, but he would "deplore far more the continuance of a Government that put Communist ideology before the good of the people."

Lyttelton conceded that the suspension damaged the commitment shared by all British political parties to give "the peoples in the Colonial Territories an increasing responsibility for the management of their own affairs"; but, the British government retained responsibility for insuring "that peace and order, good government, and conditions of social and economic advance are promoted." Irrefutable evidence demonstrated that a "deadly design" had existed "to turn British Guiana into a totalitarian state dominated by Communist ideas, whose whole political, industrial and social life would be concentrated in the hands and in the power of one party."[3]

Hoping to be fully exonerated when James Griffiths rose to speak, Burnham and Jagan were dismayed when the former Labour colonial secretary expressed his grievous disappointment at the great opportunity "missed" by the PPP. Though British Guiana had been "shamefully neglected" in the past, there was still no reason to permit the establishment of a totalitarian regime. Could it be proven that the PPP had planned a communist-style seizure of power? Griffiths retained bad memories of the Conservative party manufacturing "red scares" about the British labor movement; however, after talking with Jagan and Burnham and despite their protestations, Griffiths acknowledged that they were probably "associated with communist organisations in the industrial and political field." The actions and policies of the PPP resembled those "which have led in other countries to the establishment of a totalitarian Communist State."

Why, though, when other less extreme steps were available, had the constitution been suspended? Was it not true, Griffiths inquired, "that the police, and all matters of defence, are in the hands of the ex-officio officers responsible to the Governor and to the Secretary of State and not to the People's Progressive Party or the elected Ministers?" The most serious charge resided in Paragraph Thirty of the White Paper; it alleged "a conspiracy to set fire to business property and the residences of prominent Europeans." Jagan and Burnham had denied these charges to Griffiths. Having made the accusations, the British government was obligated "in fairness to the men, hostile as I am to their views and disliking as I do the things they do," to bring them to trial so that sworn evidence might resolve the issue of guilt or innocence. Would it not have been sufficient

for Lyttelton to have dispatched additional troops without eliminating constitutional government? There were
"ample safeguards in the Constitution" that might have
been employed before the ultimate act of suspension.
The colonial secretary could have invited the extremists
to Whitehall for a talk; he might have travelled to
British Guiana for a personal inspection. Griffiths,
despite his distaste for Jagan and Burnham, demanded the
resignation of the colonial secretary; for this incident was another in a series of failures which blanketed
Kenya, Malaya, and Central Africa. Griffiths' formal
motion was rather tepid, and hardly pleasing to Jagan
and Burnham. It criticized the government, but it also
"deplored" the actions of the PPP leaders as elaborated
in the White Paper and condemned "methods tending to the
establishment of a totalitarian regime in a British colony." Obviously, the Labour leadership sympathized with
the evidence in the White Paper. It only objected to
the conclusion: the suspension of the constitution.[4]

     As the debate continued and Labour's leftists joined
the fray, Jagan and Burnham could muster a smile. Here
they finally found some support for the policies they
had pursued. Only very few members, however, deviated
from the theme struck by Griffiths--that the governor
ought to have tried a number of his reserved powers before suspending the constitution.

     Winding up for Labour, former Prime Minister Cle-
ment Attlee referred to the PPP ministers as "Communist
stooges." "It is quite clear that they speak the language of the Communists and they feed on Communist literature." Having garnered only 51 percent of the total
vote in April, could, Attlee asked, the PPP win a new
election? To Attlee, the PPP seemed to be losing support because of its radical tactics. "They had fulfilled none of their promises. . . . Therefore, the important thing was not to give them a rallying cry." But
this is precisely what the British government had succeeded in doing. "A possible rallying cry for them is
nationalism, or anti-colonialism, and one is also provided if they, as Communists, are left to appear as the
champions of democracy against alien rule." The government had failed to prove any subversion of the police,
or that Georgetown might have been burned to the ground.
It was unfortunate that new elections had not been tried.

     Attlee harbored no illusions about Jagan and Burn-
ham; conversations with both had persuaded him that
"they were either Communists or Communist dupes." Troops
may very well have been necessary, but why suspend the
constitution? "Our indictment is that there were other
methods: that the Government brought in the last thing
they should have done and that they brought it in first."[5]

     Concluding the debate for the government, Harold
Macmillan, minister of housing and local government, argued: "It may be true, and I think it is true, that none

of these separate accusations against the People's Progressive Party leaders could be held sufficient in itself to justify the course which Her Majesty's Government have had to adopt; but surely, taken together, they are really conclusive." Macmillan brought out that British Guiana's constitution did not permit the governor to remove the PPP ministers from his Executive Council. Dissolving the Legislative Assembly would have placed the governor in peril since a new electoral campaign would then have revolved around this issue rather than around the policies of the PPP ministers.

> The Governor would in fact have announced in advance that he was unwilling and unable to co-operate with the leaders of one of the parties, and that the larger party. That would be the most complete interference with the whole spirit of the Constitution.

Macmillan affirmed that there had been no alternative to suspension; now a Royal Commission must be sent to investigate and report. As expected, the Conservatives won the debate by a vote of 294 to 256.[6]

Sitting in the gallery, Cheddi Jagan was scandalized by Lyttelton's forthright denial of pressure from the United States: "I might add on this point that no representations of any kind were received from the United States Government before Her Majesty's Government made their decision." Jagan did not believe him: "The troops came to our shores not because of disorder but to quell anticipated disorder after our dismissal and the suspension of our Constitution." He was absolutely convinced there were two main reasons for the suspension of the constitution.

> First, if we had remained in office more than a few months the position of the Governor and the whole constitutional machinery would have been thoroughly exposed in the eyes of the people. Second, American pressure must obviously have been exerted on the British government.[7]

Several constitutional clauses, Jagan noted, would have embarrassed the governor. Although the State Council could delay legislation for one year, the constitution allowed the governor to summon a joint meeting of both Houses to act immediately if a bill was judged to be of vital importance. The PPP ministers had already indicated to the governor that they would request joint meetings for the Labour Relations Bill if it was voted down in the State Council. A refusal by the governor would have exposed him as an enemy of a recently elected government; agreement would mean victory for the PPP as it could outvote its opponents by twenty to sixteen. Anticommunist hysteria in the United States and the governor's apprehensions, therefore, had buried the PPP government.

It does appear that the British government acted much too hastily; numerous alternative tactics might have been pursued under the governor's reserve powers. Admittedly, the PPP ministers could be obnoxious, but that does not justify suspension of the constitution. Three years later, Cheddi Jagan conceded: "We allowed our zeal to run away with us, we became swollen-headed, pompous, bombastic."[8]

The British government's inconclusive evidence that the PPP was conspiring to burn Georgetown was not even uncovered until several days after the decision to suspend the constitution. Why, then, destroy constitutional government in British Guiana if there were no plans for violence and a Communist-controlled seizure of power? A subtle mix of three key elements brought the decision to intervene: overreaction on the part of Governor Savage, the British government's determination to show the entire empire and the world that it retained the capacity to act, and pressure from the United States which saw British Guiana--like Guatemala--marching to the left.

President Eisenhower and Secretary of State Dulles had been delighted when the Central Intelligence Agency toppled a nationalistic Iranian prime minister, the troublesome Mohammed Mossadegh, during the summer of 1953. Even closer to the United States was the left-leaning regime of Colonel Arbenz in Guatemala. Colonel Arbenz was veering even further in the direction of radical change than his reform-minded predecessor, Juan José Arévalo, for both men followed long years of reactionary dictatorship. Arbenz had his eyes upon the enormous unused acres of the United States-owned United Fruit Company. Hysterical company officials looked to the Eisenhower administration for comfort as Guatemala started to expropriate their land. Unable to obtain further assistance from the United States, Arbenz turned towards Eastern Europe for aid and weapons. Could this action be the start of a trend in the American sphere of influence, in spite of the Monroe Doctrine which had been redesigned to give the United States a dominant position in the hemisphere? And now, added to Guatemala where the CIA was already plotting with conservative military men to depose Arbenz, the United States had to confront what appeared to be a communist regime in British Guiana.[9]

Was there anything to really cause alarm about British Guiana? Here the answer is certainly negative. Even one of the PPP's more hostile critics, the editor of The Daily Argosy, acknowledged that there was no "organized plan" for a revolution. Seemingly, Jagan and Burnham wanted a "political and constitutional crisis" to force new elections and give them an even greater mandate from the people.[10]

The PPP ministers had been noisy agitators, but

they appeared to be settling down when fired after less
than six months in office. Other reserve powers ought
to have been tried before suspending the constitution;
no one ever proved that the PPP planned to burn Georgetown. Tragically, the PPP ministers failed to try a
slightly slower pace. If they had not insisted upon
"storming heaven" immediately and righting the wrongs of
three hundred years in six months, their achievements
could have been quite remarkable. Most of their proposed legislation was needed and necessary; there was
nothing specifically "communistic," or designed to turn
British Guiana into a totalitarian state. Unnecessary
and unfortunate, the suspension of the constitution led
irreversibly to racial catastrophe.

Affirming its commitment to "the promotion of democratic self-government in colonial territories," the National Executive of the British Labour party also demonstrated its traditional anticommunism by narrowly re-
solving that it would be "inadvisable for local Parties
to provide a platform for PPP speakers or to cooperate
with other bodies (which might well be Communist dominated) in supporting them." Jagan and Burnham were appalled, though Jagan was happy to record support from the
British Communist party and its newspaper, The Daily
Worker. The Bevanite weekly, Tribune, was also sympathetic, as was Aneurin Bevan himself and his wife,
Jennie Lee. Bevan commented that the Conservatives were
seemingly saying to the colonies: "You are free to have
whatever government you like as long as it is the kind
of government we like."[11]

Expressing support for the MPCA, the British Trades
Union Congress also denounced the PPP for associating
with the World Federation of Trade Unions, and for its
contacts behind the Iron Curtain. Ian Mikardo, however,
a left-wing Labour member of Parliament, disagreed with
the British TUC and accused the MPCA of supporting "capitalism in general and colonial employers in particular."[12]

Distressed by their chilly reception in Great Britain, Jagan and Burnham journeyed to India to receive
Nehru's blessing before returning to British Guiana.
When they finally flew home in February 1954, they found
the PPP shattered as a consequence of the governor's
emergency powers. Key leaders, such as Sydney King,
Rory Westmaas, and Martin Carter, had just been released
from detention camps. Travel restrictions were imposed
upon many PPP members; it was almost impossible to publish pamphlets or to hold meetings. Violators of the
emergency regulations were fined or jailed. A number of
PPP-controlled organizations were declared illegal and a
police lock closed PPP headquarters in May.

While the Labour party had disappointed the PPP
leaders, they were consoled by Labour's almost unanimous
insistence that the Conservative government bring formal
charges in court against those responsible for the

alleged criminal acts. Lyttelton wailed: "The difficulty in the present state of intimidation is to get the
actual witnesses to testify in open court." Embarrassed
by the failure to prosecute anyone, Lyttelton took refuge behind the proposition that this decision was for
the attorney-general of British Guiana. Apparently
knowing there would be no prosecutions for the allega-
tions in the White Paper, the colonial secretary reiterated, again and again, the difficulty in obtaining witnesses prepared to testify in open court.[13]

When British Guiana was discussed in the House of
Commons in early December, Labour members again bemoaned
the governor's failure to employ the reserve powers em-
bedded in the constitution. The colonial secretary
agreed that the incompetence of the PPP ministers in office had drained away some of their support, but he
grudgingly conceded "that since the PPP got a very large
majority and there was no other organised party, I think
that all the evidence so far as one can judge, and it is
a matter of judgment, is that the same party would have
been elected again." A major flaw in the suspended constitution, Lyttelton opined, had been the absence of an
official majority on the Executive Council.[14]

Fenner Brockway, a staunch Labour left-winger, disagreed thoroughly with the government's action. Only
fools, he insisted, could fail to see that the suspension of the constitution would solidify support for the
PPP.

> Foolish utterances--yes; foolish actions--yes; but the
> only evidence of a coup or of any attempt to overthrow
> democratic self-government was this arson plot, the evi-
> dence of which was not in the hands of the Government
> when the decision to suspend the Constitution took place.
> When charges of that kind are to be included in a White
> Paper for the very grave step of suspension of a Consti-
> tution; they should not be included if the Government
> cannot bring the men against whom those charges are lev-
> elled to public trial, so that they can give their an-
> swer.[15]

Brockway's comment took place during a debate to establish an interim government for British Guiana. Despite
their mixed feelings about the PPP, the vast majority of
the British Labour party detested the retrograde constitution to be foisted upon the colony.

The Labour party failed, however, to prevent the
establishment of an interim government for British Guiana entirely nominated by the Crown. An Executive Council was composed of the three ex-officio members (chief
secretary, financial secretary, and attorney-general)
plus seven nominated members; four of the nominated members were given ministerial portfolios. The three ex-
officio members and twenty-four nominated members became

the new Legislative Assembly. The colony's elite rushed
to man the dikes, sighing contentedly now that the liberal constitution had disappeared and the PPP was abused
and harassed. Among those serving in the interim government were solid members of the bureaucracy and the
bourgeoisie such as Frank McDavid, P. A. Cummings,
W. O. R. Kendall, G. A. C. Farnum, R. B. Gajraj, James
Ramphal, Rupert Tello, and Lionel Luckhoo.[16]

When this debate occurred in the House of Commons
in December, a Royal Commission had already been appointed to investigate the crisis and to make recommendations. Chaired by Sir James Robertson, a senior Colonial Office official, the commission also included Sir
Donald Jackson, a Guyanese jurist who was chief justice
of the Windward and Leeward Islands, and George Woodcock,
assistant general secretary of the British Trades Union
Congress. The commission arrived in Georgetown in early
January 1954 and remained for two months, hearing witnesses and travelling throughout the country. Its final
report appeared in September.

Although the PPP leadership refused to testify, the
commission members still insisted the PPP could be evaluated on the basis of its past and present activities
and publications.[17] Referring to the people of British
Guiana as "politically immature," the commission concluded that "no doubt" existed of a "very powerful communist element" in the PPP. It did attempt to distin-
guish between the communist Jagans and their followers,
Sydney King, Martin Carter, Rory Westmaas, and Brindley
Benn, and the moderate democratic socialists led by
Burnham, who did not toe the "party line." Acknowledging that Burnham's differences with Jagan were more racial and personal than political, the commission was
nonetheless impressed by his nonaffiliation with the international communist movement. Numerous moderate supporters of the PPP testified that "Burnham ought to have
taken a much stronger line than he did in opposition to
the more blatantly communist activities of the Jagans
and their supporters."

The commission also concluded that neither Ashton
Chase nor Clinton Wong should be branded as communists.
Conceding that the three ex-officio ministers were "im-
bued with the somewhat cautious traditions and standards
of the British Colonial Service," the commission doubted
they would sabotage the proposals of the PPP ministers.
Once the PPP leaders accepted ministerial posts, they
had implicitly agreed to enforce the constitution they
had denounced; if they harbored doubts and reservations,
they ought not to have accepted office. In essence, the
Royal Commission endorsed the British government's suspension of the constitution. So far as they were concerned, the Labour Relations Bill was not like the Wagner Act. It gave far too much power to the minister of
labour: "The Bill's omissions are as startling as its

contents."

The commission was convinced that, by 24 September, "the extremists in the PPP had managed completely to outmaneuver their more reasonable colleagues and had taken complete control of the Party." The Labour Relations Bill, deliberately designed to provoke a crisis, had generated "turmoil" in British Guiana by the end of the month. This turmoil led to a run on the banks and economic insecurity at a time when foreign investment was desperately required. The commission sadly concluded that "conditions for sound constitutional advance do not exist in British Guiana today." The report added that, although a majority of the people wished to move toward self-government, there was no grasp of "economic realities." In rather patronizing terms, the report observed that, in the past, slaves and indentured laborers had expected everything to be provided for them. This expectation was, unfortunately, still the case, and more hard work and self-reliance were required. In all likelihood, the commission speculated, the very popular PPP would win new elections; therefore, elections must be deferred. The PPP extremists remained the "sole barrier" to progress.

The report of the Robertson Commission was followed by several appendices showing the communist links of the PPP leaders. There were quotations from <u>Thunder</u> and other PPP publications, plus a list of communist literature which had been distributed by the PPP. Although little proof was presented to substantiate the accusation that the PPP was planning to burn Georgetown, the commission still asserted that some validity should be granted to the accounts provided by informers about this plan. But they also conceded that the decision to suspend the constitution had been taken two to three days before the arson plot was added to the list of charges against the PPP.

Far more devastating than its justification of British intervention, the Robertson Commission exacerbated racial discord between Africans and East Indians, as well as promoted a split between communists and democratic socialists in the PPP. The Waddington report recognized racial problems, but had been optimistic about the present and the future. Robertson differed:

> Education is now eagerly sought by Indian parents for
> their children: many Indians have important shares in
> the economic and commercial life of the Colony; the rice
> trade is largely in their hands from production to mar-
> keting. Their very success in these spheres has begun
> to awaken the fears of the African section of the popula-
> tion, and it cannot be denied that since India received
> her independence in 1947 there has been a marked self-
> assertiveness amongst Indians in British Guiana. Gui-
> anese of African extraction were not afraid to tell us

that many Indians in British Guiana looked forward to
the day when British Guiana would be not a part of the
British Commonwealth but of an East Indian Empire. The
result has been a tendency for racial tension to increase, and we have reluctantly reached the conclusion
that the amity "with which" as the Waddington Report
said, "people of all races live side by side in the villages" existed more in the past; today the relationships
are strained; they present an outward appearance which
masks feelings of suspicion and distrust. We do not altogether share the confidence of the Waddington Commission that a comprehensive loyalty to British Guiana can
be stimulated among peoples of such diverse origins.
There is little evidence of any coalescing process in
inter-marriage between the Indian and African components
of the population.

These conclusions certainly did not reflect the
quite remarkable agreement on issues that had brought
blacks and East Indians together in the PPP. The commission also encouraged division by distinguishing between the communist and socialist sectors of the PPP;
Burnham was designated, despite his flamboyant rhetoric,
the leader of the "democratic socialists." Such statements increased the pressure on Burnham--if it was re-
quired--to try, once again, for the leadership.

Writing for the magazine Encounter, Dr. Rita Hinden,
one of the three authors of the Waddington constitution
and a long-time advocate of the rights of the colonial
people within the British Empire, remembered how disturbed she, Harlow, and Waddington had been by the brash
views of the PPP leadership.[18] Although the Waddington
report had indicated that "fully developed party organisations" did not yet exist, Hinden recalled that all
three commissioners "were perfectly aware of the growing
power of the People's Progressive Party with its Communist leadership." Opposition to the PPP was weak "and it
was more than likely that they would win in any popular
election. That their idea of democracy was not ours was
made only too plain."

In a democratic public session before a crowded audience,
the Commission debated the meaning of democracy with the
P.P.P. leaders. We talked of democracy as government by
consent, by the consent even of the opposition. We talked
of the need for constitutional checks--recognised by almost every democratic government in the world--in order
to protect the rights of minorities and the freedom of individuals, and to allow an opposition to operate. They
could see no point in all this. If a party wins a majority of the seats, they asserted, it had the right in the
name of the people to do just what it thinks fit. "The
voice of the people is the voice of God," we were told,
and when we protested, showing how the voice of the people

might change from one election to another, even that a party may win a majority of seats without a majority of votes, they were deaf to our arguments. "Do you want to put a check on God" someone shouted at us.

But, Hinden argued, this knowledge was not sufficient to withhold self-government; that act would only increase enthusiasm for the communists. Only self-government and responsibility would turn agitators into statesmen, as it had with Pandit Nehru and Kwame Nkrumah. Unfortunately, the PPP failed to become responsible when it assumed power. Hinden ultimately justified intervention, by asserting that Britain's aim was "not just self-government but democratic self-government." The "crude racialism" of South Africa had already hurt the Commonwealth and was "bad enough, but a Communist member, whose real loyalty was to Russia . . . would be inassimilable, and provoke tensions which would threaten to destroy the whole structure."

Some contended, Hinden acknowledged, that the British government ought not to have acted because British Guiana had not yet become a communist state. This argument, she asserted, neglected the whole history of the international communist movement; it was essential to act in time, even though an elected government might be ejected. The people of British Guiana had voted for social reforms, not communism. The usually anti-imperialist Dr. Hinden concluded with marvellous ambiguity that she remained "an unrepentant believer in colonial self-government."

Astonishingly, Jagan and Burnham failed to return from their world wanderings until February 1954. The "revolutionary" leaders seemed to have deserted the scene of the expected "revolution." The simple truth was that there were no plans for a revolution in British Guiana. Assuming they could twist the British Lion's tail at will, the PPP chieftains had never anticipated that the beast might turn about, growl, suspend the constitution, and eject them from office. New policies and tactics were now desperately required in the PPP.

Under the governor's emergency powers, Cheddi Jagan was prohibited from leaving the city of Georgetown. On 3 April 1954, Jagan ignored the restriction order and broke the law by going to Mahaicony, about thirty-five miles away, where he had established a second dental office. Promptly arrested and brought before a magistrate empowered to hear the case without a jury, Jagan was placed on bail after a preliminary hearing. Leaving the court, his supporters demonstrated; the police intervened. Arrested a second time, bail was denied. Jagan and some of his followers spent the night in prison. Brought before the magistrate on the following day, he delivered a fiery speech:

> Today Guiana is a vast prison. Whether I am outside or
> inside matters little. Prison holds no terror for
> me. . . . I expect no justice from this or any other
> court. Justice has been dead since the British troops
> landed.[19]

Even some of Jagan's political enemies were shocked
at his sentence of six months at hard labor. Because of
his bout with tuberculosis, he was assigned to the prison hospital. Unhappy with the sermons delivered during
the Sunday "Uplift Hour" by churchmen and other prominent figures, Jagan encouraged the prisoners to request
that he be allowed to address them. The prison authorities finally capitulated and he spoke on the topic:
"Thou Shalt Not Steal." His summary indicates why the
prison authorities removed him from the hospital.

> I concluded my talk by stating that the biggest thieves
> were outside of the gaol; that under imperialism and
> capitalism, the foreigners and local capitalists, land-
> lords, bankers and middlemen extracted surplus value--
> profits, rent, interest and commission--from the working
> people; that so long as the system of imperialism and
> capitalism prevailed there would always be prisoners,
> and the gaols would become bigger and bigger.

He then organized a partially successful attack on
the wretched prison diet. Breakfast and supper had consisted of a large cup of coffee and a small loaf of
bread, while luncheon alternated salt fish and beef;
there were no greens. After he organized a socialist
study group, and as a consequence of demonstrations outside the prison by his followers, the government decided
to move Jagan and several others to the Mazaruni Prison
Settlement. Here he was kept busy scrubbing floors and
developing a new hobby, carpentry. Articles for the
party newspaper were smuggled out on toilet paper.[20]

One month of his sentence was suspended for good
behavior. He returned to freedom in early September
only to find that his wife had just been imprisoned for
six months on charges of being in possession of a secret
Police Riot Manual and for holding a public meeting. According to Cheddi Jagan, the manual had been "planted"
in their house, and the political meeting was actually a
Bhagwat, an Indian religious festival. Janet Jagan suffered dreadfully in adjusting to prison food, and sur-
vived her five months in jail on a bread diet.

The leaders of the PPP faced the painful task of re-
appraising the strategy and tactics which had led to the
suspension of the constitution. They had denounced the
constitution, but what they now had was worse: direct
rule by the governor. Little support had materialized
when they called for a general strike. Influenced by
their journey to India, Jagan and Burnham now advocated

civil disobedience and passive resistance, although several extremists still talked wildly of violent revolution. Of even greater significance, some moderates, convinced the Jagans were Stalinists, had already deserted the party. So far as they were concerned, the Jagan policies had led to disaster. Burnham had become their man even before the publication of the Robertson report. In April 1954, the conservative newspaper, Clarion, urged Burnham to "cease being a figure-head and become the effective leader of his Party." In July, the Clarion told Burnham that he should forge an alliance with Dr. Lachhmansingh and purge the extremists.[21]

Wanting the leadership, the ambitious Burnham carefully evaluated his chances. While rhetorically violent himself, Burnham considered the constant communist jargon of Jagan and company unwise. Jockeying for the top rung continued throughout 1954. Burnham's position was fortified as many of the more militant Jaganites were in prison or suffered from a variety of restrictions. To the surprise of many, two prominent East Indians, Dr. J. P. Lachhmansingh and Jai Narine Singh gravitated into Burnham's moderate orbit. But most militant blacks, Sydney King, Martin Carter, Ashton Chase, Rory Westmaas, and Brindley Benn, were with Jagan. There was thus a nice mix of East Indians and Africans in both camps as the leadership struggle became more intense.[22]

It had been resolved in March 1953 that the PPP's next annual Congress would convene in Berbice, since the first three had met in Georgetown. Jagan preferred a meeting in East Indian territory rather than the capital, where Burnham could always mobilize his African supporters. As a result of the suspension of the constitution and the restrictions imposed upon the leaders, the Congress scheduled for March 1954 had been cancelled. Burnham now pushed for a party conclave. Only ten members of the Executive Committee were present in November 1954 when Burnham used his casting vote to schedule a Congress for mid-February. A short while later, with only seven members of the Executive Committee in attendance, it was decided to hold the Congress in Georgetown. Cheddi Jagan objected and noted the agreement to convene the next Congress in Berbice. Bitter words flew about the room as Jagan and Burnham committed themselves to a struggle for the soul of the party.

Delighted by the signs of dissension within the PPP, the police granted Burnham permission to hold the annual Congress in Georgetown on 12 and 13 February 1955. Jagan tried vainly to thwart Burnham by mobilizing the General Council; and Janet Jagan, released from jail on 18 January, rushed to her husband's assistance. Frantic negotiations took place during the first days of February as pamphleteers from both sides exacerbated the split. Most of the key leaders inclined to Cheddi Jagan; in the General Council, Burnham could only rely upon his wife, his sister, Ulric Fingal, and Dr. Lachhmansingh.

Talks continued, since all knew that a split would gravely weaken the independence movement. Evidence for those rebutting the view that the Jagans were trying to manipulate Burnham out of the party includes Cheddi Jagan's conciliatory telephone call to Burnham on the morning of Friday, 11 February. Six hours of negotiation followed until a truce was hammered out; Burnham obtained numerous concessions. A Special Conference, not a Congress, would take place on Saturday and Sunday. The Executive Committee further stipulated "that the following agenda be discussed exclusively."

1. Chairman's opening address
2. Reports of Party Members on their visits abroad
3. Resumé of the Party's activities since 1953
4. The role of Trade Unions in the National Movement
5. The role of Youth in the National Movement
6. The role of Women in the National Movement
7. The Party and Race
8. The amendment of rules to provide for the election of officers and members of the General Council by ballot of members in each constituency at such places as the General Council shall decide.[23]

Peace failed to endure, and hostilities resumed before the day was over. By Friday evening, pamphlets prepared by Dr. Lachhmansingh and Jai Narine Singh were circulating the streets, and they referred to a Congress, rather than a Special Conference. Cheddi Jagan opposed a formal Congress since that would mean an agenda which automatically included "Members' Motions," and "Any Other Business." He feared that Burnham might have support from a majority of the delegates at a Georgetown meeting and could seize control of the party. One suspects the Jaganites overrated the extent of Burnham's support.

At the insistence of Jagan, Burnham agreed to convene a special meeting of the Executive Committee just prior to the opening of the Special Conference in order to discipline Jai Narine Singh. Shortly before noon, Burnham reneged, and the emergency meeting of the Executive Committee was scuttled. The Jagans and their supporters retaliated by boycotting the Saturday meeting of the party, but reversed course and appeared for the Sunday morning session at the Metropole Cinema.

Burnham opened the Sunday proceedings by calling for the reports of the members who had been abroad. Clinton Wong promptly rose to move the suspension of the standing rules and orders. Having resigned as senior vice-chairman of the PPP just after the 1953 elections because of his objections to the leftward drift, he was determined to purge the communists. Feigning surprise, Burnham queried Wong as to the motive behind his motion. Wong replied that he intended to move a vote of "No Confidence" in the policies and tactics pursued by the Executive Committee.

Burnham polled the thirteen members of the Executive Committee surrounding him on the platform. Seven argued that Wong's motion to suspend was contrary to the exclusive agenda compromise. Burnham reflected for a moment, then rejected the advice of the majority, and allowed the motion. Cheddi Jagan objected, but the chairman persisted even as Janet Jagan pleaded: "The unity of the party is in your hands now. If you go ahead as you are doing, the party will be split. I place the full responsibility in your hands." When Burnham accepted Wong's motion, the Jagans, Martin Carter, Rory Westmaas, George Robertson, Fred Bowman, Lionel Jeffrey, and two hundred floor members walked out. The Burnham rump immediately elected him leader with Dr. Lachhmansingh as chairman. Cheddi Jagan was demoted to senior vice-chairman while Clinton Wong became junior vice-chairman. Jai Narine Singh was elected secretary and Burnham's sister, Jessie, became assistant secretary. Janet Jagan was designated treasurer while Sydney King was placed on the General Council.[24]

The marvellous years of unity, despite a normal amount of internal tension, had come to a disastrous end; a long fracture cut right through the Guyanese independence movement. No fool, Burnham recognized his exposed position and the dangerous gamble he had made. He was betting that Dr. Lachhmansingh's support would bring him the East Indian sugar workers. Since Burnham was already president of Critchlow's British Guiana Labour Union and had solid trade union support in Georgetown, he was reasonably confident of votes from both the black and East Indian working class. But most black militants remained with Jagan. These included Sydney King, Martin Carter, Rory Westmaas, and Brindley Benn. Potentially, the Jagans were in a far stronger position than Burnham when they convened a Congress of their PPP at Buxton a few weeks later, with Sydney King in the chair. The Georgetown Special Conference was declared illegal; portrayed as bourgeois opportunists prepared to appease imperialists and the local elite, Burnham and his faction were expelled from the PPP. Between 1955 and 1958 there were two PPP organizations, as Jagan and Burnham struggled to retain the name meaning so much to the ordinary working people of British Guiana.

Writing in his version of _Thunder_ on 16 April 1955, Forbes Burnham assessed recent events. While searching for moderate support, he still stressed his pledge "to fight for the establishment of socialism in this country, cost what it will." But first on the agenda must be independence.

> At this point it is perhaps essential to reiterate what
> has been stated in the past, that ours is not a communist

party nor is the party affiliated to any communist organisation outside or inside the country. This does not mean
that this party is prepared to launch a witch-hunt against
persons who call themselves communists or who are in fact
communist. What it does mean is that we will not and cannot permit persons who consider an international reputation for being communists more important than the success
of our struggle to thereby slow up our movement and weaken
it. Such persons who seem to be geniuses at isolating
themselves and the cause they espouse are liabilities unless they are prepared to discontinue their wanton conduct and put the movement above their personal fancies.
We are fighting right now to get the British off our backs
and will direct our energies and efforts to that end instead of having them diverted to irrelevant issues.

Burnham insisted that East Indian and African must
continue to cooperate. This cooperation was "one of the
greatest achievements" of the PPP. Burnham recalled
"that prior to the advent of our party we had African
politicians appealing to Africans, and Indian politicians appealing to Indians, and neither set appealing to
Guianese. When we brought the races together our mas-
ters trembled." Though socialist and "worker-based,"
the PPP must try to attract "all sections of Guianese;
workers, farmers, businessmen, intellectuals and civil
servants, regardless of their race." Unlike the Jaganites, Burnham's PPP was not automatically "hostile to
foreign capital."

If foreign capital is to be invested here we welcome it
but the Guianese workers must get their just deserts.
Proper wages must be paid and human conditions granted.
We have no desire to chase or scare foreign capital but
we have no intention of allowing anyone to further grind
the faces of the workers, or exploit our resources still
leaving us poor. It is a matter of business. Capitalists want to invest here, we agree for them to invest
here but on fair terms to our country.[25]

At first, many Guyanese felt the split would be only temporary; perhaps Burnham and Jagan were scheming to
trick the British. By the end of 1955, with verbal
knives being hurled more frequently at one another by
the two PPP's, the public realized the division was both
real and permanent. What now would happen to the Guyanese dream of independence, racial harmony, and social
justice? Was this yet another example of that most successful of British policies, divide and rule?

NOTES

1. Suspension of the Constitution in British Guiana, Colonial
Office, Command 8980, 1953.
2. Ibid., p. 11.
3. Hansard's Parliamentary Debates, 518 (22 October 1953),
pp. 2159-62.
4. Ibid., pp. 2182-95.
5. Ibid., pp. 2261-68.
6. Ibid., pp. 2268-79.
7. Jagan, Forbidden Freedom, pp. 83-85; and idem, The West on
Trial, pp. 138-46. Lyttelton's comment about the United States is
in Hansard's Parliamentary Debates, 518 (22 October 1953), p. 2175.
8. Despres, Cultural Pluralism, pp. 222-27.
9. For a good discussion of international relations at this
time see Walter LaFeber, America, Russia, and the Cold War 1945-
1980 (New York, 1980), pp. 128-72.
10. The Daily Argosy, 11 October 1953.
11. Jagan, Forbidden Freedom, pp. 90-91; and idem, The West
on Trial, pp. 132-37. See also Hansard's Parliamentary Debates,
518 (22 October 1953), pp. 2170-72.
12. As quoted in Jagan, The West on Trial, p. 135. See also
William H. Knowles, Trade Union Development and Industrial Relations in the British West Indies (Berkeley, 1959).
13. Hansard's Parliamentary Debates, 518 (28 October 1953),
pp. 2796-2800.
14. Hansard's Parliamentary Debates, 521 (7 December 1953),
pp. 1649-50.
15. Ibid., pp. 1656-57.
16. See Robert D. Tomasek, "British Guiana: A Case Study of
British Colonial Policy," Political Science Quarterly, 74 (September 1959), pp. 393-411.
17. Report of the British Guiana Constitutional Commission,
Colonial Office, Command 9274, London, 1954.
18. Rita Hinden, "The Case of British Guiana," Encounter, 2
(January 1954), pp. 18-22.
19. Jagan, The West on Trial, pp. 155-56.
20. Ibid., pp. 157-59.
21. Clarion, 25 April 1954 and 25 July 1954.
22. There is still much disagreement over the motivation of
both Jagan and Burnham as they approached the historic party meeting of February 1955. The following account uses information found
in Simms, Trouble in Guyana, pp. 125-32; Despres, Cultural Pluralism, pp. 210-16; Jagan, The West on Trial, pp. 162-75; Smith, British Guiana, pp. 179-80; Glasgow, Guyana, pp. 106-10; Newman, British Guiana, pp. 77-81; and Lewis, Modern West Indies, pp. 271-78.
23. Jagan, The West on Trial, p. 171.
24. Simms, Trouble in Guyana, pp. 130-31. See the coverage
in The Daily Argosy of 13 and 14 February 1955.
25. Nascimento and Burrowes, eds., A Destiny to Mould, pp. 3-8.

5
Return to Constitutional Government

By the end of 1955, Burnham's great expectations had been punctured by the inability of Dr. Lachhmansingh and Jai Narine Singh to deliver the sugar workers. Although wishing to maintain his socialist commitment, Burnham refused to ignore potential support from Guyana's bourgeoisie, horrified by the Jagans's radicalism. Neither Burnham nor Jagan wished to make a strictly ethnic appeal, but given the reality of Guyana's plural components, a good chance always existed, especially if demagogues replaced statesmen, that race might overshadow class.

Although Burnham had departed, Jagan still retained the endorsement of such militant black Guyanese as Ashton Chase, Sydney King, Martin Carter, Rory Westmaas, and Brindley Benn. Altogether, Jagan was far more secure than Forbes Burnham at the end of 1955. But he urgently required a careful analysis of past mistakes, and an estimate of what the Jagan PPP should do in the period prior to new elections. Instead, Cheddi Jagan disappeared into the Marxist-Leninist clouds, for 1956 was a difficult year for international communism.

In February 1956, Nikita Khruschev denounced a significant part of Joseph Stalin's ambiguous legacy. A central part of the communist faith had been ripped to pieces. After Khruschev's catalogue of crimes, numerous supporters of the Soviet version of communism reconsidered their political orientation. Demonstrations in Poland led to Gomulka and a small amount of liberalization; but, the Soviet Union rejected the neutrality schemes of Imre Nagy in Hungary, and Russian troops poured in during the first days of November. Many Soviet sympathizers were appalled by the brutal repression of the Hungarians. As the Russians moved on Budapest, Britain was forced to confront her own weakness. Conniving with the French and the Israelis to topple Nasser and regain control of the Suez Canal, the British were compelled to give way when the Eisenhower-Dulles team--with a presidential election in progress--prepared to destroy the

pound sterling if the British did not stop their march
along the canal.

If Cheddi Jagan had played his cards a little more
wisely, the loss of Forbes Burnham could have been mini-
mized and racial violence might not have replaced class
struggle in the politics of Guyana. But when the Jagan
PPP convened its annual Congress in the fall of 1956,
Cheddi Jagan embarked on a long, tortuous, Marxist-
Leninist-Stalinist-Maoist assessment of recent events in
British Guiana.[1] Jagan execrated Burnham as a pro-
imperialist, middle-class opportunist. "The Burnham
clique were prepared to deviate to the right, to sacri-
fice our proletarian working class, internationalist
outlook for narrow nationalism."

Influenced by the Robertson report, Jagan realized
the colossal blunders committed in 1953. The rhetoric
about revolution and general strike had proven to be
idle chatter when British troops arrived. Impressed
during his visit to India, and remembering Gandhi's
skillful use of passive resistance and civil disobedience, the PPP attempted to implement these tactics in
1954 and 1955. No more successful than appeals for revolution and general strikes, the pacifist approach only
antagonized some extremists in the party. Indicting the
Burnham group for trying to "degrade the revolutionary
movement and submerge the Communist elements in the general welter of bourgeois nationalists," Jagan, nonetheless, conceded that "up to October 1953, we committed
deviations to the left. We definitely overrated the
revolutionary possibilities of our Party." They had
been "bombastic" and "were attacking everybody at the
same time." A tendency had emerged towards what Mao
Tse-tung called "all struggle and no unity."[2]

Stung by these charges, the extreme leftists, Sydney King, Martin Carter, and Rory Westmaas, concluded
that Jagan was blaming them for the suspension of the
constitution. They were further irritated by Jagan's
volte-face on the proposed West Indies Federation. The
PPP had pledged "to work for the eventual political
union of British Guiana with the Caribbean territories."
King, Carter, and Westmaas wished to formally commit
British Guiana to membership in the federation, due to
be inaugurated in 1958, but Jagan doubted the wisdom of
such a move. Other key Caribbean political leaders,
such as Norman Manley and Alexander Bustamante of Jamaica, and Eric Williams of Trinidad, had already broken
with the communists. There was also another disturbing
factor: the East Indians of British Guiana. Expecting
shortly to be a majority in British Guiana, they would be
submerged in an African sea in the federation. Jagan
condemned the leftists for "adventurism"; they retorted
he only opposed the federation to retain the tribal loyalty of the East Indians. Believing that proletarian inter-
nationalism had been betrayed, King, Carter, and Westmaas,

thoroughly disillusioned, bolted from the PPP before the
end of 1956. This split, far more than the break with
Burnham, ushered in the era of racial politics in British Guiana. Ashton Chase and Brindley Benn remained
with Jagan, but the loss of King, Carter, and Westmaas,
in addition to the hostility of Burnham, suggested to
many blacks that the national liberation movement was
splitting into two ethnic blocs.[3]

Ordinary life continued in the colony during the
four years of the interim government. Frightened by the
radicalism of the PPP, the British hastened to make
amends for past deficiencies by putting additional funds
into British Guiana. Planning for economic development
really began in British Guiana when the Colonial Development Welfare Act of 1945 allocated some G$12 million
for this purpose.* By 1947, a rather primitive ten-year
plan had been put together. Estimating that some G$28
million would be spent by 1956, with about two-thirds of
the total expended in the first five years, the tentative plan designated G$6.5 million for three major
drainage and irrigation projects, G$11.2 million for so-
cial welfare, justice, and public buildings, and G$10.3
million for economic services, including agriculture,
forestry, transport surveys, and research. Administrative delays, however, led to only G$2 million being
spent by 1950. This delay necessitated a revision of
the plan and a request for experts from the International Bank for Reconstruction and Development. In 1953,
the bank prepared a Five-Year Development Programme for
the period from 1954 to 1958. It proposed to increase
national income by 20 percent, and income per head by 6
percent at the conclusion of five years; G$66 million
would be invested, most of the money going to agriculture, transport, and communication. The emphasis remained the same as in the rudimentary plan of 1947--im-
prove and expand the coastal lands. Neglecting the interior of the country, only a small sum was earmarked
for surveys of mineral and agricultural possibilities.
This neglect offended those who believed passionately
that the future would be in the interior rather than on
the coast. Some also argued that rice cultivation received too much money while industrialization had been
slighted.

Hoping to entice the Guyanese people away from the
PPP, the British government now decided to provide G$44
million for 1954-1955, G$33 million for economic devel-
opment and the rest for social services. This represented

*Before 1967, one United States dollar was equivalent to 1.7 Guyan-
ese dollars. Between 1967 and 1981, the exchange rate was one
United States dollar to 2.5 Guyanese dollars. After 1981, the exchange rate became one United States dollar to three Guyanese dollars. In January 1984, the Guyanese dollar was again devalued,
this time by 25 percent.

more than three times the money normally available, but
shortages of equipment and skilled personnel made it impossible to realize the optimistic forecast. This large,
one-year appropriation, however, laid the basis for a
new plan covering the period from 1956 to 1960 which
called for a total expenditure of G$91 million, G$61
million for economic development and the remainder for
social services.[4]

Unfortunately, the real growth rate for the years
between 1953 and 1960 was a disappointing 3 percent per
annum. This rate kept real income intact, and, by com-
parison with much of Asia, Africa, and Latin America,
was fairly good. In the Caribbean, however, Jamaica and
Trinidad roared ahead of British Guiana with growth
rates of 9 percent and 11 percent. The economy remained
totally dependent on exports of sugar, bauxite, and rice;
however, much of the profit in bauxite and sugar, being
foreign owned, went abroad and did not enter the Guyanese economy.

A significant jump in sugar production from 240,000
tons in 1953 to 350,000 tons in 1960 could be applauded,
but increased mechanization cut employment from 26,300
to 20,500 at a time of growing population. Unemployment,
estimated at 20 to 25 percent, and underemployment were
high, and growing higher. Rice production also surged
forward; output expanded from 75,000 tons in 1953 to
126,000 tons in 1960 as acreage increased from 113,000
to 220,000 acres. Bauxite production, hampered by high
production and shipping costs, remained static; British
Guiana had been second to Surinam in 1952, but by 1960
she ranked fourth behind Jamaica, the Soviet Union, and
Surinam. It was hoped that the start of manganese ex-
traction in 1960 would boost mining exports.[5]

The dawn of 1957 heralded the approach of new elections. Governor Savage had been replaced after only two
years in British Guiana. Understandably, the British
government knew that his replacement was mandatory if
the march to self-government was to be resumed. Instead
of rewarding Savage with a new appointment of comparable
importance, he found himself relegated to the London office of the Crown Agents for Overseas Governments. This
appointment lends support to those who believe that Governor Savage may have panicked when he recommended immediate suspension of the constitution. On the other hand,
his chief secretary, Sir John Gutch, was made high commissioner for the Western Pacific in 1954.

Sir Patrick Renison was appointed the new governor
in the fall of 1955. Promptly opening negotiations with
the different political groups, the governor tried to
create a united anti-Jagan front; but this effort proved
impossible. By this time, John Carter's National Democratic party had resurfaced as the United Democratic party, but was little more than the political arm of the
wealthy blacks and mulattoes dominating the League of

Coloured People. Lionel Luckhoo had deserted the National Democratic party in order to organize the National Labour Front. He was trying to corral all the East
Indians who disliked Jagan, plus all those with wealth
who opposed socialism.[6]

An all-party meeting had already taken place on 5
April 1956 in Georgetown. Organized by moderates, it
refused to entertain Jagan's motion that unity was required to end the emergency and to force new elections.
The Waddington constitution now looked much more attractive to Jagan than it had in 1953. Acting in a statesmanlike fashion, Jagan pleaded, unsuccessfully, for the
political parties to contest the next election as a unified bloc that would form a national government if successful. Representatives of the parties met with Governor Renison on 28 July. When pressed to end the emergency, the governor turned to Jagan and announced: "This
question of communism was the whole crux of the matter;
communism can do this country no good." The meeting
ended in failure.[7]

The governor knew, however, that marking time was
no policy. After consultations in London, Governor Renison announced in October that a new election would be
held in 1957. The Colonial Office decided to reconsti-
tute the fourteen seats from the 1947 general election.
To the fourteen elected members of the new Legislative
Assembly would be added the three ex-officio nominated
members; the governor could then designate a maximum of
eleven more. The British were trying, not very artfully,
to rig a defeat for the Jagan PPP. The elections of
1947 had been conducted prior to the introduction of
universal suffrage. Now the distribution of voters in
those constituencies was as follows:

Constituency	Number of voters
Eastern Berbice	31,947
New Amsterdam	5,897
Berbice River	5,429
Western Berbice	8,324
East Demerara	18,295
Central Demerara	25,135
Georgetown North	10,444
Georgetown Central	12,472
Georgetown South	22,241
Demerara River	26,972
Demerara-Essequibo	15,182
Western Essequibo	13,649
Essequibo River	11,215
North West District	3,450

In the 1953 elections, the PPP had been very strong in
the East Indian areas of Eastern Berbice. At that point,
there were the equivalent of 3½ seats representing that

area; now they were reduced to one. An all-party conference in British Guiana denounced Renison's proposals
and demanded, as a minimum, a return to the Waddington
constitution. But the governor pushed ahead, determined
to hold elections by the summer of 1957.[8]

Both Jagan and Burnham were invited to the Ghana
independence day celebrations in 1957. Although Jagan
had some travel problems, he eventually arrived in time
for the festivities. The event was as important for the
blacks of British Guiana as Indian independence, ten
years before, had been for the East Indians. Jagan
searched out some key West Indian leaders--Norman Manley
of Jamaica, Grantley Adams of Barbados, and Patrick Sol-
omon of Trinidad--and urged them to use their influence
on Burnham. He still hoped to reunite the PPP, or to
obtain Burnham's agreement to the formation of a united
front government. Kwame Nkrumah, Ghana's leader, was
also asked to help, but no meeting ever materialized between Burnham and Jagan. The West Indian leaders met
with Burnham, but were unable to bring the two antagon-
ists together. The West Indians ideologically sympathized with Burnham, and were no doubt influenced by Burnham's assurances that he would win the next election and
bring British Guiana into the West Indies Federation.[9]

As the August election day approached, excitement
increased in British Guiana. The two PPP's, John Carter's UDP, and Lionel Luckhoo's NLF waged a bitter struggle. Burnham was optimistic because his followers had
performed reasonably well in the 1956 Georgetown municipal elections. Luckhoo's party anticipated support from
the East Indian middle class and hoped to acquire some
of Jagan's following by vigorously opposing entry into
the West Indies Federation. The UDP still depended upon
the votes of the black and mulatto bourgeoisie.

Jagan tried to entice Sydney King back into the PPP
by proposing to support him in the Central Demerara constituency. Declining the offer, King ran as an independent, but Burnham, seeing an opening, rushed to his support. King, embarking on the most troubled phase of his
career, astonished everyone when he began to make racially oriented speeches. The doctrinaire King had often criticized Burnham's opportunism; however, now he
was not unhappy to receive aid and comfort. A prominent
East Indian businessman, Balram Singh Rai, was endorsed
by the PPP as King's opponent. Elements of racism were
bubbling furiously to the surface. The word circulating
in the East Indian community was "Apan Jhaat"--vote for
your own kind. Black and East Indian were growing more
agitated over just who would govern when the English
packed their bags.[10]

When the votes were tallied, the Jagan PPP stood
triumphant, winning nine of the fourteen elected seats.
Cheddi Jagan's vote was larger than the total number of
votes obtained by all five opposition victors, while

Balram Singh Rai had defeated Sydney King. Realistic in defeat, Burnham promptly conceded the PPP name to Cheddi Jagan and renamed his own group, the People's National Congress (PNC). He was demoralized by winning only three Georgetown seats, two of which (including his own) had been close. Lionel Luckhoo and the wealthy business-man, John Fernandes, both of the NLF, had nearly upset the Burnhamites.[11]

The ever-popular Stephen Campbell acquired one seat for the NLF in Amerindian territory; New Amsterdam's fa-vorite son, W. O. R. Kendall, was victorious for the UDP, even though he had served in the interim government. Confused by the suspension of the constitution and the Jagan-Burnham split, many eligible voters failed to par-ticipate--56 percent voted compared to 75 percent in 1953. The PPP received 47 percent of the vote, four points less than before. Even though the turnout was lower and he lacked a majority of the votes cast, Jagan had still obtained a sweeping victory. He met with Gov-ernor Renison on 17 August, and ten days later the gov-ernor yielded to the popular will. While the governor could nominate as many as eleven members to the Legisla-tive Council, he agreed to limit himself to six. Reni-son insisted upon Rahman Gajraj and Rupert Tello, both members of the interim government; but the other four, Martin Fredericks, H. J. M. Hubbard, Anthony Tasker, and R. E. Davis, were selected only after consultations be-tween the governor and Jagan. Hubbard was, of course, a founding member of the PAC and the PPP, while Tasker was a liberal-minded member of the Bookers' administra-tion.

In the Executive Council, five PPP ministers could outvote the three ex-officio members. Unlike 1953, no controversy developed over the spoils: Cheddi Jagan be-came minister of trade and industry, Janet Jagan took Labour, Health, and Housing, Ram Karran obtained the Min-istry of Communications and Works, Edward Beharry accept-ed Natural Resources, and Brindley Benn, one of the few well-known blacks still with Jagan, was appointed minis-ter of community development and education.[12]

Many British officials who abhorred Janet Jagan's politics, nevertheless attest to her great administra-tive skills as a minister. The Village Health Centres established during her years in office were of tremen-dous assistance in improving the lives of the Guyanese people. Most eyes, however, turned toward the key minis-ter, Cheddi Jagan. Would there be a repeat of 1953? Initially, Jagan adopted his most statesmanlike manner. Newspaper reaction was fairly favorable; some long-time opponents prepared to wait and see before launching an attack. The governor's powers were, however, quickly employed--a plan for constructing a government-owned glass factory with Hungarian aid was vetoed, as was a scheme for a rice-bran oil factory to be built by the

German Democratic Republic. Jagan's desire to bring in
a left-leaning French economist as an economic advisor
was also rejected.[13]

Relying upon a recent ILO survey showing that 18
percent of the labor force was unemployed and another 9
percent underemployed, the PPP insisted that the current
five-year development plan was inadequate. Jagan argued
that the G$91 million plan must be replaced by one allo-
cating G$200 million over the next five years. The gov-
ernor was negative, and Jagan suspected the United States
was probably involved when the British government refused to approve a planned £8 million loan from a Swiss
bank in London.

By 1961, the Jagan administration could show some
considerable achievements and, most important, it had
demonstrated that it could govern the country. The
United Nations had been generous in providing funds, and
some important surveys had been completed with respect
to soil, hydroelectric power, timber, aluminum, and
fisheries. The inefficiency of the privately owned Demerara Electric Company produced many blackouts in Georgetown; therefore, Jagan found the funds to nationalize
this public utility, even though he regarded the compensation arrangement as exorbitant considering the profits
derived by the company over the years.

Feeling that his industrialization schemes were being frustrated, Jagan turned to agriculture. No doubt
influenced by the fact that his East Indian supporters
were primarily in the countryside, Jagan was also correct in believing that proper drainage and irrigation
would open up an additional two-thirds of the coastal
plain. Development was undertaken at Tapakuma and Black
Bush Polder. By 1960, 3,300 applications for land in
the Black Bush Polder area were being processed, less
than 200 of which were from blacks. Of course, this
project, located deep in East Indian territory on the
Corentyne, was unlikely to attract many blacks.[14]

Delighted at being able to place a majority of
rice producers on the Rice Marketing Board, Jagan also
appropriated money to remove the squalid barracks on the
sugar estates and to improve the housing of the workers.
Wage councils were established in some industries, and
the weekly hours for shop assistants were reduced from
47 to 41. More workers came under the protection of
Workmen's Compensation Laws, and a paid annual vacation
was provided for many more people.

The PPP ministers were making a genuine effort to
ameliorate the living conditions of the Guyanese people.
Frustrated over the limitations imposed upon his industrialization schemes, Jagan, despite Burnham's objections, allocated significant sums of money for agricultural development by unveiling a new G$100 million eco-
nomic plan for the period from 1959 until 1964. Slightly more than 50 percent of the money was earmarked for

agriculture, rice receiving the largest portion. It should always be remembered that rice can both feed the Guyanese and be sold abroad. Cuba had already agreed to purchase surplus rice at a very good price.

While Jagan participated in the governing of the country, Burnham hastened to rejuvenate his battered followers after the electoral drubbing of 1957. Little East Indian working class support had emerged for his new PNC; so he turned, hesitantly at first, toward the moderate middle class, especially the blacks and Portuguese. A tactical retreat from socialism might also be required. By 1959, John Carter's UDP had been absorbed by the PNC, but the Portuguese middle class proved more intractable. The 1957 election had revealed glaring deficiencies in the PNC local organizations. Money was necessary to build up constituency parties to match the PPP. The merger with the UDP brought additional funds, but it also resulted in the departure of a key East Indian leader, Jai Narine Singh, convinced that Burnham was becoming an advocate of black supremacy.[15]

Nor did harmony always exist among the PPP ministers. In 1959, Jagan fired Edward Beharry, minister of natural resources. Beharry, representative of the East Indian shopkeeping and medium-sized farming interest, had criticized Jagan's emphasis upon socialist planning and, more specifically, the additional taxes proposed for the sugar industry. Accusations were hurled that Beharry's company was too closely associated with foreign capitalists. To Jagan's surprise, a long-time ally, the black militant, Fred Bowman, left the PPP at the same time. Jagan retains a fatal tendency to lose important supporters at critical moments. Brindley Benn replaced Beharry and Balram Singh Rai, a moderate East Indian, assumed Benn's old position.[16]

The PPP and the PNC continued to demand independence from the British. Burnham insisted, however, that new elections, based upon proportional representation, must first be conducted. As the PPP had garnered less than 50 percent of the vote in 1957, the PNC could scent victory if it mobilized the entire anti-PPP vote in a proportional-representation style election. The PNC would then constitute the largest group among Jagan's opponents and dominate any government that was formed.

In 1959, Patrick Renison moved on to manage the affairs of Kenya and was replaced as governor by the New Zealand-born, Sir Ralph Grey. Grey, educated for the law before entering the colonial service of the British Empire, had served in Nigeria for some twenty years before being posted to British Guiana, a governor for the first time.[17]

In March 1960, Iain Macleod, colonial secretary in Prime Minister Harold Macmillan's Conservative government, presided over a new constitutional conference for British Guiana. Among those present were Cheddi Jagan,

Brindley Benn, Forbes Burnham, W. O. R. Kendall, Jai
Narine Singh, and Rahman Gajraj. After three weeks of
discussion and argument, the colonial secretary rejected
Burnham's demands for proportional representation. Neither the Conservative party nor the Labour party has
ever evinced much sympathy for this method of election.
It is, however, passionately advocated by the Liberal
party and other smaller political organizations, as it
would usually mean a significant increase in their number of parliamentary seats.[18]

Macleod, a very liberal-minded Tory, made numerous
concessions to the Guyanese, designed to bring them back
to where they had been in 1953. New elections were
scheduled for 1961, and it was clearly implied that the
electoral victor would bring British Guiana to independence. The country was to be divided into thirty-five,
single-member constituencies that would elect representatives to a Legislative Assembly. An upper house, the
Senate, would be composed of thirteen senators, eight
designated by the prime minister, three by the opposition, and two by the governor. The leader of the winning party would form a government and be regarded premier; he would be in full charge of all internal matters.
Defense and foreign affairs were still reserved for the
governor.

Burnham, disappointed by Macleod's decisions, returned to British Guiana determined to increase the size
of the anti-PPP vote. His most important catch could be
the wealthy Portuguese middle class, but only if he did
not antagonize his own militant socialist supporters,
already unhappy over the merger with the bourgeois UDP.
They had been partially pacified when the Marxist, Sydney King, was snared by Burnham and appointed general
secretary of the PNC and editor of its magazine, New Nation. Negotiations with the Portuguese and other middle
class elements, however, proved fruitless, and the reins
were now seized by the usually quiet and taciturn Peter
d'Aguiar, about to embark upon ten frantic years of activity that would end in personal catastrophe and a political disaster.[19]

D'Aguiar's family had been in British Guiana for
more than one hundred years. His grandfather, Jose
Gomes d'Aguiar, arrived from the Madeira Islands and set
up a small rum business. Soon a chain of retail shops
had been established, and a cocoa and chocolate factory
were added. Trained as a doctor, Peter d'Aguiar's father eventually joined his three brothers in running the
firm. In 1896, they purchased the assets of the Demerara Ice House, an organization importing ice from Canada.
The assets included a hotel and a soft drink plant. After the death of his father and his uncles, the company
declined until Peter d'Aguiar assumed control in 1933.
A devout Roman Catholic, d'Aguiar had attended Stonyhurst
College and the University of Birmingham in England.

Dissatisfied with his studies, he travelled to the con-
tinent, returning to British Guiana in 1931. Searching
for adventure and gold, he became a "pork knocker," or
prospector. Finding illness rather than gold or diamonds, he left the interior and finally decided to manage the family company. Hard work and attention to detail made him a very successful businessman. By 1940,
the company's delivery system was transformed as motor
trucks replaced donkey carts, and a fully automatic soft
drink plant was installed in 1942 and expanded in 1952.
Bank Breweries Ltd. was established in 1956, even though
a British firm had recently concluded a brewery would
not be profitable in Guyana. Ten years later, the private family business became a public company, and numerous Guyanese rushed to buy shares. By 1970, the rum,
beer, wine, and soft drink operation had moved to a new
modern complex, Thirst Park, in the suburbs of Georgetown. D'Aguiar's business achievements have been steady
and continuous, but his political course was destined to
be much bumpier and irregular.[20]

Throughout the fall of 1959 and during most of 1960,
talks took place between d'Aguiar and the PNC. D'Aguiar
was supported by members of the well-to-do Portuguese,
Chinese, black, and East Indian middle class; they wanted neither Jagan's Marxism nor Burnham's moderate socialism. Burnham had, however, moderated his socialist
proposals when he merged with the UDP, and he was clearly preferable to Jagan. D'Aguiar's extravagant demands,
however, made Burnham recoil in anger. To join the PNC
along with his followers and to provide ample funds,
d'Aguiar demanded nine seats on the fifteen-member Executive Committee. Burnham could remain party leader and
become prime minister if they won the next election, but
d'Aguiar must be minister of trade and industry.

Burnham was indignant; apparently d'Aguiar was
treating him as an inferior. The black leader complained:
"He wanted to buy the party as though it were a box of
empties being returned to his brewery." Upon reflection,
the PNC leaders offered a compromise: d'Aguiar could
have six seats on the Executive Committee, but four must
be East Indians from the Rice Producers Association.
D'Aguiar asserted that many wealthy East Indians had
cast their lot with him, but the six names submitted included only two from the Rice Producers Association.[21]

This deal was deemed inadequate by the PNC; a number of prominent East Indians might have enabled the PNC
to detach some of Jagan's East Indian enthusiasts.
D'Aguiar's present proposals gave the impression of a
PNC capitulation. Acceptance of the proposal could lose
the black working class and provide support for Jagan's
slashing charges that the PNC leaders were bourgeois opportunists. Burnham had always to remember his overwhelming strength in Georgetown's trade union movement;
if he became too cozy with the bosses, his working class

support would evaporate.

To the surprise of the PNC, d'Aguiar, tiring of the endless discussions, seized the initiative and formed a party of his own in early October 1960. Calling his movement the United Force (UF), d'Aguiar could rely upon the Guyanese middle class, especially the Portuguese, and he also won the backing of the East Indian MPCA leaders--Richard Ishmael, Rupert Tello, and Cleveland Charran. The endorsement of the MPCA chieftains, however, attracted few sugar workers, since the latter still regarded the MPCA a company union.

Many Guyanese still yearned for a rapprochement between Burnham and Jagan. This desire was also prominent among third world countries, particularly Ghana. In early 1961, however, compromise attempts were again unsuccessful. Jagan was usually more conciliatory than Burnham, but he could afford this luxury since a reconciliation would undoubtedly have left him in the first position.[22]

Elections were now planned for August 1961, and the constituency boundaries were redrawn by Sir Hugh Hallett, a retired British High Court judge. Anticipating a cold official reception, Jagan nevertheless denounced (with some accuracy) Sir Hugh's boundary lines as gerrymandered to give an edge to his opponents. While liking Jagan personally, the British would still have preferred to see him defeated because of the complications caused by his communist leanings. The PNC and the UF prepared to fight all thirty-five constituencies, while the PPP ran for twenty-nine. Conceding the Rupununi constituency of Amerindians and ranchers to the United Force, the PPP also doubted that anyone could beat W. O. R. Kendall, now of the PNC, in New Amsterdam. The four Georgetown seats it chose not to contest would inevitably go to the PNC or the UF. PPP supporters, however, might still be able to influence the elections in these constituencies by voting in a bloc for either the PNC or the UF nominee, most likely the latter as a lesser of two evils.[23]

Burnham carefully cultivated a moderate image. Speaking over the radio in late March 1961, the PNC chieftain called for "a properly planned programme of industrial development." Guyana, Burnham stated, would require an economic planning unit, an industrial development corporation, a finance corporation, and a central bank. But private enterprise would not be discouraged. "We will not seek to confiscate or expropriate; we shall merely firmly insist on proper labor practices and the observance of the principle of Guianisation at all levels and all times." Everything was linked to the particular version of socialism the PNC projected as its alternative to Jagan's communism and d'Aguiar's capitalism. This alternative was "cooperative" socialism; it would emphasize the establishment of producer and consumer cooperatives, and give "social size to the little man."

No one will be herded into the cooperative but direct government aid, financial and advisory, and encouragement
will be given to establishing cooperatives not only amongst
farmers, but also in marketing and the distribution trades.
There will be such institutions as cooperative banks, res-
taurants, garages and firms. The cooperative will be for
all, not for one group or race, but for all Guianese.

Burnham stressed the commitment of the PNC to all
the basic freedoms, including free elections. Turning
to the intensification of racial tension during the
heated election campaign, he reminded his listeners that
all Guyanese, including the Amerindians, must work together in unity. "The People's National Congress is interested in the Guianese people and has no time and will
have no truck with those who talk about remaining separate and distinct and maintaining their identity." [24]
Suddenly, Burnham reeled before an onslaught from a
prominent member of his own party. The mercurial, un-
corruptible, but temperamental Sydney King had been a
marvelous prize for Burnham when he collared the young
activist after his departure from the PPP in 1957. King,
PNC general secretary and editor of its journal, New Nation, had become progressively disgusted with what he
regarded as Jagan's East Indian racism. King now quarreled with Burnham when the latter announced in May that
after the election--which he expected to win--he would
immediately demand independence. Burnham thundered that
he would insist upon a British departure, even if Jagan
retained office. This idea was intolerable to King, who
had nightmares of blacks being exploited by East Indians.
In July, King advocated a joint premiership for Jagan and Burnham after the election. Convinced that the
PPP would win the election and that Jagan would refuse a
joint premiership, King suggested partitioning the country into a black zone, an East Indian area, and a third
region in between for those who wished to live together.
Stung by this completely unacceptable racist formula that
none of the three parties would accept, Burnham expelled
King from the PNC. [25]
Only a few independents were involved in this election; the three major parties dominated the political
scene. All three tried valiantly to prove they were
multiracial while their opponents were racist. The
United Force ran 14 East Indians, 12 Africans, 3 Chinese,
3 Portuguese, 2 Amerindians, and 1 Englishman. The PPP
put forward 14 East Indians, 12 Africans (8 of them were
given safe seats), and 3 Portuguese. The PNC did not
manage quite so well: 24 Africans, 6 East Indians, 3
Portuguese, 1 Chinese, and 1 Amerindian.
Adopting a more moderate line on many major issues,
Jagan did not swerve from his socialist beliefs. Only
through socialism, he argued, could there be a better

life for all Guyanese. Yet, Jagan insisted, parliamentary democracy must be retained and a section on fundamental rights was essential in British Guiana's independence constitution. Bringing up the accusations that he
was a communist, Cheddi Jagan observed:

> As the colonial peoples rose to freedom, have not their
> leaders always been dubbed communist. Were not Nehru,
> Nkrumah, Soekarno, Sekou Toure, Jomo Kenyatta, Lumumba
> all called communists? This is illustrious company. If
> these are communists, then I take my place beside them
> gladly.

Jagan pointed with pride to the four-year development plan that would span the years from 1960 to 1964.
Although emphasizing agricultural improvements, some
funds were to be made available for industrialization.
Jagan agreed with Burnham on foreign investments--it was
necessary to acquire all available funds even if it meant
capitalist investors in British Guiana. Ultimately, Jagan planned to nationalize the country's major industries, but this proposal was left rather vague. Neither
the PPP nor the PNC was very precise about bringing sugar and bauxite under public ownership. While <u>Thunder</u>,
the quarterly theoretical organ of the PPP, could be
quite doctrinaire, Jagan was much more pragmatic about
governmental policies and the conduct of an electoral
campaign.
   During the first half of 1961, the PPP injected the
entire educational system into the campaign. Since its
formation, the PPP had advocated a national system of
secular education in place of the dual system of primary
education which really gave control to the Christian religious denominations. The PPP government of 1953 had
advocated the elimination of dual control, and Minister
of Education Forbes Burnham had been a forceful advocate
of government schools. East Indians were doubly unhappy-
many of their children were being educated in Christian
schools, and East Indian teachers believed they were being denied promotion in these schools. School teachers
had become the largest professional group within the
East Indian community, a reflection of a growing commitment to seize every educational opportunity. The East
Indian teachers accused the mainly black headmasters,
senior teachers, and Christian school boards of discrim-
inating against them. Indeed, the leadership of the
British Guiana Teachers Association had joined with most
of the trade union movement (except for the sugar workers) in actively supporting the PNC.[26]
   After the suspension of the constitution in 1953,
the government continued to provide funds for denominational schools while building new public schools under
government supervision. This solution failed to satisfy
either the East Indians or the secularists and national-

ists who believed that religious schools were a divisive
force in society. In 1960, Balram Singh Rai, the minister of education, introduced an Education Amendment Bill
allowing the government to take over fifty-one denominational schools constructed with government funds, some
of them built on church-owned land.

Jagan's opponents have argued that he produced this
bill a month after the formation of the United Force because he feared East Indian teachers and professionals
might defect to d'Aguiar's side. Although this consideration may have been a minor factor, it seems far more
likely that Jagan simply wished to secularize education.
There is nothing more important than education in creating a sense of national unity and purpose, and, to Jagan,
the church schools were a source of division. Burnham
repudiated his 1953 views and criticized Jagan's bill.
In early 1961, debate raged over the issue and, by the
time the bill became law, the PPP had demonstrated its
commitment to secular education, increased its support
among the East Indians, but antagonized black teachers
and the Christian denominations. Jagan was denounced
with gusto as an atheistic communist who hated private
property.[27]

As spring gave way to summer and the election date
approached, the entire nation was alive with excitement.
While the rhetoric was vigorous and some violence occurred, the election itself was conducted in a comparatively calm atmosphere on Monday, 21 August. As the
votes were tallied it became apparent that the PPP was
victorious, but that its popular vote would only be
about 3,000 over the PNC; however, the PPP had not provided candidates in six constituencies. The PPP won
twenty seats with 42.6 percent of the vote, while the
PNC garnered 41 percent of the vote but only eleven
seats. D'Aguiar's UF acquired four seats with 16.3 percent of the vote. Two of these seats were in the interior, and the other two were in Georgetown. The two
Georgetown seats were won by the UF in constituencies
without a PPP candidate; no doubt many PPP supporters
voted UF as the lesser danger. Burnham deserted the
Georgetown Central constituency when d'Aguiar decided to
stand for that seat. It was left to the party chairman,
Mrs. Winifred Gaskin, to battle d'Aguiar and to lose by
some 800 votes.

The results indicated the continued strength of the
PPP, the new power of the PNC, and the quite respectable
position of the UF. Jagan lacked a majority of the popular vote; therefore, a coalition of his opponents might
defeat him. Some members of the UF, fearful of black
violence in Georgetown from the unemployed, still hoped
to modify Jagan's policies by supporting the property-
conscious East Indian groups among his followers. But
most UF supporters now saw only one way to power--coop-
eration with Burnham in order to defeat the menace of

communism. This coalition would necessitate forcing new
elections prior to independence, despite an apparent
British indication that this election was to be the last
test of public opinion before their departure.[28]

Jagan, delighted with the results, was promptly
designated premier by the governor. Brindley Benn became minister of natural resources, Balram Singh Rai accepted Home Affairs, Ram Karran went to Works and Hy-
draulics, and Fenton Ramsahoye became attorney-general.
C. R. Jacob was appointed minister of finance, and the
old Marxist, H. J. M. Hubbard, took over Trade and Industry. Strangely, Janet Jagan was not in the government, for it was decided that she was the only person
capable of running the party machine. Her absence could
also have been a concession to United States opinion,
which regarded Janet Jagan as a communist Machiavelli,
dominating her weak husband.

Crusading anticommunist groups from the United
States had travelled to British Guiana to work against
Jagan during the election campaign, and several congress-
men and senators lamented the possibility of another
Castro in the Carribean. A youthful President Kennedy,
traumatized by the shattering fiasco at Cuba's Bay of
Pigs in April 1961, gazed apprehensively at events in
British Guiana. Was there about to be another indepen-
dent state in the Caribbean area administered by a com-
munist? Would this form of government be contagious?
Castro, unrepentant, dreamed of a hemisphere-wide revolution against Yankee imperialism.

British officials, somewhat more blasé, were not
all that agitated by Jagan's fuzzy communism, suspecting
that power would bring responsibility and realism. While
disliking Jagan's ideological pronouncements, they rather preferred him to Burnham as a human being. Burnham's
arrogant opportunism had convinced the British that he
was an antiwhite, black racist. Since Jagan was premier,
cooperation seemed worth the gamble. The alternative
might be to antagonize him and drive him irretrievably
into the arms of Moscow.

Although very suspicious, Washington was half inclined to go along with the British. When Jagan requested meetings in the United States to discuss economic assistance, the Kennedy administration agreed. It was a
decisive moment in the career of Cheddi Jagan. Washington was undecided; its impression of Jagan would determine future policy. Initially, Washington had earmarked
about $5 million for aid to British Guiana--not much,
but something--and infinitely better than official hostility to a Jagan government.

Regrettably, though he enjoys the question, Cheddi
Jagan's instinct for self-destruction erupts when he is
asked about his political creed. Able to escape when he
generalizes, he cannot resist the urge to verbalize and
define. This verbosity leads to lengthy discussions

about communism, Marxism, and Leninism. The listener often concludes that Jagan is a species of communist who lacks the courage to admit his real beliefs.[29]

Invited to appear on the United States television program, "Meet the Press," on 15 October 1961, Jagan was pressed relentlessly by the fiercely anticommunist, permanent panel member, Laurence E. Spivak, about his communist commitments.[30] While the other panelists elicited information about Jagan's policies, Spivak hammered away at the communist theme. Early in the show, Spivak inquired if there was really "freedom" in the Soviet Union and China. Jagan responded:

> All I can say—I haven't been to China, I haven't been to Russia, but the experts who have been there who have said—for instance, you have this chap who is a writer on this question, an expert, apparently, who writes for the London Observer—I can't recall his name right now, but he has said in his latest book that life in the Soviet Union is growing day by day better and better. The standards of living are improving, and as such, we are concerned. We want to know how this is done.

Returning to the attack later in the program, Spivak quoted from a 1953 Jagan speech:

> Those who know anything about economic theory know that Communism according to the definition of Marx, Engels, Lenin and Stalin is only the advanced stage of socialism. My idea was to show the members of the Council that in theory socialism and communism are the same.

Spivak demanded to know if Jagan still subscribed to those words. Harassed and irritated, Jagan replied:

> If I may elaborate that a little, I would like to say from what I have read from the text books, socialism means, or the slogan under socialism is, from each according to his ability, to each according to his labor, the work that he gives. Under communism as under the early Christian set-up, all persons were supposed to share equally, and so I see the Communists say in that period to come there will be distribution according to needs. Each one will contribute according to his ability, and from my point of view this is good. This is a good thing that all persons should get from society what they need, regardless of whether he is a cripple or whether he is able to produce more or less.
>
> This I believe you will believe in too, because I am sure you don't agree that some people should own vast sums of money and others should be wallowing in poverty. You have in many countries today the terrible distribution of wealth. Even in my country if you will study the statistics you will find—in most capitalist countries you will find the same thing: very unequal distribution of wealth.

You have conspicuous consumption of those who are wealthy
with the result they dissipate the surplus of the country,
and nothing is there for development.

Truth, error, and ambiguity can be found in Jagan's
statements. There was no ambiguity in the reaction of
President Kennedy, who tuned in for the last part of the
program. Appalled at Jagan's unwillingness to speak
critically of the Soviet Union, the president promptly
decided to reexamine United States policies toward British Guiana. No pledges of aid should be made until he
had talked to Cheddi Jagan. An interview was arranged
for 25 October.[31] Jagan realized the importance of the
occasion, but he refused to be intimidated by Kennedy
and his advisers. Socialist planning, he told them, was
absolutely essential for the economic development of
British Guiana. Kennedy responded that this policy was
no problem, for the United States was not trying to impose private enterprise throughout the world. The United
States wanted national independence for all states; after that, it preferred as much individual and political
freedom as possible. "This is the basic thing. So long
as you do that, we don't care whether you are socialist,
capitalist, pragmatist or whatever. We regard ourselves
as pragmatists." The United States would expect compensation when industries were nationalized, but such had
been achieved with Mexico and Bolivia and could be negotiated with British Guiana.
Recalling his own studies at the London School of
Economics, the president began a general discussion of
political ideas. Kennedy and his advisers were impressed
when Jagan called himself a Bevanite, for they remembered that Aneurin Bevan, dead for just over one year,
had been a forceful socialist, but also a champion of
personal freedom and quite critical of Soviet communism.
Jagan affirmed his belief in parliamentary government,
but then added expressions of admiration for the Marxist journal, Monthly Review, edited by Paul Sweezy, Leo
Huberman, and Paul Baran. To the Kennedy people, Monthly Review was as procommunist as Pravda. Jagan was revealed as much more than an admirer of Aneurin Bevan and
the left wing of the British Labour party. Trapped by
his expansive nature, Jagan retreated: "Well, Bevanism,
Sweezyism, Hubermanism, Baranism--I really don't get
those ideological subtleties." Arthur M. Schlesinger,
Jr., remembered that Kennedy later noted "that this was
the one time when his exposition rang false."
Kennedy had even indicated the United States would
not object to a trading arrangement between British Guiana and the Soviet Union if it did not lead to a loss of
national independence. Becoming more precise, Jagan requested some $40 million in United States aid. This
amount was far more than the United States had ever contemplated, and Kennedy remained noncommittal. After

Jagan left, it was decided that no concrete commitments would be made to British Guiana. Each separate request would be judged on its own merits. Informed of this decision, Jagan appealed for another interview with the president, but was informed that Kennedy was too busy.

Not wanting Jagan to be too disconsolate, Kennedy prepared a pleasant letter which was delivered by Schlesinger. Designed only to save face for Jagan, it provided nothing specific. A final statement affirmed that Jagan would "uphold the political freedom and defend the parliamentary democracy which is his country's fundamental heritage," while the United States would send a mission to explore how it could best assist British Guiana's economic development.

Jagan's words had convinced Washington that even if aid were given, a good chance still existed that Jagan would gravitate to the communist bloc; however, if assistance was denied, he would surely issue an invitation to Moscow. Congressional criticism was a certainty if funds were appropriated for British Guiana. Officials at the Agency for International Development observed that their ability to obtain funds for other countries might be compromised if United States money and equipment were invested in a Jagan-led government. But the State Department, impressed by the British argument that no alternative to Jagan existed, was prepared to work with the PPP, until, as Arthur Schlesinger wrote: ". . . Rusk personally reversed this policy in a stiff letter to the British early in 1962." The government of the United States had decided to subvert the legally elected government of British Guiana.[32] In order to save democracy, democracy must first be destroyed.

NOTES

1. See The Daily Chronicle, 22 December 1956. This issue contains a copy of Cheddi Jagan's "Address to the 1956 Congress of the People's Progressive Party."

2. Jagan's speech is evaluated in Despres, Cultural Pluralism, pp. 215-20; and in Simms, Trouble in Guyana, pp. 134-39.

3. Jagan, The West on Trial, pp. 174-76. For a broader perspective on the significance of the party split, see Ralph Premdas, "Party Politics and Racial Division in Guyana," Studies in Race and Nations, 4 (1972-73), a publication of the Center on International Race Relations at the University of Denver; and Raymond T. Smith, "Race and Political Conflict in Guyana," Race, 12 (1971), pp. 415-27. Smith concludes (p. 427):

> that political conflicts have indeed lined up with racial differences and activated a sense of group identity in the major races, but that is not the cause and origin of political conflict. That must be sought in the social and eco-

nomic structure and in the external political environment of these poor, small, and weak ex-colonial territories.

4. For Guyana's economy, see Wilfred L. David, The Economic Development of Guyana, 1953-1964 (Oxford, 1969).

5. Newman, British Guiana, pp. 54-76; and Smith, British Guiana, pp. 58-97.

6. Smith, British Guiana, pp. 180-81.

7. Jagan, The West on Trial, pp. 180-82.

8. Ibid., pp. 182-83.

9. Ibid., pp. 183-84.

10. Despres, Cultural Pluralism, pp. 228-51.

11. The New Statesman, 24 August 1957, p. 216; and 7 September 1957, p. 263. The Economist, 17 August 1957, p. 258; 24 August 1957, p. 264; and 7 September 1957, p. 749.

12. Jagan, The West on Trial, pp. 186-89; Smith, British Guiana, pp. 180-81; Simms, Trouble in Guyana, pp. 140-42; and Newman, British Guiana, pp. 82-87.

13. For a discussion of Jagan's economic plans at this time, see Jagan, The West on Trial, pp. 188-201; Kempe R. Hope, Development Policy in Guyana: Planning, Finance, and Administration (Boulder, Colorado, 1979), pp. 103-5; and Newman, British Guiana, pp. 54-67. See also The Economist of 21 June 1958; and The New Statesman of 1 March 1958.

14. Despres, Cultural Pluralism, pp. 246-49.

15. Ibid., pp. 251-62.

16. Simms, Trouble in Guyana, pp. 143-45; and Jagan, The West on Trial, p. 204.

17. Personal interview with Lord Grey of Naunton (formerly Sir Ralph Grey) at The Travellers Club in London on 21 February 1978.

18. Report of the British Guiana Constitutional Conference, Colonial Office, Command 998, 1960.

19. Despres, Cultural Pluralism, pp. 256-60.

20. See the reprint, "A Stockholders' Meeting of Banks DIH Ltd. in Guyana," which originally appeared in the June and July 1973 issues of Brewers Digest. This article contains a fine discussion of the d'Aguiar family. The activities of Banks DIH Ltd. can be followed in its bimonthly publication, The Pacesetter, and in its Annual Reports. Personal interview with Peter d'Aguiar in his London home on 31 May 1978.

21. Despres, Cultural Pluralism, p. 257; and Simms, Trouble in Guyana, pp. 147-51.

22. Jagan, The West on Trial, p. 205.

23. C. Paul Bradley, "The Party System in British Guiana and the General Election of 1961," Caribbean Studies, 1 (1961), pp. 1-26.

24. Nascimento and Burrowes, A Destiny to Mould, pp. 9-13.

25. The Daily Chronicle, 23 July 1961.

26. Despres, Cultural Pluralism, pp. 236-39.

27. Jagan, The West on Trial, pp. 199-200.

28. Newman, British Guiana, pp. 87-91; Glasgow, Guyana, pp. 118-20; The New Statesman, 25 August 1961, p. 234; and The Economist, 26 August 1961, pp. 808-9.

29. See Serafino Romualdi, Presidents and Peons (New York, 1967), pp. 345-52, pp. 358-59.

30. <u>Meet the Press</u>, 15 October 1961. This is the published transcript of Cheddi Jagan's appearance on the NBC Television Network.

31. Arthur M. Schlesinger, Jr., <u>A Thousand Days: John F. Kennedy in the White House</u> (Boston, 1965), pp. 774-79.

32. Warren I. Cohen, <u>Dean Rusk</u> (Totowa, New Jersey, 1980), p. 204. See also Richard J. Walton, <u>Cold War and Counterrevolution</u> (New York, 1972), pp. 210-13.

6
Racial Warfare
and Foreign Intervention

Few realized that the government of the United
States had decided to eradicate the Jagan regime in British Guiana. A knowledgeable British observer, T. E. M.
McKitterick, concluded that the PPP, despite its failure
to obtain a majority of the popular votes in the recent
election, was in a stronger position than most people
realized; for there was "no alternative" to Cheddi Jagan.
Burnham had "taken his defeat badly to the point of
childishness" and could no longer be taken seriously "as
the political leader of the future." The "strange electoral mixture of ultra-conservatism, Catholicism, and
Moral Rearmament" that Peter d'Aguiar had created was
dismissed as if of little consequence. In fact, McKitterick believed, many of d'Aguiar's bourgeois followers
preferred Jagan to Burnham because they were white su-
premacists, fearful of Georgetown's black community.[1] Raymond T. Smith concluded in late 1961 that Cheddi Jagan
had "shown considerable political acumen in his efforts
to win friends." British Guiana would surely "be granted complete independence during 1962 or 1963."[2]

Undaunted by his meager success in the United
States, Jagan engaged in a flurry of activity. Stopping
in London on his return from independence celebrations
in Tanganyika (now Tanzania), Jagan insisted that Reginald Maudling, the Conservative party's colonial secretary, call a conference to grant independence to British
Guiana in 1962; but Maudling refused. The British were
stalling, and Jagan promptly appealed to the United Nations Organization.[3]

Chapter 11 of the United Nations Charter deals with
"Non-Self-Governing Territories," and calls upon member
states "to develop self-government, to take due account
of the political aspirations of the people, and to assist them in the progressive development of their free
political institutions." Although the colonial powers
had tried to interpret this clause very conservatively,
the arrival of newly freed African and Asian states in
the 1950s and the growth of neutralism and a third world

89

bloc increased the pressure to use the institutions of
the United Nations if a colonial power tried to thwart a
colony's drive for freedom. On 14 December 1960, the
General Assembly agreed unanimously to a resolution pro-
claiming "the necessity of bringing to a speedy and un-
conditional end colonialism in all its forms and mani-
festations." All people were entitled to "complete independence and freedom." Great Britain and the United
States abstained. Almost one year later, unhappy with
the response to its appeal for universal self-determination,
the General Assembly established a seventeen-member Special Committee on Colonialism. Nominated by the president of the General Assembly, this committee was assigned
the task of implementing the United Nations commitment
to abolish the last vestiges of colonialism. Enlarged
to twenty-four members in December 1962, the special committee contained an overwhelming majority of representatives from anticolonial states.

Maudling's negative response prompted Jagan's appeal to this new Special Committee on Colonialism, and
he was invited to appear on 18 December 1961. The British government objected--internal matters could not be
considered at the United Nations. When the special committee insisted on its right to hear Jagan's complaints,
the British delegate urged the PPP leader to speak from
the British chair. Jagan refused, for he intended to
castigate British procrastination on the independence issue and he wished to set a precedent that would aid the
leaders of other colonial areas wishing to appeal directly to the United Nations Organization. To avert condemnation from the special committee, the British government
capitulated in mid-January 1962. A conference was scheduled for May "to discuss the date and arrangements to be
made for the attainment of independence by British Guiana." Victory seemed imminent for Cheddi Jagan. He
would soon be prime minister of an independent Guyana.[4]

His two major domestic opponents, however, Forbes
Burnham and Peter d'Aguiar, did not waste precious moments nursing their wounds after their election defeat.
Although Burnham had supported a resolution calling for
the British to set a date for independence, he and
d'Aguiar now advocated new elections prior to independence on the basis of proportional representation rather
than single-member constituencies.

Speaking to the annual Congress of the PNC on 5 November 1961 in Georgetown, Burnham noted that the party
had recommended proportional representation as early as
1959. He acknowledged, with regret, that in the recent
election voting had been "on the basis of race"; Africans
had voted for him, the East Indians for the PPP, and the
Portuguese for the UF. But the PNC need not be discouraged. They had, after all, won only 4,000 votes fewer
than the PPP. More ominously, he remarked "that the
Legislative Assembly is not our only forum."

The People's National Congress controls the city, the People's National Congress controls the heart of the country,
the People's National Congress, as the election results
have shown, also controls all the urbanised and industrial-
ised area of Guiana and an analysis of the sources from
which we got our votes shows that of the three parties
which contested, the People's National Congress had the
most widely distributed support.

Turning to the PPP, Burnham argued it was constructed on sand. Its left-wing extremism "does not so easily
and readily mesh with the economic aspirations of the Indian community from which it draws support." The PNC
must work to overcome its own deficiencies. It was "a
question of war and the People's National Congress must
do battle," never forgetting its roots in the working
class and its commitment to socialism.[5]
Despite his bombastic rhetoric, Burnham seemed resigned to British Guiana becoming independent in 1962
under the leadership of Cheddi Jagan. The PNC members
of the Legislative Assembly had just joined the PPP in
"calling upon the British government to fix a date in
1962 when Guiana should be independent." No nationalist
leader could survive if he opposed independence. Burnham further noted that constitutional safeguards would
be required to keep Jagan from instituting a dictatorial
regime. Certain fundamental rights and freedoms, including the freedom to organize politically, "must be enshrined in the constitution, enshrined not only by statement but also by its being made impossible for those
rights to be removed or changed in any way unless there
is at least a two-thirds majority, not in the legislature, but amongst the voters of the country."
The British were also prepared to accept the electoral decision of 1961. What now became crucial was
President Kennedy's decision to win British support for
the destruction of the Jagan regime. Anticommunist
United States trade unionists had already begun the
struggle against Jagan and the PPP. During the 1961
election campaign, they were joined by the CIA, but a
sustained campaign to remove Jagan had not been mounted.
Washington's distaste for Jagan, however, was ultimately
decisive--the Marxist must be ousted prior to independence. There would be no more Castros in the Americas.
A number of avenues required exploration. One very
promising approach to subversion might be the black-
controlled trade unions of Georgetown.[6]
After the suspension of the constitution in 1953,
right-wing and anti-PPP elements had taken over the British Guiana Trades Union Council. Aid quickly arrived
from British and United States trade unionists who opposed Jagan's communism. Support was channelled to the
MPCA to prevent GIWU from displacing it. In 1955, the
TUC joined the International Confederation of Free Trade

Unions and the following year entered the Inter-American
Regional Organization of Workers (ORIT), the regional affiliate of the ICFTU. The key United States personality
in these organizations was the passionately anticommunist
Serafino Romualdi, an exile from Mussolini's Italy and a
close associate of David Dubinsky, head of the International Ladies Garment Workers Union. Romualdi had been
designated interamerican representative of the AFL-CIO
and vice-president of ORIT.[7]

Romualdi represented a United States trade union
movement which had jumped far to the right. The former
communist, Jay Lovestone, and his ally, Irving Brown, had
been actively working against communism for some years in
the AFL. The CIO had purged its communist unions in 1949-
1950. The deaths of William Green and Philip Murray, respective leaders of the AFL and the CIO, encouraged re-
unification of the United States labor movement. Walter
Reuther, auto worker leader and new president of the CIO,
agreed to step aside and allow George Meany of the AFL to
assume the presidency of a unified AFL-CIO in 1955. Meany,
a dedicated trade unionist, was rigidly anticommunist.

Knowledgeable about Jagan and the PPP since he visited British Guiana twice a year, Romualdi had greeted
the suspension of the constitution in 1953 with enthusiasm as "the only recourse left to prevent the setting up
of a Communist totalitarian state." Romualdi later remarked: "Having become convinced of Dr. Jagan's subser-
vience to the Communist movement since my first visit to
British Guiana in 1951, I did everything in my power to
strengthen the democratic trade union forces opposed to
him and to expose Jagan's pro-Communist activities from
the day he was elected Prime Minister."[8]

The CIA was already active in British Guiana,
through its infiltration of a United States trade union,
the American Federation of State, County, and Municipal
Employees (AFSCME). Presided over by Arnold Zander,
this not particularly wealthy union possessed little in
the way of an international department when it was approached by the CIA in 1958-1959. Funds were promised
to enable the AFSCME to become more active in the Public
Services International (PSI), a body to which it belonged.
The PSI, a comparatively weak international organization
associated with the ICFTU, attempted to bring trade
union skills to the less-developed countries of the
world. It especially tried to aid civil service unions.
Short of capital, the PSI was delighted when Arnold Zander appeared with bags of money in 1959. He urged that
the funds be employed for a trade union recruiting drive
in the northern part of South America, and that William
J. Doherty, Jr., later identified as a CIA contact, head
the campaign. The PSI would also be required to send
Howard McCabe, a man with no trade union background but
with CIA ties, as its representative to the region. Not
wishing to discover distasteful details, the PSI leaders

neglected to inquire about the source of Zander's fortune. Some years later, the secretary of the PSI admitted: "We did not ask where the money came from because I think we all knew." In 1967, Arnold Zander confessed that his union had been financed by the CIA between 1958 and 1964 through a New York City-based, CIA front known as the Gotham Foundation.[9]

Plotting the downfall of Cheddi Jagan was not difficult, but the deed itself might prove more demanding. The British government and British security services must necessarily authorize CIA subversion on territory still part of the British Empire, and the end in sight was the removal of a freely elected government. Prime Minister Harold Macmillan and Colonial Secretary Duncan Sandys hardly thought twice; much could be tolerated to maintain the "special relationship" with the United States.

Not content with the anticommunist activities of ORIT and the PSI in the Western Hemisphere, the AFL-CIO decided to sponsor a new organization in 1961, the American Institute for Free Labor Development (AIFLD). This body received funds from the United States government through the Agency for International Development, and from the business community. George Meany assumed the presidency, while the wealthy capitalist J. Peter Grace of W. R. Grace & Co. became chairman of the board. Romualdi appeared as full-time director of the organization.[10]

Ostensibly, the AIFLD was an educational project committed to "the development of the democratic trade union movement in Latin America and the Caribbean." It soon branched into other fields like community development, and certainly demonstrated a desire to improve living conditions in Latin America. Alas, the organization was even more deeply committed to working against radicals, Marxists, socialists, and communists, and to furthering the interests of the government of the United States. The AIFLD brought selected trade union leaders from Latin America and the Caribbean to three-month training courses at a center in Front Royal, Virginia.

J. Peter Grace summarized the approach of the AIFLD:

> We must bear in mind that we cannot allow communist propaganda to divide us as between liberals and conservatives, or between business and labor, or between the American people and their government. . . . In this organization we have a joint venture that the communists cannot hope to match--one of free men from all walks of life working together in consensus for a common goal without selfish purpose.

An unstated goal for 1962 was the overthrow of Cheddi Jagan and the PPP in British Guiana.

The road to catastrophe began with the introduction

of the most sensible budget in British Guiana's history
on 31 January 1962. Constructing roads and irrigation
canals would require significant sums of money; therefore, consumption of nonessentials must be curtailed.
Charles Jacob, the finance minister, received assistance
from Nicholas Kaldor, a Cambridge economist of socialist
inclinations who had provided advice to many less-
developed countries trying to industrialize and modernize. The entire nation faced an increase in taxes, but
the rich would clearly pay more. New taxes were proposed on net wealth, gifts, capital gains, and the turn-
over on sales. Import duties on nonessentials were aug-
mented, and an interesting scheme for compulsory saving
was proposed. Five percent of salaries over G$100 a
month and 10 percent from the incomes of the self-
employed and companies would be placed in government
bonds paying 3.75 percent interest. The interest would
be tax free and the bonds could be redeemed in seven
years. Anticipating controversy, the finance minister
postponed debate on the budget until 12 February. This
delay would provide time to explain these serious issues
to the nation. Jagan disliked the tax increases on the
poor, but felt the burden of modernization must be shared
by all.[11]

While The New York Times and The Times of London
praised the budget, Burnham and d'Aguiar perceived a
marvelous chance to make trouble for the PPP government.
Cheddi Jagan never fully appreciated how exposed he was
in black Georgetown. The trade unions of the city plus
the civil service and police were overwhelmingly black.
Unanimously opposed to the PPP, the Georgetown newspapers
pounced upon the budget, arguing, inconsistently, that
the proposals were both Marxist and anti-working class.

Demands increased for Burnham and d'Aguiar to cooperate. Jagan was howled down at a public meeting in
Georgetown when he tried to explain the budget proposals.
Demonstrations became more frequent and excitement intensified. Jagan pleaded with the people not to withdraw their savings from the banks. On 6 February, the
Georgetown Chamber of Commerce criticized the budget.
The TUC also opposed the budget, and rather than discuss
the matter it planned a general strike for the following
week. On 9 February, the government retreated and agreed
to postpone the budget debate for a few days. A bois-
terous audience in the public gallery made it difficult
for Jagan to speak. Burnham and d'Aguiar withdrew from
the Legislative Assembly with their followers after dis-
paraging the budget and calling upon the government to
resign.

Finally beginning to realize his awkward position,
Jagan spoke, angrily, to a half empty chamber:

It has come to the knowledge of the Government that violence is actually being planned on a general scale by

> certain elements acting for a minority group. In addi-
> tion, it is understood, that attempts against the Pre-
> mier's life and the lives of certain of his Ministers
> and supporters are contemplated. These acts of violence
> are intended to secure the overthrow of the legally
> elected Government by force, and the tax proposals in
> the budget are being used as a screen for the general
> strike for Monday, February 12. Since there is no
> likelihood of this strike call being widely supported
> by the workers, certain elements of the business commun-
> ity plan to shut down their business houses. The inten-
> tion is in effect to stage a general lockout on the ex-
> cuse that the strike has created conditions which pre-
> vent continued business operations. Every step possible
> is being taken to bring the Civil Service in on this
> strike and if these designs are successful, the total
> result will be to cause widespread dislocation of the
> colony's economy.

He was convinced his opponents knew they could "depend on foreign support."[12]

The situation deteriorated rapidly during the weekend. Jagan was enveloped by Georgetown's hostility to him and the PPP. Burnham fired up his black supporters, while d'Aguiar rallied the middle class. The TUC leadership responded to Burnham's appeals, and, highly significant, the black-dominated civil service unions prepared to join the antigovernment campaign.

British Guiana's civil servants were convinced that their wages had failed to keep up with inflation. They had received a pay increase in 1954, but had rejected the proposals of a PPP-sponsored inquiry in 1957 as inadequate. The lower grades of government workers were organized in a Federation of the Unions of Government Employees (FUGE) while the higher ranks had formed a Civil Service Association (CSA). Not originally affiliated with the TUC, the CSA had joined the TUC in 1959, becoming more radical and embarking upon a struggle to Guyanize the entire civil service.

In July 1961, another government commission proposed salary and allowance increases for the civil service totaling about G$2.5 million. This proposal seemed much too high for a government so short of money and Jagan procrastinated, though part of the tax increase in the Kaldor budget was earmarked for civil servants. But the government had made no specific commitments, and the civil servants grew more irritated as negotiations continued through January.

A frantic weekend of activity brought together the PNC, UF, and TUC. Mass demonstrations were held in Georgetown and a general strike was scheduled for Tuesday, 13 February. The CSA indicated it would join the strike. This situation could be a desperate affair for the PPP. Throughout Monday and into Tuesday, Georgetown

was alive with speeches, marches, and demonstrations.
     In an effort to keep the civil servants from parti-
cipating, Jagan leaked word that those who went on strike
would be fired and lose their pension rights. Undeterred,
the CSA joined the TUC in a general strike that would
continue through the week. Jagan, hoping for an armis-
tice, capitulated--striking civil servants would not
lose their jobs.
     On Wednesday, the PPP government prohibited public
meetings near the Legislative Assembly, but also announced concessions on the budget. The TUC had opposed
indirect taxes, and, except for a few minor items, these
were to be withdrawn. The compulsory saving scheme lower limit would be raised from G$1200 to G$3600. Designed
to detach the TUC and the PNC from the UF, these concessions proved insufficient. Burnham and d'Aguiar could
sense victory, and the budget was not that important.
The real goal was to eject Jagan and the PPP. On the
following day, Thursday, 15 February, Burnham and d'Aguiar
ignored the prohibition on demonstrations in the area of
the Legislative Assembly. They marched through with
their followers on the way to PNC headquarters where
Burnham and d'Aguiar shook hands.
     D'Aguiar's newspaper, The Daily Chronicle, and the
other newspapers of British Guiana hammered away at the
government. In a radio speech, d'Aguiar thundered:

> If any budget has to be substantially changed because
> pressure has been brought by the people who are being
> taxed, then it amounts to a vote of no confidence. The
> government must stand or fall by its budget. In a de-
> mocratic country, in such circumstances, the normal
> procedure would be for the government to withdraw their
> budget and resign. (Jagan 1972: 218)

Demonstrations against the government continued into the
evening as Burnham worked his followers into what the
Commonwealth Commission, which investigated the incident,
called a "state of frenzy." Governor Grey urged Burnham
to restrain his followers, but the PNC leader refused to
accept responsibility.
     Ambiguity existed about the relationship of the po-
lice commissioner to the minister of home affairs. The
commissioner, with Governor Grey's approval, insisted he
must retain operational control of the police. By Thursday, as fears mounted that police officers and prison
guards would join the strike, the commissioner realized
that Georgetown had slipped from his control:

> I am of the opinion, as a result of the events of the
> past four days, that the present government can resist
> the demand to resign by the opposition political par-
> ties which have today shown definite signs of uniting,
> only by the ultimate use of physical force. The dis-

persal of a crowd by the use of tear smoke is of a temporary nature only, and will not prevent the ultimate need
for the use of more extreme measures. Having reached
this conclusion, I must give it as my considered opinion
that the only means of maintaining the government without
the loss of life will be the presence of a sufficient
number of troops.[13]

At 6:00 P.M. on the evening of 15 February, Jagan,
the Home Affairs minister, the governor, and the com-
manding officer of the British troops at Atkinson Field
met to discuss alternatives. Jagan wanted troops immediately. The governor countered that British troops
should not maintain Jagan in power since British Guiana
had full, internal self-government. There was an implication that Jagan should resign. Faulty memories and
biased reporting provide conflicting interpretations of
what was finally decided. Governor Grey recollected
that he had agreed to bring troops to Georgetown by 1:00
A.M. on Friday morning if the police and prison guards
went on strike. Since they did not, the troops were
kept at their base. Jagan remembered insisting that the
army be sent immediately, and claimed he departed from
the governor's office convinced the troops would be in
Georgetown when dawn broke on what was to become another "Black Friday."[14]
        The demonstrations resumed with the rising of the
sun. No soldiers appeared in Georgetown, and the situation rapidly deteriorated. Attempts were made to close
down the electricity corporation. The riot squad arrived, filled the air with tear gas, and the agitators
fled. Several children were bothered by the tear gas.
D'Aguiar, speaking to a crowd outside his soft drink
factory across the street from Jagan's office in the
public building, where the Legislative Assembly met, received word that one or two children had died from the
gas. Believing this inaccurate report, d'Aguiar announced the news to the crowd. The Commonwealth Commission concluded:

A number of witnesses appearing before us stated that what
Mr. d'Aguiar told the crowd was that the child had in fact
died. We are inclined to the view that Mr. d'Aguiar did
not exercise any restraint upon himself and that he, in
fact announced the death of the child to the crowd and not
its mere illness. We are constrained to observe that his
being wedded to truth did not impose so stern a cloisteral
isolation upon him as not to permit an occasional illicit
sortie, in order to taste the seductive and politically rewarding adventure of flirting with half-truths.

The crowd, overcome with rage, marched around the
parade ground and set off for PPP headquarters on Robb
Street. Police officers worked desperately to assert

control. Suddenly, a shot was heard and Superintendent
D. G. McLeod fell to the ground. A short time later, he
died from his wound. More shots filled the air. Then
the shouting and cursing turned to looting and arson,
and Georgetown's central shopping district disappeared
in flames and smoke. The mob seized everything of value. Most of the police were overwhelmed, although some
probably felt a certain sympathy with the demonstrators.

Not until 2:30 P.M. did British troops finally arrive in Georgetown to end the rioting and to reestablish
order. Fifty-six buildings had been destroyed; many
more were damaged and looted. Insurance claims totalled
G$11 million. Five people were killed and fifty were
injured.

The fatal weakness of the PPP in the nation's capital city was revealed to the opposition parties. They
had almost toppled the Jagan government. One could easily predict that they would try again. The PPP fell
back in disarray, and the budget proposals were further
modified. Jagan caved in completely to the civil service: salary and allowance increases were approved, and
even the days lost by striking were counted as a part of
annual leave. The general strike was called off, but at
a dreadful cost to the Jagan government.

What a colossal victory it had been for those
strange allies, Forbes Burnham and Peter d'Aguiar. Their
tactics on the budget had worked perfectly--they had demonstrated Jagan's inability to control Georgetown. The
passionate anti-British nationalist had been forced to
call upon British arms to keep him in office. On 1
March 1962, the PPP government moved the establishment
of a Commission of Inquiry "to investigate the events
which resulted in death, robbery, arson, malicious damage to property and other offences, and the severe economic loss which the country has suffered." Burnham
taunted the prime minister about his dependence on British troops, and blamed the government's "blundering" for
creating "an atmosphere in which anything was likely to
happen." Burnham argued that Jagan ought to have declared a state of emergency and then relied upon the
British Guiana Volunteer Force and the police. Now, he
continued, there was only one option left--Jagan must
resign, for his government had "collapsed."[15]

The Commission of Inquiry was chaired by a British
judge, Sir Henry Wynn Parry, and included Sir Edward
Asafu-Adjaye of Ghana and Gopal Das Khosla of India. It
arrived in Georgetown on 17 May 1962, conducted a vigorous investigation, and reported two months later. The
commission rejected the views of the cultural pluralists.

> We found little evidence of any racial segregation in the
> social life of the country and in Georgetown. East Indians
> and Africans seemed to mix and associate with one another
> on terms of the greatest cordiality, though it was clear

that the recent disturbances and the racial twist given
to them by some of the unprincipled and self-seeking politicians had introduced slight, but it is hoped, transi-
ent over-tones of doubt and reserve. Among the inhabitants of Georgetown there is, of course, always present
the danger that hostile and anti-racial sentiments may be
aroused by a clash of the hopes and ambitions of rival
politicians. We draw attention to this possibility because there have been indications of such friction in the
past, although, as will appear in the course of this report, the disturbances of February 16th did not originate
in a racial conflict, nor did they develop into a trial
of strength between the East Indians and the Africans.
(Colonial Office, No. 354, 1962:7)

The commission concluded that "there was nothing
deeply vicious or destructive of economic security in
the budget"; and, attacking the budget had been a tactic
employed by Burnham and d'Aguiar to depose Jagan. Since
the split between Burnham and Jagan, admittedly "signs
of racial awareness have been observable, though happily
so far this awareness had not developed into conscious
or active hostility between the East Indians and the Africans." Even the dreadful events on Black Friday were
"not a manifestation of racial rivalry or hatred. There
were no clashes between exclusively racial groups."
Though most East Indians followed Jagan and most Africans supported Burnham, the commission found that the
grievances separating the ethnic groups were "not really
racial, but economic and vocational."
The PNC and UF had no precise plans to overthrow
the Jagan government. Opposition to the budget had been
exploited by Burnham and d'Aguiar to discredit the PPP.
It was ridiculous that they denounced the budget in one
breath as "communist" inspired, and in the next as too
harsh on the working class.

A careful reading of the evidence, therefore, shows that
although there was a certain element of racial conscious-
ness which promoted the tension among the different political parties, the disturbances were not racial riots in
the sense that members of one race strove to do injury to
the personal property of the members of the other race.
The real origin of the riots lay in political rivalries
and jealousies which finally found expression in the criminal acts of a few groups of hooligans.
(Colonial Office, No. 354, 1962:50)

The February riots postponed the new Constitutional
Conference until 23 October 1962. Unable to reach agreement, the conference collapsed two weeks later. Jagan
demanded a date for independence. D'Aguiar retorted
that independence under Jagan meant communism for British Guiana. How, d'Aguiar asked, could Britain contem-
plate such a bizarre notion when the PPP did not even
have the support of a majority of the population? New

elections based upon proportional representation were
required prior to independence. Burnham followed
d'Aguiar; independence was necessary, but it should not
be granted until a proportional representation election
took place. Even though he had angrily rejected any
thought of a coalition with d'Aguiar during the summer
of 1962, Burnham was now advancing in that direction.[16]

Responding to the lack of agreement among the Guyanese leaders, Colonial Secretary Duncan Sandys informed
them that Britain might be compelled to impose a solution. The three Guyanese leaders rejected arbitration
by Sandys. Knowing that the anticolonial powers at the
United Nations would be disturbed by the collapse of the
Constitutional Conference, the British government announced that talks would resume immediately in British
Guiana under the chairmanship of Governor Grey; Jagan,
Burnham, and d'Aguiar must achieve a compromise.

With d'Aguiar absent from the country, Jagan and
Burnham met with the governor on several acrimonious occasions; but, by 11 December, the discussions had disin-
tegrated. Jagan actually conceded new elections prior
to independence, but insisted they must still be conducted on the basis of first-past-the-post. He was
willing, however, to establish a second chamber selected
by proportional representation. Burnham, surprised by
the concessions, doubted that an emerging country could
afford the luxury of a second chamber. Having drawn
blood in February and realizing the extent of United
States support, Burnham was unwilling to compromise. He
wanted one thing, and one thing only--new elections
based on proportional representation. Jagan, growing
desperate as his 1961 election victory slipped away, suggested a coalition government to the PNC. A protracted
correspondence developed, but Burnham would accept no
arrangement that left Jagan in the first position. He
was growing more confident that Jagan could be removed
before independence.[17]

Searching frantically for institutionalized strength,
Jagan turned, once again, to the sugar workers. The
MPCA must be ousted, and replaced by the PPP's GAWU
(Guyana Agricultural Workers Union--the old GIWU of 1953).
Jagan certainly had a very strong case, and no one doubt-
ed that the sugar workers would vote overwhelmingly for
GAWU.

Georgetown was a tense city during the early months
of 1963. Rival demonstrations were continuous; political and racial epithets filled the air. Jagan committed
his dwindling resources and introduced a Labour Relations
Bill, similar to the one of 1953 which had caused him
such trouble. Ten years before, Burnham had endorsed
the proposed legislation, but now he vilified it. The
bill did give considerable power to the minister of labour, but its major purpose was to ensure that workers
were represented by a union of their choice through the

use of a secret ballot. Sixty-five percent of the vote would be required for an established union to be ousted as a bargaining agent. The anti-PPP forces mobilized for action when the TUC joined Burnham and d'Aguiar in opposing the bill.

In late March 1963, Ranji Chandisingh, minister of labour, health, and housing, introduced the Labour Relations Bill without having had full discussions with either the TUC or the PNC. Demonstrations and picketing against the bill started immediately. A fight between quarreling trade unionists at the Rice Marketing Board turned violent on another Black Friday, 5 April. Hooligans joined in and a part of central Georgetown was again looted. Richard Ishmael, president of both the MPCA and the TUC and a prime contact with the various United States groups working to subvert Jagan, decried the bill and threatened another general strike. Moving quickly, the TUC issued an appeal for a general strike on 18 April, to start two days later.

Much depended, once again, on the reaction of the Civil Service Association. At a packed meeting, it endorsed participation in the strike. Never expecting the CSA to join a political strike since it had won its salary demands the previous year, Jagan still calculated the strikers could never hold out for more than thirty days. He failed to consider the strike support funds--estimated at close to $1 million--that would pour in from the AFL-CIO and the CIA. The strike lasted eighty days, a catastrophe for Jagan and the PPP. Top civil servants played a key role in organizing and maintaining the strike. When threatened by Jagan with the loss of seniority, they refused to be intimidated. The tradition of service was sufficiently strong, however, among most of the very senior civil servants that they remained at work to maintain essential services. The permanent secretaries reported for work, but many of the principal assistant secretaries joined the strike. Below the top echelon, most East Indians continued working, while the black civil servants participated in the labor stoppage. With a few exceptions, class had been superseded by race.[18]

The PPP sugar workers wanted to work, but found themselves locked out. Employers chortled at this splendid opportunity for all anti-Jaganites to unite. Critical shortages of food and oil soon developed, and the major airlines ceased service to British Guiana. On 9 May, at Jagan's request, the governor declared a state of emergency. This condition would only last fourteen days, but could be extended by either the governor or the Legislative Assembly. Not wishing to rely too heavily upon the British governor, the PPP sponsored legislation on 20 May to continue the state of emergency. But the Speaker of the Legislative Assembly, Rahman Gajraj, had broken with Jagan after the Kaldor budget. A wealthy, East Indian businessman, he had bitterly opposed the marriage of his daughter to Cheddi Jagan's brother, Derek.[19]

By failing to intervene, Gajraj allowed the opposition to talk the state of emergency measure to death. Jagan and several other PPP legislators were beside themselves with rage and cursed the Speaker. Gajraj promptly suspended them and demanded an apology. Refusing to recant, Jagan had no alternative but to ask the governor to prorogue the Assembly, even though the Labour Relations Bill would be killed and would have to be reintroduced when the Assembly met again. This action ought to have terminated the strike, but it continued for another six weeks. No one could doubt any longer that the general strike had been designed not merely to thwart the Labour Relations Bill, but to destroy the PPP government.

Violence became a daily occurrence throughout the strike, and racial relations deteriorated. In mid-June, Jagan asked for troops but the governor hesitated and the British Army commander demurred. The police chief insisted he could maintain order despite the many incidents.

The strike finally dragged to a bitter end on 8 July. CSA strikers were decisive in negotiating triumphant terms for the pickets. There would be no reprisals against striking civil servants, and the government agreed to consult both the TUC and the employers before introducing a new Labour Relations Bill.[20]

Nine people were dead, and many more had been injured. Ten years after the united electoral sweep of 1953, British Guiana's working class was tearing itself to pieces. Just as the strike was finally being resolved, President John F. Kennedy dropped in to visit with Harold Macmillan, Britain's prime minister. Kennedy had already stopped in West Germany, Berlin, and Ireland, when he arrived for a twenty-four-hour visit with Macmillan on 29 June. Twelve hours were devoted to work. Macmillan was delighted with the results and called it "a great success from our point of view. . . . We got all we wanted." The test ban talks with Moscow were "to be No. 1 priority," and agreement had been reached to "go slow on Multi-Manned." Macmillan concluded: "On other difficult but really less important matters we were in agreement. . . ."[21] Macmillan neglected to mention British Guiana, even though it was high on President Kennedy's list of priorities. Arthur Schlesinger's comments are much briefer, but infinitely more revealing. After discussing West Germany, Berlin, and Ireland in some detail, Schlesinger wrote: "Then to Birch Grove in England, where Macmillan said no on the multilateral force and yes on British Guiana; and to Italy for the last lap." One of America's finest historians would appear to have succinctly described the final decision to remove Cheddi Jagan and the People's Progressive Party.[22]

But without Cheddi Jagan's help, the foul deed would have been much more difficult to execute. Jagan continued to receive support from third world countries at the United Nations. He also counted heavily on assistance from his friend, President Nkrumah of Ghana. Arguing that British Guiana was an internal matter, the British denied United Nations inspection teams entry to the country. Both Burnham and Jagan appeared before a subcommittee of the United Nation's Decolonization Committee. Guinea and Ghana urged a compromise; so, Jagan offered five of eleven Cabinet seats to the PNC. Burnham, however, insisted on a five-five split, the PNC to pocket both Finance and Home Affairs. Jagan objected, arguing that the PPP had, after all, won the general election. Unable to agree, they discussed the possibility of inviting a Commonwealth Committee to investigate and make recommendations. Burnham eventually vetoed this proposal.[23]

Duncan Sandys visited British Guiana in July to make certain the Birch Grove arrangements were being implemented. The entire country was dreadfully troubled; the long general strike had resolved nothing. All eyes now turned to the latest Constitutional Conference, which opened under the chairmanship of Duncan Sandys, at Lancaster House, on 22 October 1963. Burnham and d'Aguiar were adamant, even though Jagan offered a series of compromises--they could see victory. Jagan even conceded a version of the Surinam voting system, which would have mandated twenty-four, single-member constituencies elected by first-past-the-post, with twelve more determined by proportional representation.

Burnham and d'Aguiar demanded Israeli-style proportional representation, with the entire nation a single voting unit. Several days of fruitless talks failed to produce anything substantial. Recognizing his own desperate weakness, Jagan decided upon a reckless gamble which led to his destruction. Relying upon British fair play, but tempting providence, he urged d'Aguiar and Burnham to allow Sandys to impose a solution. Hardly believing Jagan could be so foolish as to sign his own execution decree, d'Aguiar and Burnham hastened to join the PPP leader in asking the British government "to settle on their authority all outstanding constitutional issues, and we undertake to accept their decisions." The letter specifically stated the key issues to be resolved: "The electoral system, the voting age, and the question whether fresh elections should be held before independence." Subversion was no longer necessary; Cheddi Jagan had delivered himself to his enemies.

On 31 October, Sandys announced his decision--it was a total triumph for Burnham and d'Aguiar. New elections were scheduled for 1964, prior to independence. They would be conducted on the basis of proportional representation with the entire nation a single constitu-

ency. The voting age remained twenty-one, and, after
the new elections, another independence conference would
be scheduled. Trying to justify his extraordinary decision, Sandys argued that proportional representation
would "encourage coalitions between parties and would
make it easier for new political groupings to form on a
multi-racial basis." Still hoping to resolve the racial
issue, the colonial secretary concluded that British
Guiana was "faced with an acute crisis of confidence.
While this manifests itself primarily in a racial form,
the cause is basically political. It is therefore a
political solution which must be sought." He was confident the three leaders would accept his decision since
they had requested it. What a coup it had been for
Sandys, Burnham, and d'Aguiar![24]

D'Aguiar smiled broadly; the magnitude of the victory was astonishing. Burnham's position required
greater delicacy. He must not appear to be a puppet of
the British and the Americans. Although recognizing the
scope of Jagan's disaster, he initially jabbed at Sandys
for failing to provide a specific date for independence.
Then he stopped talking, for he realized that with such
luck, the future belonged to him.[25]

A bitter Jagan was staggered by the decision. His
reliance upon the honor of Duncan Sandys had produced
nothing but proof of his own political naiveté. Thrashing about to vindicate his original trust in Sandys, Jagan wailed that, by the fall of 1963, he had had no alternative.

> Our position as a government had become untenable and hu-
> miliating. In actual fact, although we were in office we
> were without any of the real power which a government or-
> dinarily has, as had been shown, especially during the
> 1963 disturbances when our government was under siege. . . .
> In addition, it was my firm belief that had we returned
> home without a decision on independence, the opposition
> would have found some new pretext to stir up riots and
> disturbances, as it had done in 1962 with the budget and
> in 1963 with the Labour Relations Bill, and bloodshed
> would have continued. I have no doubt that the British
> government would have imposed its will in any event. And
> its will, in accordance with the wishes of the U.S. gov-
> ernment, was to unseat us and install the opposition in
> power either by suspending the constitution or by calling
> for a referendum on proportional representation.[26]

Several British newspapers agreed that Sandys had
not been fair, and the opposition British Labour party
noted its own distaste for proportional representation.
Harold Wilson, Labour's leader, referred to the Sandys
proposals as "a fiddled constitutional arrangement." By
10 November, Jagan, determined to fight, was back in
British Guiana mobilizing the PPP for action. He appealed

to his friends from Ghana for assistance. Ghana's United
Nations delegate, Alex Quaison-Sackey, visited British
Guiana in January, and a mission arrived in February.
For a moment it appeared the Ghanaians might be successful. Jagan retreated on a wide front--parity in the
Council of Ministers was accepted, and a single chamber
legislature could be elected by a mixed system of voting.
After considerable procrastination, Jagan even agreed
that the PNC might have the Ministry of Home Affairs if
Burnham would concede that a party should have no representation if it acquired less than 12 percent of the total poll. Confident that a proportional representation
election would give the anti-Jagan parties a majority,
Burnham objected and raised his terms even higher. He
was sure he would become prime minister, with d'Aguiar a
dependent of the much larger PNC. Any compromise with
the PPP would mean a second position for Burnham in a
Jagan government. British Guiana was crying out for a
coalition to unify the races, but Burnham betrayed this
national need as he grasped for power and skillfully evaded
every attempt to bring him together with Cheddi Jagan.[27]

The Ghana mission was troubled by the political
demonstrations. Seemingly, Jagan had lost almost all
black support. Swindled in London, ruined at home by
the budget violence in 1962 and the general strike of
1963, Jagan played his last possible trump card: the
sugar workers.

GAWU had already submitted forms to the Sugar Producers Association indicating that 14,000 of 25,000
sugar workers wished to resign from the MPCA. The SPA
procrastinated, and anger among the workers intensified.
In addition, PPP activists wanted a show of strength after their recent setbacks. A dispute at Plantation
Leonora in early February 1964 quickly spread. By the
end of the month, GAWU had brought most work on the
sugar estates to a halt. When blacks from Georgetown
were transported to work on the plantations, violence
erupted throughout the country. Conditions deteriorated
throughout March, April, and into May. Sir Ralph Grey
heaved a sigh of relief and departed early in the year.
His replacement, Sir Richard Luyt, a South African with
previous service in Ethiopia and Kenya, had been chief
secretary in Northern Rhodesia before being posted to
British Guiana. He arrived to find racial violence, an
economy in ruins, and a prime minister unable to control
the opposition.[28]

Disagreement with Jagan over government and party
policies led to the departure of the moderate minister
of home affairs, Balram Singh Rai. Cheddi Jagan promptly turned to his strongest supporter, and Janet Jagan
accepted the challenge. Daily life in British Guiana
was now marked by bombings, arson, mutilation, and murder. Clearly racial in context, blacks and East Indians
fought out, in a more primitive fashion, the issues di-

viding their leaders. By the middle of July, nearly 150 people had died, and the injured numbered almost 800.[29]

Overshadowing all other incidents was the horrible destruction of the East Indian community of Wismar, just across the Demerara River from the black-dominated bauxite town of Mackenzie. The mutilation of two blacks on 23 May near the village of Buxton had triggered a surge of anti-East Indian feeling. In Georgetown, sixty people were beaten and robbed. Rumors spread that PNC activists were terrorizing the countryside. Janet Jagan heard that atrocities were planned for the Mackenzie-Wismar area. At 2:00 P.M. on Monday, 25 May, the police and army, convinced they were adequately prepared there, refused to send reinforcements to Mackenzie and Wismar. Certain that the local volunteer force would join an anti-East Indian demonstration, Janet Jagan predicted the worst. A call from Wismar confirmed her fears an hour later. She reported to Commissioner of Police P. G. Owen that the situation "had gone beyond control, that a large number of buildings were burning, and that people were being attacked, raped and murdered." Owen responded that he had already requested British troops. It was too late! East Indians had been beaten and chased from their homes. The once pleasant East Indian village of Wismar now contained 200 ruined houses and 2,000 homeless people. Janet Jagan resigned in protest, denouncing the police for partiality to the PNC. On 27 May, the governor agreed to Cheddi Jagan's request for the declaration of a state of emergency.[30]

Violence, outrage, and atrocity swept the tiny colony. Burnham suggested an immediate, all-party coalition government to serve until the election. Realizing his chances of winning a proportional representation election were slight, Jagan recognized that only an accommodation with Burnham could resolve the crisis in favor of the PPP. He responded favorably to Burnham's proposals, but tried to twist them to the advantage of the PPP by insisting the coalition be maintained beyond the election and that the UF be excluded. Except for Jagan's retention of the premiership, the counterproposal included massive concessions to Burnham. The PNC chief would be deputy premier and leader of the Legislative Assembly. After the election, the leader of the largest party would become prime minister, while the head of the smaller party would assume the post of deputy prime minister. Jagan also recommended a United Nations presence in British Guiana to help restore public confidence. His scheme was designed, Jagan concluded, to allow the PPP and the PNC to shape "an agreed program based on a domestic policy of democracy and socialism, and a foreign policy of non-alignment."[31]

Burnham scoffed at Jagan's attempt to harness the PNC after the election. Neither he nor the British government had any interest in salvaging the PPP. At the

Commonwealth Conference in London in July 1964, Dr. Eric
Williams of Trinidad advocated a United Nations presence
in British Guiana. He argued a New Zealander would make
a fine commissioner during the transition period to independence. Williams had already failed on several earlier occasions to ease racial rivalry in British Guiana.
He had hoped that the reasonably good relations existing
between blacks and a very large East Indian minority in
Trinidad might serve as a good example for British Guiana.[32] The British government, however, frowned upon the
Williams plan. Sir Alec Douglas-Home, prime minister
since the retirement of Harold Macmillan the previous
October, was committed to ousting Cheddi Jagan before
independence. Jagan's inability to control the country
provided the British government with a fine pretext for
further limiting his power; therefore, the governor's
authority was enlarged. The PPP leader remained in office, but power was in the governor's hands.

Sandys had to defend his October 1963 decision in
the House of Commons; perhaps, Jagan hoped, the Labour
party would provide some assistance. Most members of
the Labour party opposed proportional representation on
principle because it could lead to numerous small parties.
They especially objected to the form of proportional
representation selected by Duncan Sandys. Regarding the
entire nation as a single constituency would deny the
Guyanese people any sense of being represented by a particular individual. Other types of proportional representation which divided the nation into several electoral areas or linked proportional representation to single-
member constituencies might have been tried. Then there
would have been a more effective link between the people
and their elected representatives.

Speaking for the Labour party on 27 April 1964,
Arthur Bottomley conceded that Conservative tactics to
limit Jagan's authority were better than suspending the
constitution but the British government was now intervening too much. The PPP was being told it could "stay
in power and keep responsibility for running your country, but we are going to interfere to the extent that we
think necessary." Bottomley agreed with Sandys that
proportional representation might lead to a number of
splinter parties obtaining representation, but he feared
they would still be based on race. If Jagan lost the
forthcoming election, the basic racial clash dividing
the Guyanese people would not be resolved. Burnham and
Jagan would simply reverse roles. A constitution was
required that "would have ensured, as far as possible,
that no Government of British Guiana was able to ride
rough-shod over the Opposition." Bottomley also charged
that the new system of registering voters would damage
the PPP's strength in rural areas.[33]

Iain Macleod, one of the few Tories to resign office when Douglas-Home replaced Macmillan, rose to defend

the Sandys proposals, even though they repudiated Macleod's policies as colonial secretary in 1960. Making much of Jagan's pledge to abide by Sandys's decision, Macleod acknowledged they were "highly unusual." Still, they might just work. Ridiculing the United States for its absurd anticommunist hysteria, Macleod recalled that in the past the United States had advocated the dissolution of the British Empire as quickly as possible. Now the United States wanted Britain to hold back independence so long as Jagan retained power. Macleod thought President Kennedy's fears about the PPP were "exaggerated."

> I do not think, for example, that Dr. Jagan himself is a Communist. . . . The American attitude seems to me to be dangerous in this respect. If one puts off independence because one fears that one may get a Left-wing Government, in my experience, the most likely thing to happen is that one will get a Government still further to the Left.[34]

Conservative spokesmen warned Labour members of the Commons that a vote against the Sandys proposals might convince Jagan that a Labour victory in the forthcoming British general election would bring a reversal of British policy. British elections were anticipated in October, while British Guiana's were not scheduled until December. Jennie Lee, Aneurin Bevan's widow and a fiery socialist, was not convinced:

> I do not think that this situation would have arisen if British Guiana had been handled more sympathetically since the end of the last war. I had my own quarrels with my party about this. I do not think that this situation would have arisen if we had been a little kinder to Dr. Jagan and to Mr. Burnham when they first came here. It says something for Dr. Jagan that after the treatment that he received from us from time to time he was such an innocent as to give the Colonial Secretary a blank cheque. I certainly would not have done that. Is that the behaviour of a theoretical Communist? Of course not. It is the behaviour of a rather too innocent fellow. Instead of concentrating fire on Dr. Jagan, I think that we ought to pause and think of what will follow after him if the impression is given that the leadership of the P.P.P. is too soft, and not too hard.[35]

Fenner Brockway, another left-winger, noted Sandys had created the impression that he was

> . . . seeking to reach an agreement between the two sides by impartiality, and this led to the leaders of both sides concluding that if the matter were put to him for decision one would be made which would accommodate the views of all those who were there. If there has been

shock in British Guiana, it has been due to the fact that
those expectations were not realised, that a decision was
made by the right hon. Gentleman which has been acceptable
to one side and entirely unacceptable to the other--a
feeling that he did not act as an arbitrator but acted as
an exponent of the point of view of one party.[36]

Sandys reiterated the arguments he had employed
when he first presented his decision to Jagan, Burnham,
and d'Aguiar, and concluded that proportional representation would give the most accurate representation of
public attitudes in British Guiana.[37] The Conservative
majority remained firm, and the Orders in Council which
had been prepared further increased the governor's powers. Acquiring much of the authority previously dele-
gated to ministers, the governor was in full charge when
the state of emergency was declared on 27 May. Money
could be withdrawn from the Treasury without legislative
approval, and the governor obtained complete control of
arrangements for the 7 December election.

The death by arson of Arthur Abraham, a senior civil
servant, and seven of his children on 12 June provoked a
prompt response by Governor Luyt. Two weeks before, the
British government had agreed that the governor could
use the emergency powers at his own discretion; advice
from the PPP ministers was no longer required. The day
following Abraham's death, the governor arrested some
thirty members of the PPP. Among those placed in detention were Deputy Premier Brindley Benn and four other
PPP members of the Legislature, including Hary Lall, also president of GAWU. Only two PNC activists were taken
into custody, and no UF followers were detained. By a
stroke of the governor's pen, the PPP had lost its majority in the Legislature. The constitution was, in effect, suspended. The governor had openly joined the opposition.[38]

Although the sugar strike finally ended during the
summer, bombings, arson, and mutilations continued. It
was a dreadful atmosphere in which to conduct an election campaign. Then, suddenly, a ray of hope appeared
for Cheddi Jagan. The British Labour party squeaked
through to a very narrow victory in mid-October. Now,
the same person who had ridiculed "fiddled constitutions"
was Britain's prime minister. Unfortunately, Cheddi Jagan did not comprehend that Harold Wilson, elected as
the left-wing candidate to succeed Hugh Gaitskell, was
plunging to the center as he planned new elections to
gain a decisive majority. Anything that might antagonize the United States was bound to be among the last
items on Wilson's list of priorities.

Wilson's foreign secretary, Patrick Gordon Walker,
journeyed to Washington at the end of October to ascertain if the "special relationship" was functioning properly. The United States, delighted with its successful

plot to destroy the elective democracy in Brazil in early
1964, continued to fear both Fidel Castro and Cheddi Jagan. The New York Times reported on 31 October that,
"Mr. Rusk had left Mr. Gordon Walker in no doubt that
the United States would resist a rise of British Guiana
as an independent Castro-type state."[39]
    Colonial Secretary Anthony Greenwood and Secretary
for Commonwealth Relations Arthur Bottomley, old acquain-
tances of Cheddi Jagan, informed the PPP leader that the
clock could not be turned back. The proportional representation election would be held on 7 December. Harold
Wilson granted a small concession--a Commonwealth team
would observe the conduct of the election. From the joy
of his electoral victory in 1961, Cheddi Jagan had journeyed a sad, bitter road during the last three years.
Still, the PPP just might gain 50 percent of the vote;
then, not even the British could refuse independence.[40]

NOTES

    1. T. E. M. McKitterick, "The End of a Colony: British Guiana
1962," The Political Quarterly, 33 (January–March 1962), pp. 30–40.
    2. Smith, British Guiana, pp. 207-8.
    3. See Basil A. Ince, Decolonization and Conflict in the
United Nations: Guyana's Struggle for Independence (Cambridge, Mas-
sachusetts, 1974).
    4. Jagan, The West on Trial, pp. 267-69.
    5. Nascimento and Burrowes, eds., A Destiny to Mould, pp.14-23.
    6. See Colin V. F. Henfrey, "Foreign Influence in Guyana: The
Struggle for Independence," in Emanuel de Kadt, ed., Patterns of
Foreign Influence in the Caribbean (London, 1972), pp. 49–81.
    7. Romualdi, Presidents and Peons, pp. 345-52.
    8. See also Stanley Meisler, "Meddling in Latin America: The
Dubious Role of the AFL-CIO," The Nation, 10 February 1964, pp. 133-
38; and Sidney Lens, "Labor and the CIA," The Progressive, April
1967, pp. 25-29.
    9. This arrangement is discussed by the insight team of the
Sunday Times of London in articles on 16 April 1967, pp. 1, 3; and
on 23 April 1967, p. 3.
    10. Romualdi, Presidents and Peons, pp. 415-33. For a very
critical assessment, see Fred Hirsch, An Analysis of Our AFL-CIO
Role in Latin America or Under the Covers with the CIA (San Jose,
California, 1974).
    11. For the controversy over the budget, see Simms, Trouble in
Guyana, pp. 155-63; Jagan, The West on Trial, pp. 207-14; Nascimento and Burrowes, eds., A Destiny to Mould, pp. 24-35; Newman,
British Guiana, pp. 91-93; Rawle Farley, "Kaldor's Budget in Retrospect: Reason and Unreason in a Developing Area, Reflections on the
1962 Budget in British Guiana," Inter-American Economic Affairs, 16
(Winter, 1962), pp. 25-63; The Economist, 24 February 1962, p. 693;
and The New Statesman, 23 February 1962, p. 252.

12. Jagan, The West on Trial, pp. 213-14. See also Peter Newman, "Racial Tension in British Guiana," Race, May 1962, pp. 31-62; and Raymond T. Smith, "British Guiana's Prospects," New Society, 1 August 1963, pp. 6-8.

13. Report of a Commission of Inquiry into Disturbances in British Guiana in February 1962, Colonial Office, No. 354. See also Nath, A History of Guyana, vol. 3, pp. 55-70; and Ved Prakash Vatuk, British Guiana (New York, 1963).

14. Jagan, The West on Trial, pp. 259-61. Personal interview with Lord Grey of Naunton (formerly Sir Ralph Grey, governor of British Guiana, 1959-1964) at the Travellers Club, London, 21 February 1978.

15. Nascimento and Burrowes, eds., A Destiny to Mould, pp. 24-35.

16. Report of the British Guiana Independence Conference, 1962, Command 1870.

17. Jagan, The West on Trial, pp. 268-75; and Nascimento and Burrowes, eds., A Destiny to Mould, pp. 77-86.

18. B. A. N. Collins, "The Civil Service of British Guiana in the General Strike of 1963," Caribbean Quarterly, 10 (June 1964), pp. 3-13; and Nascimento and Burrowes, eds., A Destiny to Mould, pp. 36-42.

19. Jagan, The West on Trial, p. 244. For the UF view of events, see Peter d'Aguiar, Chaos in Guiana (Georgetown, British Guiana, 1963).

20. Jagan, The West on Trial, pp. 222-47. See also Philip Reno, The Ordeal of British Guiana (New York, 1964); The Economist, 22 June 1963, p. 1247, 13 July 1963, p. 117, 2 November 1963, p. 452; and The New Statesman, 14 June 1963, p. 888, 12 July 1963, p. 35, 19 July 1963, p. 68, 8 November 1963, p. 640.

21. Harold Macmillan, At the End of the Day, 1961-1963 (New York, 1973), pp. 471-72.

22. Schlesinger, A Thousand Days, p. 886. The muckraking journalist Drew Pearson soon became aware of United States activities in British Guiana. See his article of 22 March 1964 in The Washington Post where he concluded that the "main thing" agreed upon by Kennedy and Macmillan "was that the British would refuse to grant independence to Guiana because of the general strike against pro-Communist Prime Minister, Cheddi Jagan. The strike was secretly inspired by a combination of United States Central Intelligence Agency money and British Intelligence." In a letter to the author of 15 May 1978, President Kennedy's secretary of state, Dean Rusk, indicated he did "not recall details of the Guyana matter" and had no "recollection that the matter figured prominently when President Kennedy and Prime Minister Macmillan met at Birch Grove in 1963."

23. Ince, Decolonization and Conflict in the United Nations, pp. 59-90; and Jagan, The West on Trial, pp. 275-78.

24. Report of the British Guiana Conference of October-November 1963, Command 2203. See also The New Statesman, 8 November 1963, p. 640; and The Economist, 2 November 1963, p. 452.

25. Nascimento and Burrowes, eds., A Destiny to Mould, pp. 98-109.

26. Jagan, The West on Trial, pp. 278-87.

27. Ibid., pp. 312-17. For a more critical view of Jagan, see

Simms, Trouble in Guyana, pp. 172-75; and Despres, Cultural Pluralism, pp. 264-67.

28. Ernst Halperin, "Racism and Communism in British Guiana," Journal of Inter-American Studies, 7 (January 1965), pp. 95-134.

29. B. A. N. Collins, "Acceding to Independence: Some Constitutional Problems of a Poly-ethnic Society (British Guiana)," Civilisations, 15 (Brussels, 1965), pp. 376-96; Elizabeth Wallace, "British Guiana: Causes of the Present Discontents," International Journal, 19 (Autumn 1964), pp. 513-44; and Leo Despres, "The Implications of Nationalist Politics in British Guiana for the Development of Cultural Theory," American Anthropology, 6 (October 1964), pp. 1052-72.

30. Jagan, The West on Trial, pp. 307-11; Nath, A History of Guyana, vol. 3, pp. 96-103; Chase, A History of Trade Unionism in Guyana, pp. 297-305; and Hansard's Parliamentary Debates, 696 (9 June 1964), pp. 44-45.

31. Jagan, The West on Trial, pp. 317-19; The Economist, 27 June 1964, pp. 1461-62; and The New Statesman, 15 May 1964, p. 754.

32. Eric Williams, Inward Hunger: The Education of a Prime Minister (London, 1969), pp. 249-300.

33. Hansard's Parliamentary Debates, 694 (27 April 1964), pp. 97-106.

34. Ibid., pp. 106-11.

35. Ibid., pp. 125-28.

36. Ibid., pp. 135-41.

37. Ibid., pp. 155-64.

38. Jagan, The West on Trial, pp. 310-15; Simms, Trouble in Guyana, p. 175; Glasgow, Guyana, pp. 128-30; and Hansard's Parliamentary Debates, 696 (15 June 1964), pp. 937-43, and (16 June 1964), pp. 1096-99.

39. See also Ronald Radosh, American Labor and United States Foreign Policy (New York, 1969), pp. 393-405; and Richard J. Barnet, Intervention and Revolution (New York, 1968), pp. 237-43.

40. Jagan, The West on Trial, pp. 320-23.

7
Government by Coalition

Though the PPP leaders reiterated their criticism of Duncan Sandys, they had no alternative but to mount a massive campaign aimed at achieving an electoral majority. After being buffeted about so much since the 1962 budget fight, most PPP activists were eager to lock horns with the PNC. Every East Indian would be registered to vote.[1]

Burnham, fearful of losing his militant socialists if he moved too close to d'Aguiar, talked optimistically of winning a clear majority for the PNC. A studied vagueness surrounded his comments on the course of action he would pursue if no party garnered a majority and a coalition government was required. The PNC did not deviate from its socialist commitments, but stressed it never received instructions from Moscow. The party would always welcome foreign capital if used in the interests of the Guyanese people.[2]

Denouncing Jagan's atheism, Peter d'Aguiar referred to the PPP leader as a Soviet puppet who would build an iron curtain around British Guiana. No society could exist without a religious foundation, he argued. Basic political and social freedoms would disappear under communism. Only free enterprise, competition, and capitalism could release the creative energies of the Guyanese people.[3]

The state of emergency remained in effect throughout the entire electoral campaign. British troops joined the police in calming the country,[4] but sporadic acts of violence continued as the election approached. Foreign interest intensified. Some could not comprehend the apprehension felt by the United States toward the naive communism of Cheddi Jagan. John Hatch wondered: "How the Americans can deceive themselves that Jagan is a dangerous communist when his seven years of office have not led to any socialist planning and when he has no armed forces, passes my understanding."[5] Hatch regretted the British failure to force a coalition between Jagan and Burnham. Both men were "inadequate in office but

113

dangerous in opposition."[6]

The Sugar Producers did their best to defeat the PPP. On 18 November 1964, Richard Ishmael of the MPCA announced a G$6 million bonus for the sugar workers. Four days later, Fidel Castro's anticommunist sister, Juana, arrived in Georgetown to denounce her brother and Cheddi Jagan. Forbes Burnham had the further advantage of being Georgetown's mayor in 1964; he was also president of Hubert Nathaniel Critchlow's old union, the British Guiana Labour Union. Pouring money into the battle and hoping to influence the public, Peter d'Aguiar reported that a secret poll gave twenty-six seats to his United Force, fifteen to the PNC, only ten to the PPP, with two seats going to minor parties.[7]

A constitutional issue arose when Cheddi Jagan asserted that the leader of the largest party must automatically be given the first chance to form a government if no party had a clear majority. Governor Luyt intervened with a statement on 2 December contradicting the premier. Acknowledging that he would have no choice if one party acquired twenty-seven seats since the leader of that group would obviously become premier, the governor maintained that the situation would be very different if no party had a majority. Then his constitutional duty would be to designate as premier the individual most likely to obtain majority support in the Legislative Assembly. Jagan, convinced this interpretation could only help the opposition, criticized the governor for failing to remain impartial.[8]

A sudden quiet descended upon the country as the Guyanese trekked to the polls on Monday, 7 December. The excitement and fears engendered by three years of crisis were reflected in the turnout--more than 95 percent of the registered voters went to the polling booths. Counting was slow in some constituencies, but it soon became clear that the PPP had not cornered the elusive 50 percent of the vote, even though its share of the vote had increased. The PPP soared to just under 46.0 percent with 24 seats, the PNC received 40.5 percent and 22 seats, and the UF, 12.4 percent and 7 seats. An analysis of the voting pattern demonstrates that, with a few exceptions, it followed racial lines. The various minor parties staggered in with just over 1.0 percent of the vote and no representation; Duncan Sandys had been mistaken about assisting the smaller parties. Unlike 1953, a frightened, tormented people had overwhelmingly voted racially. Only some wealthy East Indians and blacks broke ranks and supported the antisocialist UF.

The British Labour government had made only one concession to Cheddi Jagan; it had appointed a Commonwealth team of observers under the chairmanship of India's Tek Chand to observe the election and to make a report. Composed of eleven members--two each from India, Canada, Ghana, Malta, and Trinidad, and one from Nigeria--the group arrived in British Guiana on 30 November. The team concluded that the "administrative arrangements were fair and proper," though the "proxy system is liable to abuse." Proxy voting was fine for those incapacitated or prevented by their professional duties from voting, but abuses could develop by permitting overseas residents to participate in this manner. No fraud had been observed, though there had been numerous accusations. Understandably, Jagan opposed proxy voting—the PPP secured only 8.6 percent of the 6,665 proxy votes. The observers also criticized the governor for his 2 December statement. "The Governor may be within his rights to construe the intention and language of this provision but the premature disclosure as to how he would exercise these discretionary powers in certain circumstances might have the effect of not merely informing the public but also influencing them." Despite these minor reservations, they unanimously concluded that the "election reflected the political conviction of the Guianese electorate."

While all members of the team signed the final report, Bakar Ali Mirza of India added some personal reflections. He believed the people of British Guiana had passed through "the gateway of fear" before they voted. In reality, Mirza stated, a "racial census" had just been taken. "Where fear exists, freedom is nominal." But the elections had been peaceful. Mirza speculated that, "the significant quietness may even lead to the conclusion that previous racial riots were perhaps engineered." Brooding over the tragic partition of the Indian subcontinent, he observed that "no election, however well conducted can be called fair when it leads to division, racial conflict and creates a sense of fear and insecurity." Proportional representation had been a catastrophe. Mirza conceded that it did provide "room for minorities," but "it also sharpens divisions and creates new ones."

> When there are two almost equal racial groups the appeal
> of P. R. is on racial lines. When it was as in British
> Guiana without the transferable vote the sense of insecur-
> ity, that I have referred to also heightens. The situa-
> tion is further intensified by treating the whole country
> as one Constituency. Voting is not for an individual but
> for the whole part, and for the whole life of the Legisla-
> ture. It is doubly cursed, as it prevents the differences
> from being localised. It also prevents good men from se-
> curing the good will of the other races. It makes the
> race conflict and sense of fear country-wide.[9]

Two days after the election, Gene Meakins, his wife, and children left British Guiana and returned to the United States. Meakins, a United States trade unionist, had worked in British Guiana during the previous year as

public relations officer for the British Guiana Trades
Union Council. Helping to edit the MPCA's weekly paper,
Labour Advocate, he also broadcast a daily radio program,
"Voice of Labour." Convinced Meakins was a CIA agent,
Jagan instituted deportation proceedings, but Meakins
won in the courts. Philip Agee, a former CIA agent, re-
ferred to Meakins as "one of our main labour agents in
the operation." The "operation" was designed to depose
Cheddi Jagan. On 18 December 1964, Agee wrote that
Burnham's victory was "largely due to CIA operations
over the past five years to strengthen the anti-Jagan
trade unions, principally through the Public Services
International which provided the cover for financing
public employees strikes."[10]

Despite a nice increase in support, Cheddi Jagan
and the PPP had failed to obtain a majority of the total
votes. A desperate Jagan now offered Burnham the premiership in a coalition government. Burnham, smelling
blood, refused to negotiate. He would be premier anyway
with UF support, and his bitter enemy of the past ten
years would be out in the cold. Jagan must step down,
and the governor would then send for Burnham, the leader
of the next largest party. One last card remained in
Cheddi Jagan's hand--he refused to resign. To the governor's consternation, the constitution was silent on
this issue. Finally, after an embarrassing interlude,
Jagan was removed by an Order in Council from London.[11]

Since Peter d'Aguiar had announced his intention to
sustain the PNC, Governor Luyt invited Burnham to form a
government on Sunday, 13 December. Some UF members urged
d'Aguiar to aid Burnham but not to enter a coalition.
The majority, however, were thirsty for office, and
d'Aguiar was convinced that coalition would provide the
most effective way to control Burnham and the PNC.
D'Aguiar demanded the Ministry of Finance, confident
that he would then control the country's economy. Two
other UF members were awarded cabinet seats.[12]

Like Jagan, Burnham has a tendency to alienate key,
independent-minded associates. Both seem to prefer syco-
phants. Most PNC members of Burnham's 1964 cabinet have
either quarreled publicly with him or been eased from
office. Only Ptolemy Reid, a United States-trained vet-
erinarian and former employee of Bookers, has been a
permanent ornament in all Burnham's administrations.
Reid, one of the few people Burnham seems to trust, assumed the Ministry of Home Affairs and later became deputy prime minister.

In a radio address to the nation on 19 December,
Burnham, premier at last, emphasized his commitment to
racial harmony. First on his list of priorities would
be the establishment of a consultative assembly so that
all groups might be heard. Speaking again on Christmas
day, he stated that independence was imminent; all Guyanese must remember their "common heritage and goals."[13]

Forbes Burnham was now leading a nation which had
endured ten years of uncertainty and confusion, culmin-
ating in three years of crisis and violence. His government started with a burst of activity, and a sympathetic
United States government responded to d'Aguiar's appeal
for development funds. Some detainees were released as
Burnham made a real effort to bring the ethnic groups
together. He travelled throughout the country and, in
July, summarized the achievements of six months in power.
The country was calm and the economy was improving. Of
most importance, Burnham exclaimed, was "self-help" and
the establishment of producer and consumer cooperatives.
Only through cooperative efforts would each Guyanese
citizen have the chance "of coming together with so many
more other Guyanese in a grand effort for building something of economic significance and importance."[14]

The PPP members of Parliament, hesitant and uncer-
tain, boycotted the Legislature until May; then, not
knowing what to do, they crawled back to their seats.
In a further effort to conciliate the East Indians and
to convince the British that independence was justified,
the Burnham government agreed to a visit by the International Commission of Jurists (ICJ) to investigate alleged racial imbalances in the public services. Recognized by the United Nations Organization, the ICJ is
nongovernmental and nonpolitical. Even though the PPP
had been denouncing the paucity of East Indians in the
public services, Jagan refused to cooperate with the ICJ,
arguing that the PPP had not been properly consulted.
The PPP doubted that any recommendations would be implemented anyway.

The Burnham government accumulated a great mass of
evidence for the commission. The data covered the members of each race in the public service, the security
forces, and the Land Development Schemes.[15] The commission, chaired by Seamus Hendy of the Irish Republic, also included Felix Ermacora of Austria and Peter Papadatos
of Greece. In order to hear testimony, they visited
British Guiana for two weeks in August and, by October,
had completed their report. Although regretting the
PPP's failure to participate, the commission concluded
that all necessary information had been obtained.[16]

The police force statistics showed that there was a
"marked preponderance of Africans." The commission recommended that 75 percent of new recruitment for the next
five years should be composed of East Indians. While
not advocating a crash program or the establishment of
permanent racial quotas, some action was clearly required
to win back the confidence of the East Indian community.
Of 1600 policemen, some 1200 were Africans, and about
300 were East Indians. The number of East Indians in
the police force had increased since 1961, when the Jagan government had decreed that recruitment for the security services must be 50 percent African and 50 percent

all other races. The commission did note that the para-
military Special Service Unit, established in February
1964, was equally divided between East Indians and Africans.

In the volunteer forces, it was obvious that four
of the five companies were overwhelmingly African. "We
find the practice whereby, until 1964, every single Company of the Volunteer Force was established in an area
of predominantly African population does amount to racial discrimination." The commission recommended that
more units be established in the East Indian regions.

The civil service also indicated that Africans were
doing much better than East Indians. But this was partially the fault of history; conditions were improving.
Some East Indians were moving into the higher grades,
but the Africans monopolized the lesser positions. This
imbalance was caused by the African majority in Georgetown and by the fact that, until recently, East Indians
had not been attracted to civil service jobs. East Indians were functioning effectively in the judiciary and
in the teaching profession, but the commission suggested
that something be done to assist East Indian teachers
working in Christian schools. On the other hand, the
Land Development Schemes involved few Africans; they
were dominated by the East Indians.

The report noted that in 1931 only 8.8 percent of
the civil service had been East Indians; however, the
number was now 33 percent. The commission did not believe that rigid quotas in all categories were the answer. Only equal opportunity could resolve the controversy. Good will could be created through education and
by opening the courts to all who felt the sting of discrimination. British Guiana had been wise to agree to
the appointment of an ombudsman; for, he would be very
helpful in responding to accusations of racial unfair-
ness. Ultimately, economic development, the commission
believed, would improve the racial situation by providing jobs.

In certain occupations the East Indians more than
held their own. Almost 70 percent of government-employed
doctors were East Indians, while only 13 percent were
Africans. Likewise, East Indians comprised 42 percent
of government-employed lawyers, while only 23 percent
were Africans. Seemingly, East Indians marched nicely
up the ladder of success when a university education was
required.

Burnham accepted the commission's report and discussed it with the nation on 20 October 1965.[17] Delighted with the commission's view that independence would
improve race relations, Burnham promised to implement
the recommendations "subject only to the restrictions
which our limited financial resources impose on us."
Without early independence, "the community will not find
the common purpose and cohesion of nationhood that are

necessary for the successful pursuit of a racially integrated society." The report only strengthened Burnham's
position as he prepared for independence talks in London
in early November.

The PPP was in disarray throughout 1965. Having
refused to testify before the International Commission
of Jurists, it now proposed to boycott the forthcoming
independence talks. Jagan had often employed the rhetoric of revolutionary communism, and, now that capitalist
tricks had swept the PPP from office, some stalwarts demanded violent action, even though twenty activists were
still in detention.

Only with reluctance had the Jagans finally decided
to participate in that December election. There had
been strong support for a PPP boycott. Brindley Benn,
chairman of the PPP and one of the few important Africans still with Jagan, had never wavered in his opposition to participation in the electoral process; he favored increased industrial agitation. Moses Bhagwan,
East Indian leader of the Progressive Youth Organization,
was convinced the election could not be won. He thought
the PPP should cease acting as a regular political party
and should immediately transform itself into a disciplined, vanguard, Communist party with a militant hard
core functioning both openly and in secret.

The PPP met for its annual Congress in April, and
recriminations were hurled through every corner of the
hall. Jagan struggled successfully to maintain control,
but at an enormous cost. Bhagwan, suspended in July,
resigned in August. In the following year, the purge
fell upon Benn. The Jagans remained supreme but they
had lost more key followers and seemed hopelessly at sea
when it came to defining their policy.[18]

Colonial Secretary Anthony Greenwood's peace mission to British Guiana in February 1965 had been aimed
at obtaining PPP participation in independence talks.
Before agreeing to participate, however, Jagan demanded
an end to the state of emergency and the release of all
detainees. He also demanded that the police and security forces be promptly reconstructed so that they reflected the ethnic distribution of the country. Finally,
there must be a new constitution with a different electoral system. Jagan challenged Greenwood's contention
that Burnham was a socialist and vilified the PNC leader
for serving with the antisocialist d'Aguiar. The peace
mission was a failure.[19]

Once the constitutional and independence talks were
set for early November, Jagan did meet with Burnham.
Jagan reiterated his final terms: the state of emergency
must be terminated and all political detainees released.
When Burnham refused, Jagan responded that the PPP would
boycott the independence talks. The PNC leader was
probably delighted with Jagan's decision. Without the
presence of the PPP, the independence talks were sure to

proceed to a smooth and rapid conclusion.[20]

A personal appeal from Greenwood to Jagan was again rejected by the PPP chieftain. Jagan cut his own throat by refusing to participate. Many significant constitutional concessions might have been won, which could have prevented Burnham's swift moves to despotic government after independence. With Jagan absent, the independence conference completed its deliberations between 2 November and 19 November. S. S. Ramphal, a distinguished East Indian lawyer and nonparty member of the coalition government in which he served as attorney-general, had drafted a constitution for an independent Guyana.[21]

Ramphal's constitution proposed that the Legislature remain a single house selected by nationwide proportional representation. It was suggested, however, that members be linked to particular regions. Impartial commissions were to be maintained to supervise the judiciary, police, and public service. An ombudsman would be appointed to assist citizens who felt they had received unfair treatment. Certain clauses designed to protect citizen rights would be entrenched in the constitution, and a two-thirds vote of the Legislature or a nationwide referendum would be required to alter them.

To overcome ethnic suspicion and fear, this constitution designed an independent Guyana as a genuine consultative democracy. The leader of the opposition was formally recognized in the constitution, and he had to be consulted on certain matters. The constitution further provided for an election commission to supervise the conduct of future elections. It would be presided over by a judge or ex-judge and contain one representative from each party with more than five members in the Legislative Assembly. Private property was guaranteed by the constitution. If the government demonstrated a need to requisition private property, then prompt and adequate compensation was required.[22]

Independence was set for 26 May 1966. Burnham was overjoyed, d'Aguiar, apprehensive. Jagan sarcastically noted that the designated day was the second anniversary of the Wismar Massacre. Anxiety intensified; what would happen when the British departed and the Guyanese began to handle their own affairs? Queen Elizabeth II visited the country in February and received a warm reception. And then, finally, the fateful day arrived; British Guiana became the independent state of Guyana.[23]

Guyana, like most former parts of the British Empire, decided to remain within the Commonwealth of Nations. Peter d'Aguiar had been particularly insistent that the monarchy be retained and that Guyana not become a republic. Agreement was reached that new elections be held by December 1968. Only then would a decision be made on whether to establish a republic. But d'Aguiar was becoming increasingly disturbed by his lack of real power and by the governmental corruption which seemed to be increasing at an extraordinary rate. His optimistic first budget on 14 April 1965 demonstrated his belief in free enterprise capitalism; however, it appalled Burnham and his socialist followers. The finance minister, confident of United States aid, increased capital expenditures by 266 percent over the previous year. Manufacturers and traders obtained numerous concessions; foreign exchange controls were relaxed. Inheritance and corporation taxes were also reduced.[24]

The United States poured in more than $5 million worth of equipment plus assistance for road repairs and airport renovation. Professor Sir Arthur Lewis and other expert economists provided advice in the preparation of a new, five-year plan covering the first years of independence. By the end of 1966, however, d'Aguiar sensed that all was not well; he had underestimated Burnham. The PNC leader had not abandoned his socialist ideas. Even worse was the staggering amount of corruption as the PNC rewarded the Georgetown faithful. The sound business sense and efficient mind, which had made d'Aguiar's business a model for the entire Caribbean, were outraged. Had he cast out the Devil only to bring in the Devil?[25]

With independence, Burnham replaced the governor as chief of the security forces. During the violence, the British garrison had, at one time, consisted of two infantry battalions, a helicopter unit, and support services. With the exception of some senior officers and a small training unit of about thirty men, they were all removed in October 1966. The Guyana Defense Force and the Guyana police were now responsible for internal security and for protecting the frontiers against border incursions from Brazil, Surinam, and Venezuela. Anthony Verrier, defense correspondent of The Observer, visited Guyana for five weeks in 1966 and wondered:

> For the biggest question hanging over Guyana is what will happen in 1968. General elections are due then, and from Mr. Burnham downwards few expect his party, the African People's National Congress, to retain power through the ballot box. Guyana's constitution provides for proportional representation, and it is no secret that this was devised by the British Government in 1964 in the hopes of permanently excluding Mr. Burnham's opponent, the allegedly communist Dr. Cheddi Jagan, who leads the Indian People's Progressive Party.
>
> Unfortunately for these calculations, it now appears that the past, let alone present, fertility of the Indian population is such that its voters in 1968 are likely to outnumber the P.N.C. and its coalition partners put together.[26]

Forbes Burnham was as aware as Anthony Verrier of the fact that he would probably lose a free election in

1968. But Burnham was not merely in office, as Cheddi
Jagan had been. He had real power and, with the departure of the British, could mobilize all the influence
and patronage of the state in order to make sure that
the votes were counted before the election took place.
Burnham had the guns, and he was prepared to use them to
insure his retention of power. Despite his pledges to
implement the recommendations of the International Commission of Jurists, Burnham maintained the overwhelmingly African composition of both the Guyana Defense Force
and the police. He intended to take no chances with
East Indians, whose loyalties might be open to doubt.
Shortly after independence, the coalition regime passed
a severe National Security Act. It gave the government
the right to suspend habeas corpus and to detain Guyanese when necessary for national security.[27]

Matters grew worse for Peter d'Aguiar in 1967. He
felt adrift in a sea of corruption, and he wondered if
he would drown. More than G$1 million had been spent
illegally on the East Coast highway, and the director of
audits was unable to produce proper vouchers for almost
G$20 million of government expenditures. The PNC even
thrust the party faithful into the supposedly impartial
civil service, judicial, and police service commissions.
Burnham was moving more rapidly than even his most bitter opponents had contemplated toward one-party control
of the state. One possible source of embarrassment
still existed--he lacked a majority in the present Legislative Assembly.

By September 1967, rumors surged through Georgetown
that an open quarrel between Burnham and d'Aguiar had
erupted. D'Aguiar drew back from a complete break, for
Jagan still seemed an even worse alternative than Burnham. In an incredibly inept performance, d'Aguiar resigned from the cabinet over an issue that could not
conceivably win him much support. He opposed Burnham's
choice for income tax commissioner, insisting that as
finance minister he must have someone in this post upon
whom he could rely. D'Aguiar's position was further
compromised by his preference for an expatriate rather
than a Guyanese for the vacant position. Reasonably
pleasant letters were exchanged between d'Aguiar and
Burnham, and d'Aguiar left as an individual while maintaining UF membership in the coalition government.[28]

Ptolemy Reid succeeded d'Aguiar as finance minister,
and introduced a new budget in the last days of December.
Jagan pounced upon it for not being sufficiently socialist, while d'Aguiar exploded for opposite reasons.
D'Aguiar stated it was "unrealistic," providing too much
"lavish and wasteful expenditure." Why spend money on a
Guyana Defense Force which passed the days losing its
equipment? Increasing taxation would be disastrous,
d'Aguiar continued, for it would limit investment from
the private sector.[29]

The death of the Speaker of the Legislative Assembly led to a furious battle between the PNC and the PPP over the choice of a successor. Once again, d'Aguiar caved in. He joined Burnham in designating an East Indian, Rahman Gajraj for the position. In 1961, Gajraj had won the Speakership with Jagan's blessing. A short time later, however, forgetting the traditional impartiality of the Speaker, he turned into an opponent of the PPP. He had been responsible for Jagan's failure to extend the state of emergency during the general strike in May 1963.

By early 1968, opportunists could sense the direction the wind was blowing. Several desertions to the PNC had already occurred. The defectors may have believed the PNC was best equipped to govern the country, maybe they had been bought, perhaps a combination of both. Two PPP parliamentarians, Mohamed Saffee and George Bowman, joined the PNC as did Mohamed Kasim of the UF. Burnham could almost taste a majority of his own. [30]

At the PNC annual Congress in April 1968, Burnham thundered against coalitions. The PNC, he complained, was constantly thwarted by the UF. After the next election, the PNC must have a clear majority so that its program could be properly implemented. [31] In 1967, the PNC began to register all Guyanese, both in Guyana and overseas. Help was obtained from Shoup Registration Systems Inc. of the United States, accused by some of having links to the Central Intelligence Agency. By mid-1968, the registration activity had intensified; it was obvious that elections would be held, as required, in December. The PPP accused the PNC of fraud and irregularities as registration proceeded. A National Registration Center had been officially established in April, and its lists would be used in the next election.

In October, legislation was introduced to give the party leader authority to designate the individuals to serve in the next Legislative Assembly. In 1964, the candidates were ranked from number one to number fifty-three (the total number of seats). Victorious candidates were taken from the list in numerical order depending upon the percentage of votes obtained by each party. Now, with the names listed in alphabetical order, the party leader could designate, after the election, who would serve. The change was a massive increase in power for the party leader. Legislation was also brought forward to permit voting by overseas Guyanese and to allow a greater use of proxies. Any "good cause" would be sufficient to permit a proxy vote. The Elections Commission was being ignored. Contrary to the constitution, the government was seizing control of the electoral machinery. By-elections would disappear; the party leader could simply designate a replacement from the list of candidates nominated at the election. [32]

Such drastic legislation required a constitutional
majority of twenty-seven votes. D'Aguiar was outraged;
debate was fast and furious. PNC pressure on UF member
Rupert Tello, also Deputy Speaker, began to have an effect. If he went with the PNC, Burnham had his twenty-
seven votes.

D'Aguiar attacked the bill, for it would lead inevitably to a one-party dictatorship. On 24 October 1968,
d'Aguiar finally withdrew the UF from the coalition government. After an animated debate on the following day,
the vote was taken. Rupert Tello marched into Burnham's
arms, and Burnham had his twenty-seven votes. Burnham
stood victorious; but Guyana lost something it has still
not recovered. Cheddi Jagan stomped out in anger. He
and d'Aguiar prepared to challenge Burnham in the courts.[33]

Burnham moved rapidly to consolidate his coup.
Elections were set for Monday, 16 December. A native
Guyanese, Sir David Rose, had replaced Governor Luyt
near the end of 1966. No doubt existed, however, that
Burnham would establish a republic if he won the elections. Speaking to a special Congress of the PNC on 3
November, Burnham warmed up his troops for the electoral
battle. Emphasizing the need to retain the tough National Security Act of June 1966, he reminded his listeners that all political prisoners and detainees had
been released. Burnham enumerated the PNC achievements
of the past four years: peace and racial harmony throughout the country, a strengthened economy, a decrease in
unemployment, and a significant number of self-help and
community development projects designed to implement
Burnham's strong commitment to building a cooperative
society. In response to opposition grumbling about a
PNC dictatorship, he thundered: "And may I unequivocally
state that elections will, as long as I have the last
word, always take place as provided by the Constitution
of Guyana. I shall never remain in office save by your
will--the people's will." Acknowledging the rumors that
d'Aguiar and Jagan were negotiating to construct a unified opposition to the PNC, Burnham, ignoring his own
strange marriage to d'Aguiar in 1964, observed: "Two
parties whose proclaimed, I emphasize proclaimed ideolo-
gies, philosophies and goals are miles apart now lie together in sterile concubinage. Shades of the Hitler-
Stalin pact of 1939." The PNC needed a clear, decisive
majority. He implored his audience to grant him a free
hand: "I do not have the physical capacity and stamina
to deal with another coalition government."[34]

By the end of the month, the prime minister was
worried, even though he controlled the electoral machinery and vote counting. He rediscovered the "Red Menace"
and accused the PPP of having ties to revolutionary
groups in Venezuela.[35] Venezuela was deeply into its
presidential election campaign. The Democratic Action
party, which had governed the country since the overthrow

of the Marcos Pérez Jiménez dictatorship in 1958 and
provided Presidents Rómulo Betancourt and Raúl Leoni,
was about to be defeated on 1 December by the more conservative Social Christians led by Rafael Caldera.
Events in Venezuela were always carefully watched by the
Guyanese because of the ever-present boundary dispute.

Guyana's Elections Commission failed in its constitutional obligation, and the PNC stepped in and ran the
election. Proper facilities were not provided for check-
ing names on the electoral registers. Llewellyn John,
minister of home affairs in Burnham's cabinet, actually
conducted the election, making sure the PNC would win.
The PPP and the UF had no luck in the courts; their attempts to stop the election were unsuccessful.[36] Angry
street scenes, rowdy mass meetings, and racial incidents
marred the final days before the balloting. Georgetown
remained a PNC stronghold, but Burnham and John were astonished by the depth of antigovernment feeling in the
sugar belt. Their attempts to woo the East Indians over
the past four years had failed; they turned back to
their traditional black support and to electoral manipulation.

Burnham was indignant enough at being called a
corrupt politician by Jagan and d'Aguiar. He was outraged, however, when, on 9 December, Britain's Granada
Television Company presented a thirty-minute documentary
on its "World in Action" program called "The Trail of
the Vanishing Voters."[37] Much of the program was based
upon work performed by Humphrey Taylor's prestigious
Opinion Research Centre. This organization, commissioned
by d'Aguiar, conducted a survey of the names listed by
the government as overseas Guyanese qualified to vote.
The Opinion Research Centre selected 1,000 names for investigation, indicating that, at most, there might be a
sampling error of 3 percent. It came up with the most
extraordinary results. On the basis of a survey conducted in the United Kingdom between 7 October and 20
October 1968, the Research Centre concluded that 25 percent of the addresses did not exist. When the addresses
did exist, some 41 percent failed to house the individual listed, and 1 percent were not Guyanese. Seventy-two
percent of the names examined, therefore, were not entitled to vote. Further investigation led to the conclusion that only about 15 percent of the names on the
overseas electoral register for the United Kingdom were
valid.

The television program began by showing two horses
grazing at 163 Radnor Street in Manchester, where Lily
and Olga Barton were registered to vote in the Guyana
election. Electoral lists had been prepared indicating
that 38,000 Guyanese lived in London with about 7,000 in
the rest of Great Britain. The British census figures
revealed, however, that just over 20,000 Guyanese resided in Great Britain, not 45,000. Lancelot Ferreira,

commissioner of registration, had prepared the lists under the supervision of Chief Election Officer Reginald Butler, and he insisted upon their accuracy.

"World in Action's" investigative reporters confirmed the results of the Opinion Research Centre. Of 550 names checked in London, only 100 were genuine; one-half of 350 addresses in Manchester did not exist. There had been a massive fabrication. The elderly black judge, Sir Donald Jackson, chairman of the Elections Commission which was constitutionally required to guarantee fair elections, stammered: "It is not for me to enquire and in point of fact I do not go about looking for faults. I try to find out the best in everyone so that I may improve my own imperfections." Sir Donald was neither independent nor impartial. Each of the three major parties had a representative on the Elections Commission. Regrettably, the commission was in constant deadlock because Jackson always voted with the PNC representative while Janet Jagan, delegate from the PPP, sided with the UF nominee.

The Granada television show then turned to Joe Hughes, a Guyanese citizen living in Wolverhampton. Hughes had been put in charge of registering Guyanese inhabitants of that city. When interviewed, he stated he had registered forty-one people. He could not explain why, or how, his list had suddenly grown to 225 names. Lionel Luckhoo, Guyana's high commissioner in London, declined to appear. Forbes Burnham, refusing to show embarrassment, chuckled and blandly stated he was completely satisfied that the electoral registers were accurate. The "World in Action" reporter concluded that "the scale of the discrepancies indicates something more sinister than incompetence." He wondered "whether our vanishing votes will reappear in the ballot boxes of Georgetown." They did.

Election day on 16 December passed peacefully with tight security and a good voter turnout.[38] Within Guyana the biggest initial complaint centered on the right of one individual to cast as many as three proxy votes. Some citizens appeared to vote and were told that a proxy had already been exercised for them. When the polling places closed, UF and PPP counters found themselves excluded from a number of the counting places.

Despite all the pressure employed by the PNC militants--beating the opposition, padding electoral registers, and irregular proxy voting--the PNC only received 50.4 percent of the total vote within Guyana. This vote would have given the PNC twenty-seven seats and the combined opposition twenty-six. This was not much of a victory for Forbes Burnham; an honest vote at home would clearly have removed him from office and probably given Cheddi Jagan an electoral victory without requiring any support from the UF. But this situation might well have led to civil war, as the PNC controlled the Guyana Defense Force (GDF), the police, Georgetown, New Amsterdam, and Mackenzie.

What gave the PNC a sizable victory--even if fraud-ulent--was the overseas vote. Just over 68,000 overseas citizens had been registered and some 36,000 participat-ed in the election. The PPP and the UF received about 1,000 votes each. The other 34,000 went to the PNC and, with it, a decisive electoral win.

In a pathetic performance, Sir Donald Jackson, chairman of the Elections Commission, certified the re-turns on 21 December 1968. The PNC was first with al-most 56 percent of the vote and thirty seats, the PPP acquired just under 37 percent of the vote and obtained nineteen seats, and the UF was awarded four seats as a consequence of having obtained a little over 7 percent of the total vote.

Granada television's "World in Action" team hoped to perform a follow-up to its first show now that the elections were over. On 21 December, Burnham was asked to allow the Granada people into Guyana. Within twenty-four hours they received a curt rejection; no "World in Action" reporters could enter the country. Burnham wanted no additional criticism as he was preparing to attend the Commonwealth Prime Minister's Conference in London in early January. Granada plunged ahead with the program, and Jagan and d'Aguiar were brought to London. On 6 January 1969, just as Burnham arrived for the Com-monwealth meeting, "World in Action" presented "The Mak-ing of a Prime Minister." It was a devastating perfor-mance for the Guyana government. The show began with a summary of the fraudulent proxy voting, the padded elec-toral lists, and the dishonest counting in Guyana. Once again, viewers were reminded of the fake lists of names which had been prepared in Great Britain; the majority of these individuals did not exist, yet most had voted in Guyana's election. "World in Action" then surveyed the Guyanese living in New York and concluded that, as in Britain, most of these people and many houses did not exist. Only about four names in ten were genuine, and some of these people had already become United States citizens.

The Guyana government's claim that 68,000 Guyanese were living overseas was absolutely false. At the most there were about 30,000, yet 36,000 overseas votes had been recorded. Also, between 1964 and 1968 the total electoral list had strangely increased by 21 percent while in the eleven-year period between 1953 and 1964 it had gone up by only 19 percent.[39] How odd that the voter increase should only be 10 percent in the East Indian areas on the Corentyne, while Mackenzie showed a stagger-ing jump of 109 percent. In contrast to 1964 when the votes had been tallied in more than thirty different places, all the ballots were now transported to three centers--Georgetown, New Amsterdam, and Suddie. Was

this change to provide ample time for tampering and
stuffing the boxes?[40]

While it is difficult to have much sympathy for
Peter d'Aguiar after his violent, abusive tactics in
1962, a twinge of pity may be felt as he mournfully commented: "I feel that I should have acted quicker, that I
shouldn't have been so naive, that I should have seen
what was going to happen." A "plot" to subvert the constitution began on the day Burnham became prime minister.
There had been no election in Guyana, "it was a seizure
of power by fraud, not an election." D'Aguiar reiterated his opposition to communism but concluded that "the
worst thing you can do is to give the communists a valid
excuse for a violent revolution. And I can't think of a
better excuse than a fraudulent election, than a parti-
san government that lives it up at the expense of the
people. These excuses are being presented on a platter
to the communists in Guyana."[41] Thoroughly disgusted and
humiliated, d'Aguiar announced his resignation as UF
leader and his retirement from active politics. Partially responsible for bringing Burnham to power in 1964,
he now retreated to his investments at Thirst Park.

The final word is best left with Humphrey Taylor,
director of the Opinion Research Centre. Conceding he
knew nothing personally about the electoral lists within
Guyana, he did not hesitate to affirm that the one compiled for Great Britain "was a totally dishonest and
corrupt operation," since "the great majority of people
listed do not exist." The election was "unprecedented
for a Commonwealth country" and "a pretty awful and dis-
graceful episode."

Burnham was embarrassed and annoyed by the accusations of a rigged election. But while his opponents
hurled verbal abuse, the PNC leader could afford to put
on a show of serene indifference. He was in power, controlled the army and the police, and knew that as long
as Jagan chanted the Soviet line there was nothing to
fear from the United States. Now, however, there could
be no excuses for Forbes Burnham; he could not blame his
failures on a coalition government. The PNC was solidly
entrenched in power, and it must accept responsibility
for both failures and achievements. Would Forbes Burnham be able to win East Indian support without losing
the backing of the black militants upon whose shoulders
he had been carried to power? The future of Guyana
would depend upon whether he developed into a judicious
statesman prepared to lose some black support in order
to build a unified Guyanese nation, or whether he was
simply an opportunist, ready to employ every trick to
stay in power, but unwilling to use that power in a
creative, constructive manner.

NOTES

1. See B. A. N. Collins, "The End of a Colony--II," The Political Quarterly, 36 (October-December 1965), pp. 406-16.

2. Nascimento and Burrowes, eds., A Destiny to Mould, pp. xxvii-xxviii.

3. The 1964 election manifesto of the United Force was published under the title, Highways to Happiness.

4. See Anthony Verrier, "Guyana and Cyprus: Techniques of Peace-Keeping," Journal of the Royal United Service Institution, 111 (November 1966), pp. 298-306.

5. The New Statesman, 15 May 1964, p. 754.

6. The New Statesman, 11 December 1964, pp. 913-14.

7. The very strong views of Peter d'Aguiar can be followed in The Daily Chronicle and The Sunday Chronicle. D'Aguiar owned a controlling interest in this newspaper from 1961 until he sold it to the government in 1971. The fairest and most judicious paper throughout this period and until its purchase by the government in 1974 was The Guyana Graphic and The Sunday Graphic. The Graphic organization was a part of the international chain of newspapers owned by Lord Thomson (formerly Sir Roy Thomson).

8. See the Report by the Commonwealth Team of Observers on the Election in December 1964, Colonial Office, No. 359, 1965.

9. Ibid., pp. 14-15.

10. Philip Agee, Inside the Company: CIA Diary (London, 1975), p. 406.

11. Jagan, The West on Trial, pp. 324-26; and Simms, Trouble in Guyana, pp. 176-78.

12. The Economist, 12 December 1964, p. 1231, and 19 December 1964, p. 1331.

13. Nascimento and Burrowes, eds., A Destiny to Mould, pp. 43-47, 117-19.

14. Ibid., pp. 48-58, 120-25. See also Bertram Collins, "'Consultative Democracy' in British Guiana," Parliamentary Affairs, 19 (Winter 1965-1966), pp. 103-12.

15. See the Memorandum Presented by the Government of British Guiana to the Commission of Inquiry, International Commission of Jurists, July 1965. This five-part submission contains a mass of fascinating information about the ethnic groups of the nation and the extent to which they were members of the security forces, the public service, government agencies, local government bodies, primary education, etc. For a discussion of the Guyana Defense Force, see Cynthia H. Enloe, "Civilian Control of the Military: Implications in the Plural Societies of Guyana and Malaysia," in Claude E. Welch, Jr., ed., Civilian Control of the Military (Albany, New York, 1976), pp. 65-98.

16. Report of the British Guiana Commission of Inquiry, International Commission of Jurists, Geneva, Switzerland, October 1965.

17. See B. A. N. Collins, "Racial Imbalance in Public Services and Security Forces," Race, 3 (1966), pp. 235-53.

18. Simms, Trouble in Guyana, pp. 177-82.

19. Jagan, The West on Trial, pp. 326-33. Personal interview with Lord Greenwood of Rossendale (formerly Anthony Greenwood), House of Lords, 6 February 1978.

20. Jagan, The West on Trial, pp. 333-39.

21. Nascimento and Burrowes, eds., A Destiny to Mould, pp. 110-13. Personal interview with S. S. Ramphal, now secretary general of the Commonwealth Secretariat, Marlborough House, 27 February 1978. Ramphal served under Burnham until he accepted the prestigious Commonwealth position in 1975, a post he still occupied in early 1984.

22. Report of the British Guiana Independence Conference, Command 2849, December 1965.

23. See the article by Colin Henfrey in The Listener, 2 June 1966, pp. 781-83. For a PPP view of independence, see H. J. M. Hubbard, "Guyana—Another U.S. Satellite?" New World Review, 34 (August-September 1966), pp. 35-40. There is a judicious assessment of Guyana at the moment of independence in a Special Supplement to The Times on 26 May 1966.

24. Mitchell et al., Area Handbook for Guyana, pp. 184-86; and Jagan, The West on Trial, pp. 381-89.

25. See W. M. Ridgwell, The Forgotten Tribes of Guyana (London, 1972). Ridgwell was an advisor to the United Force in 1967-1968.

26. Verrier, "Guyana and Cyprus," p. 299.

27. George K. Danns, Domination and Power in Guyana: A Study of the Police in a Third World Context (New Brunswick, New Jersey, 1982), pp. 30-33.

28. D'Aguiar's disenchantment with Burnham's policies can be followed in the pages of The Guyana Graphic and The Sunday Graphic. See especially the exchange of letters which followed d'Aguiar's resignation, The Guyana Graphic, 26 September 1967; and Carl Blackman's evaluation in The Sunday Graphic, 1 October 1967. The reports of the debates in Guyana's Legislative Assembly are also of importance.

29. The Guyana Graphic, 9 January 1968.

30. Ibid., 20 February 1968; and The Sunday Graphic, 18 February 1968 and 25 February 1968.

31. Nascimento and Burrowes, eds., A Destiny to Mould, pp. xxx-xxxii; and Nath, A History of Guyana, vol. 3, pp. 145-46.

32. See The Guyana Graphic and The Sunday Graphic for October and November of 1968.

33. Nath, A History of Guyana, vol. 3, pp. 147-49.

34. L. F. S. Burnham, It Is a Matter of Survival (Georgetown, Guyana, 1968). This reprint is of Burnham's speech of 3 November 1968.

35. See The Case of Pedro Beria. This reprint is of Burnham's speech to the nation on 30 November 1968, in which he tried to show close links between Cheddi Jagan and revolutionary groups in Venezuela.

36. See the Report on the National Assembly General Election of 1968 (Georgetown, Guyana, 1969). This report was prepared by the chief election officer, Reginald C. Butler.

37. The author wishes to thank Granada International and Miss Julie Sinclair for arranging a special showing of "World in Action's" "The Trail of the Vanishing Voters" and "The Making of a Prime Minister."

38. For a detached and scholarly assessment of the Guyanese

people at this time, see J. E. Greene, Race versus Politics in Guyana: Political Cleavages and Political Mobilisation in the 1968 General Election (Kingston, Jamaica, 1974).

39. Ibid., p. 29. Greene provides a partial explanation for the jump in numbers. Believing that the size of the registered electorate was too low in 1964, he notes that "compulsory registration in 1968 tended to redress the 1964 inconsistency, and what has therefore resulted is that the 1968 figures represent both natural increases from 1964 to 1968 together with corrections for the under registration in 1964 which was voluntary."

40. Jagan, The West on Trial, pp. 389-93.

41. Granada Television, "World in Action," "The Making of a Prime Minister."

8
King Forbes I

Hoping that the fraudulent manner in which he had won the election would be quickly forgotten, Burnham adopted statesmanlike tones when he spoke to a mass meeting a week after the votes had been counted. It had been a great triumph for the PNC; it was clear, he reflected, that many East Indians had voted for his administration. Rejecting all charges of electoral dishonesty, he called upon his followers to be magnanimous toward their defeated foes. Then, a word of warning to the opposition:

> We do not deny the right of the opposition to oppose but as a government we will not permit the disruption of our national life in any manner. We are equipped materially and psychologically to deal firmly, impartially and swiftly with all who by any means or in any guise may be so ill-advised as to seek to spoil our record of peace and tranquillity to gratify their puerile ambitions.[1]

Burnham was still preparing for his January meeting with the Commonwealth prime ministers in London. He expected some criticism from those who had viewed Granada television's coverage of the elections, but he was unprepared for the Rupununi uprising of 2 January 1969. More than a century before, some European ranchers had moved into this remote region. Life was harsh and difficult, and profits were small. The few original Amerindian inhabitants were slowly being won to Christianity by Roman Catholic missionaries. The Scottish Melville family was one of the more important ranching families. Its members soon intermarried with the Amerindians and also with an American adventurer, Ben Hart. Close to Peter d'Aguiar and the United Force, the Harts and Melvilles were disgusted by events in Georgetown.[2] With the connivance of some Venezuelan officials eager to provoke trouble in the coveted Essequibo territory, the Melvilles and Harts planned an insurrection designed to lead to a separatist state.

As British Guiana moved toward independence, Venezuela had resumed its fishing expedition in troubled waters. In 1962, the Venezuelan government repudiated the 1899 Boundary Award and claimed the entire Essequibo district, some two-thirds of Guyana's total area. Great Britain rejected Venezuela's claims, but agreed to discussions in order to avoid violent incidents on the border as Guyana prepared for freedom in 1966. Shortly before independence and with Burnham's assent, Venezuela and Great Britain, meeting in Geneva, agreed to establish a Mixed Commission charged "with the task of seeking satisfactory solutions for the practical settlement of the controversy . . . which has arisen as the result of the Venezuela contention that the Arbitral Award of 1899 about the frontier between British Guiana and Venezuela is null and void." The commission was to be in existence for four years.

Twisting the meaning of the agreement, Venezuela argued that the Mixed Commission should redraw the frontier instead of merely trying to decide on the validity of the 1899 award. Despite the negotiations, the Venezuelans swept into the Guyana half of Ankoko Island before the end of the year. Ankoko Island, about three square miles in area, is on the frontier of Venezuela and Guyana where the Venamu River joins the Cujuni River. The Venezuelans further exacerbated the conflict in July 1968 when they claimed a nine-mile belt of sea running along the Essequibo coast and reaching to within three miles of the coast. The Burnham government bitterly protested.[3]

Suddenly, word arrived of an uprising in the Rupununi, led by the Melvilles and the Harts. Could this uprising be a prelude to a Venezuelan attack? Guyana's Defense Force would be no match for the well-equipped Venezuelan army. An assault on Lethem, capital city of the Rupununi, started on Thursday morning, 2 January. Arms, equipment, and some training had been provided the rebels by the Venezuelans. The initial attack quickly routed the twelve-man police force, and hostages were seized. Lethem's small airfield and most of the other landing sites in the vicinity were covered with obstructions. Only the runway at Manari, five miles from Lethem, was left open, apparently for the use of the rebels themselves. This tactic turned out to be a fatal blunder. News of the attack reached Georgetown within an hour, much more rapidly than anticipated. Moving swiftly, the Guyana Defense Force rushed two planes loaded with troops to the grass strip at Manari. Overcoming a small amount of hostile fire, the trained troops were soon in control. Within twenty-four hours the uprising was crushed. The rebels fled from Lethem, which was retaken without casualties although several people had already been killed. The ill-conceived revolt ended in farce as the rebels fled across the border to Boa Vista in Brazil.

In a speech to the nation on 4 January 1969, Burnham insisted Venezuelans were responsible for the uprising. The incident, Burnham argued, illustrated Venezuela's determination to seize Essequibo by wooing the ranchers and the Amerindians.[4] Venezuela denied Burnham's charges, though some Venezuelans had certainly been involved. To Guyana's delight, what started as a sour overture suddenly changed to a sweet finale. The new Social Christian president of Venezuela, Rafael Caldera, proved more conciliatory than his Democratic Action predecessors. When the four-year Geneva Agreement terminated, the Venezuelans finally agreed to freeze the border issue for twelve years. While the twelve-year moratorium did not solve the problem, it left Guyana in full control of what she had always claimed. The longer the Essequibo region remained in Guyana's hands, the less likely any segment would ever go to Venezuela.

The disturbances in the Rupununi convinced Burnham more must be done to win the loyalty of the Amerindians. Should the Amerindian be integrated into Guyanese society or should his distinctive civilization be preserved? Considerable discussion had already taken place over who actually owned the land inhabited by the Amerindians.

Prior to independence the United Force had obtained the signatures of thousands of Amerindians. These petitions urged the British government to grant them title to the Crown lands where they lived and toiled. At the Independence Conference in 1965, a provision was made granting the Amerindians legal ownership of the lands on which they were settled. A commission was to be established to apportion the land. Venezuela's activities among the Amerindians prodded the Guyanese to action. An Amerindian Lands Commission was finally put to work in 1967, but little happened. The Rupununi rebellion, however, forced the government's hand. The Lands Commission eventually recommended that the Amerindians be granted legal ownership of the land they occupied. Squatters would be granted conditional rights to a maximum of thirty acres, and those leasing Crown lands could become owners of the property.[5]

On 28 February 1969, 150 chiefs and their counsellors met with the government in Georgetown. Burnham rejected the UF contention that the Amerindian culture be safeguarded by keeping them in isolation; the prime minister insisted they become fully integrated citizens. He pointed to the "inhuman treatment" suffered by Negroes in the southern part of the United States and vowed he would never "permit a similar situation here." Amerindians should not be separated from the rest of the community and treated like "second-class citizens." They "must be brought into and become an important part of the whole community." Burnham was delighted that the Amerindian leaders had pledged their loyalty to the

Guyana government and had democratically selected a representative to serve on the Lands Commission. Now the Lands Commission could prepare a final report. To prove its good faith the government would immediately "transfer to villages, as communities, the lands occupied by these villages as well as some extra lands, which they can farm for themselves and those whom they have to feed." The chiefs departed in a reasonably confident mood, but were soon disappointed by the slow and lengthy procedures involved in arranging the land settlement.[6]

Despite the electoral rigging and the Rupununi troubles, Burnham still had time for constructive policies. In full control and no longer dependent upon d'Aguiar, he turned, once again, to socialist solutions for Guyana's social and economic problems. First he was determined to make Guyana a republic, but a republic of a special type, a cooperative republic. Here Burnham would attempt to demonstrate that he had found an alternative to Jagan's communism and d'Aguiar's capitalism.

Cuffy, leader of the Berbice slave rebellion of 1763, had already been designated Guyana's national hero. The PNC decided that on the 207th anniversary of that revolt, 23 February 1970, Guyana would become a cooperative republic while remaining within the Commonwealth. Speaking to a PNC meeting on 24 August 1969, Burnham defined his conception of a cooperative society. Cooperatives must not be "a mere appendage to the economic life of the nation," nor must they be simply "a social welfare exercise." "Our basic proposition is this: the organization of our human and material resources through the cooperative movement, with government providing financial assistance, management, training and administrative direction." Only a cooperative republic would enable "the small man . . . to own large and substantial business enterprises and make decisions which will materially affect the direction which the economy takes and where the country goes." All Guyanese must "grasp the value of coming together as a group, of pooling your physical, your material and human resources, so that as small men we can become real men." A cooperative bank would be established by the government to provide funds for cooperative projects.[7]

In the midst of frantic celebrations in Georgetown, but of suspicion in the East Indian countryside, Guyana became a Cooperative Republic in February 1970.[8] Cheddi Jagan and the PPP, bitter and resentful at the course of events, though supporting the establishment of a republic, refused to permit old party stalwart, Ashton Chase, to become Guyana's first president. For that honorary position, symbolic of national unity, the Legislative Assembly eventually selected Arthur Chung, a member of the Guyanese judiciary.[9]

Speaking the year before on the third anniversary of independence (26 May 1969), the prime minister had

painted a portrait of achievements. There were more
roads, schools, hospitals, and health clinics. Per capita income had gone up along with an increase in the
gross national product. But Burnham agreed Guyana was
no utopia; there was still far too much unemployment and
underemployment. Fortunately, the Guyanese were demonstrating a great degree of independence and self-reliance
by dealing with their many problems in a cooperative
manner. They must, however, move away from the coast;
the riches of the interior were there for one and all.
"Our motto now and in years to come must be: Forward!
Go West, Go South, Go to the Land!" Before the end of
1969, he expected a report from the Interior Development Committee containing plans "for the settlement and
development of our vast inland areas." But then he wondered if Guyana's population was large enough for the
task. East Indian hearts must have paused as Burnham
observed:

> The time has come to treat as a matter of urgency the
> question of the size of our population and its relation
> to the potential of our country. The time has come to
> examine the need for a rapid increase in population and
> the sources from which that increase should come. The
> swift but ordered development of our country, both as
> regards manpower on the one hand, and agriculture and in-
> dustry on the other, is a vital necessity if our country
> is to survive.[10]

Just after the establishment of the Cooperative Republic, the prime minister asserted to the 13th Annual
Conference of the People's National Congress that Guyana's resources must be controlled by the Guyanese. Referring to foreign investments, he noted Guyana had
"seen the foreign investor in operation, especially
when he is part of an international cartel, and sells
what he extracts to himself; his insensitivity to the
interest of the nation, his unconcern for real development, his disdain for Guyanese and Guyanese institutions."
Some additional comments about the Demerara Bauxite Company indicated that, no longer hampered by a coalition
with the pro-capitalist UF, he intended to either purchase 51 percent of the stock or nationalize this important industry. The mining sector contributed to about
20 percent of Guyana's gross domestic product. In addition, 40 percent of the total investment in Guyana was
in mining, and the mining industry provided about 40
percent of gross foreign exchange earnings. Guyana ac-
counted for 15 percent of the world bauxite trade, rank-
ing fourth behind Jamaica, the Soviet Union, and Surinam.[11]
Bauxite had first been identified in British Guiana
by the Geological Survey Department in 1910. The Aluminum Company of America (ALCOA), presided over by the
Mellon family and Arthur Vining Davis, rushed to develop

this new source of aluminum. A Scottish-American, George B. Mackenzie, was put in charge of the operation. Quietly moving about the region to which he would give his name, Mackenzie bought property at a low price. In 1914, ALCOA established the Demerara Bauxite Company (DEMBA) in British Guiana as a subsidiary of its Canadian company, Northern Aluminum. Twelve years later ALCOA organized a new Canadian corporation, Aluminium Ltd. The new company owned most of ALCOA's holdings outside the United States, including DEMBA. Aluminium Ltd. was often referred to as ALCAN, and the name was formally changed in 1966 to Alcan Aluminium Ltd. In 1951, the United States courts held that the antitrust laws required a complete separation of ALCOA and ALCAN within ten years. Until the opening of bauxite mines in Jamaica in the 1950s, British Guiana had been ALCAN's major supplier.[12]

The growth of the leftist-leaning PPP in the early 1950s convinced ALCAN its mines in British Guiana were in jeopardy. Rigid segregation had reigned in Mackenzie; white expatriate managers lived in the big houses while the black laborers lived in much smaller, more primitive accommodations.[13] Recognizing that it must move with the times, DEMBA finally began training some black managers. But the very top positions remained in the hands of the white expatriates. Once the UF had been ousted from the coalition, DEMBA's officials could see the handwriting on the wall. It responded by mounting a spectacular public relations scheme to demonstrate its contributions to Guyana.

Assisted by a number of talented economists, the PNC produced conclusive evidence that ALCAN's major interest was in profits for the shareholders and not in the development of Guyana. Burnham, however, drew back from full nationalization and opted for "partial" ownership. On 28 November 1970, Burnham announced that the Guyanese government planned to acquire 51 percent of DEMBA's shares by 1 January 1971. The purchase money would be obtained from future profits.

Jagan and the PPP urged complete nationalization immediately. ALCAN officials, however, replied with a counteroffer conceding very little. They insisted that majority control remain in their hands along with the right to designate the chief executive officer. ALCAN could only promise a modest expansion of calcined bauxite production. Burnham's moment of decision had arrived. He could back down or push ahead with full nationalization.[14]

Retreat before the white bosses was inconceivable to Burnham; he had always retained his socialist commitments. The only alternative was nationalization. He knew the vast majority of the nation would rally to his standard, for Jagan would be an ally on this issue. Negotiations with ALCAN had started amidst much fanfare in

early December 1970. On 20 February 1971, the government broke off the talks. A few days later, on the
first anniversary of the establishment of the Cooperative Republic, Burnham announced that DEMBA would be
fully nationalized. Within two weeks, the necessary
legislation had been rushed through the Legislative Assembly. A "Peace Plan" was temporarily worked out between Burnham and Jagan, though it had little long-term
significance.

Compensation remained a problem. Burnham wished to
pay as little as possible and from future profits. ALCAN
objected. Former United States Supreme Court Justice
and United Nations Ambassador Arthur Goldberg helped arrange a compromise. Guyana agreed to pay $53.5 million
over twenty years at 6 percent interest with money derived from government revenues.

While the compensation negotiations were in session,
the bauxite workers, fearful of losing their pension
rights, began to demonstrate. When Burnham failed to
appear in Mackenzie, they requested Jagan's assistance.
The workers were far more radical than their union leaders whose greatest loyalty was to the PNC. By 20 April,
the rank and file were on strike. The government was
waiting for an arbitration tribunal to bring in a report,
but the bauxite workers demanded an immediate decision
on higher wages and guaranteed pension benefits. Violent demonstrations developed, and the police responded
with tear gas. By 28 April 1971, twenty-five workers
were in custody with bail refused. May Day demonstrations then took place as usual on 1 May. Tear gas was
again used on the Linden activists. The TUC leaders in
Georgetown urged the government to be conciliatory and
generous. Fortunately, the arbitration body completed
its investigation and recommended concessions. A significant retroactive pay increase was granted, and re-
trenchment and retirement benefits were improved.[15]

The government, surprised by ALCAN's refusal to accept the 51 percent proposal, now argued that full nationalization of foreign-owned industries was part of
cooperative socialism. But to the workers in the bauxite industry, the changes seemed minimal. Mackenzie,
joined now with Wismar and Christianburg, was renamed
Linden, after Linden Forbes Sampson Burnham. Otherwise
few differences appeared--black bourgeois bosses committed to profits and efficiency had simply replaced white
managers. Labor unrest would continue in the bauxite
industry. Burnham could normally keep the support of
the miners by playing the racial card, but there was
growing resentment throughout the 1970s as black bauxite
workers argued that nationalization had brought little
change in their conditions of life. The nationalized
company had been baptized the Guyana Bauxite Company
(GUYBAU), but to the workers it seemed very similar to
DEMBA. Burnham was gradually losing the support of a

black proletariat which found little of benefit in the
PNC's version of cooperative socialism. The PNC's base
of support was slowly eroded until it rested on an African tripod, composed of highly paid government bureaucrats, the police, and the army.

It does need to be remembered, however, that the
nationalization of DEMBA gave the Guyanese control of
one of their most important natural resources. Profits
would no longer be carried away by foreigners. Guyana
could now determine how to sell its aluminum and calcined bauxite to the entire world. The way was open for
participation in a Caribbean aluminum smelter project,
if sufficient regional cooperation could be achieved.[16]

The Canadian government resented ALCAN's nationalization while Reynolds, United States-owned but smaller,
had not yet been touched. But the government of Pierre
Trudeau had no desire to play the colonial paternalist
interested only in protecting Canadian capitalism; it
suggested that Reynolds also would soon be nationalized.

Taking a cue from OPEC, seven key bauxite-producing
countries met twice in 1974, first at Conakry, Guinea,
in March and then in Guyana in November. Australia,
Guyana, Jamaica, Surinam, Yugoslavia, Sierra Leone, and
Guinea--soon to be joined by Ghana, Haiti, and the Do-
minican Republic--hoped to establish a minimum price for
bauxite.[17] But this goal proved difficult. While they
controlled 75 percent of the world's bauxite, the demand
for bauxite was not as great as that for oil. It was
also possible to produce aluminum from other ores. The
defeat of Australia's Labour government in 1975 was another blow to the International Bauxite Association.

If the nationalization of DEMBA had been part of a
plan, then one might have anticipated more nationalization schemes in the immediate future, along with a more
systematic approach to economic planning. But this approach was not to be taken for several years.[18] Burnham
still hesitated to further antagonize the United States
interests which had brought him to power. Many third
world countries admired Burnham's nationalization of
DEMBA. He enjoyed their applause and intensified his
commitment to non-alignment, demonstrating his independence from both the United States and the Soviet Union.
Burnham recognized the People's Republic of China just
prior to hosting the meeting of non-aligned states in
1972. The CIA was beginning to wonder if it had wagered
on the wrong man in Guyana.

Burnham still floundered about as he sought to
place his government on a more stable foundation. Ultimately, he was in power because of the black-dominated
Guyana Defense Force and police. The civil service and
the roughnecks of Georgetown also followed their racial
brother. With the exception of a very few East Indians,
he had, however, thoroughly alienated the East Indian
majority. Attempts to follow through on his calls for

racial harmony by enlarging East Indian opportunities for advancement antagonized his black allies. The size of the pie was very limited. Some East Indian moderates were trying to woo the East Indian masses from Cheddi Jagan's Marxism-Leninism, but this task proved difficult. Jagan, on the other hand, was not sure what course to follow. He approved of Burnham's drift to the left but yearned to be in office himself.

By 1972, Burnham looked back on eight years of power and could not pretend there had been an economic miracle.[19] Far too many Guyanese were still unemployed and underemployed. From 1964 until 1968 he had been saddled with the UF's ambition to attract foreign investment by maintaining a free market. Since 1968 he had pledged himself to cooperative socialism without being sure what exactly this course meant. His schemes for economic development had thus been fundamentally altered midway through his eight years of power. Elections were legally required by early 1974 at the latest, but he was clearly planning to hold them in 1973. A new development plan was thus needed prior to the election to explain what the PNC would achieve during the next few years. Speaking to the annual Congress of the PNC on 9 April 1972, the prime minister reminded his followers that they must "Feed, Clothe, and House the Nation" by 1976 at the latest. He concluded: "We may be said to have had the Political Revolution in Guyana by virtue of having achieved independence in 1966. The P.N.C. has now embarked upon the Economic and Social Revolution."[20]

The prime minister was delighted to host the meeting of non-aligned countries in August 1972. He denounced the racial policies of South Africa's government and obviously enjoyed the limelight.[21] Later that month, Guyana was host country for the Caribbean Festival of Creative Arts (CARIFESTA). Burnham reflected: "This festival is an attempt on the part of the people of the Caribbean to identify themselves, their history, their strains, their habits, their way of life. That, no man can take from us, no bomber, no war ship."[22]

In a much less spectacular fashion, Cheddi Jagan presided over a Caribbean Anti-Imperialist Conference in Georgetown at the end of August. Jagan concluded that, "While imperialism has grown weaker vis-a-vis socialism, it is still a strong and dangerous enemy. And the leader of the imperialist camp, the United States of America, has grown more aggressive."[23]

Rickey Singh, the leading correspondent of Guyana's most independent newspaper, The Sunday Graphic, noted the decline in public morality and the increase in crime and violence. On 12 November 1972, he observed:

> Public morality is not what it should be, and it is eroding all our institutions and the very quality of our life. Our predicament is not eased by the fact of having politi-

142

cal parties which are bent on destroying each other at
all cost, irrespective of the consequences to the national life.

Hence, while the present ruling party did its very
best to encourage indiscipline among school children, policemen, civil servants, church and trade unions to embarrass and bring about the downfall of the PPP, the latter is now doing nothing to help the PNC in creating an
atmosphere of stability.[24]

By this time, 5,000 to 7,000 people a year were
voting with their feet. Having given up on Guyana, they
were emigrating to the United Kingdom, the United States,
and Canada. These emigrants were mostly middle class,
mostly East Indians, and mostly just the type of person
required for building a better Guyana. With a population growth of 3 percent per year, however, the number
of citizens continued to expand in spite of this emigration. Slow economic growth and the failure of plans for
social development, therefore, meant a decline in the
standard of living for most Guyanese.

Not surprisingly, the PNC cancelled the local government elections scheduled for late 1972. They had
last been conducted in five districts in June 1970, when
the PNC claimed a massive victory while the PPP justifi-
ably complained of misused proxies and tampering with
the ballot boxes. Burnham and the PNC endorsed a Trades
Union Congress resolution in November calling for the
reduction of the voting age to eighteen. But they were
indignant when a motion from Ashton Chase, president of
the National Association of Agricultural, Commercial,
and Industrial Employees (NAACIE), calling for free and
fair national elections was defeated by only a dozen
votes. Chase had ceased to be active in the PPP, but
many of his members supported Cheddi Jagan.[25]

In early 1973, the prime minister once again had to
confront the disturbing presence of Sydney King. By
this time, King's black racial pride had led him to take
the name Eusi Kwayana (black man from Guyana). He was
fired from the PNC in 1961 for his partition ideas, but
made peace with Burnham and returned to the government
as head of the Guyana Marketing Corporation in 1968.
Three years later, disgusted with governmental corruption, he resigned. He was constructing a reputation for
honesty, asceticism, and incorruptibility that would
serve him well in the future. Deciding that the government was beyond redemption, he opened fire on Burnham
and his policies. Kwayana made extremely effective use
of his position as head of the African Society for Cultural Relations with Independent Africa (ASCRIA) to attack the administration. He urged landless citizens to
seize the unused portions of the great sugar estates.
When the SPA and the government ignored him, Kwayana and
his followers began an occupation of the sugar lands.[26]

Burnham hesitated; he dreaded a fight with Kwayana. But the law must be enforced or dangerous precedents would be set. After ten days the police moved in and ejected the squatters. Kwayana had finally seen the fallacy of Black Power and had returned to his original socialist philosophy of working-class solidarity. He was trying, once again, to open bridges to the East Indian workers. The timing was perfect. Reaching out to him was Moses Bhagwan, a militant young PPP activist of the middle 1960s who had been expelled by Jagan because of his revolutionary zeal. Bhagwan, a lawyer, had recognized the impracticality of his revolutionary rhetoric. He was now speaking the language of democratic socialism and working-class cooperation across racial barriers.

The government denounced Kwayana's land campaign, and then tried to discredit him by announcing that land improperly used by the sugar plantations would be confiscated without compensation. At the anniversary celebrations of the Cooperative Republic in February, Burnham reported victory; he claimed the credit for the SPA's decision to acquiesce to the loss of much unused sugar land. Kwayana retorted it was really a victory for Guyana's working people. Now, he insisted, more people's committees and a Council of Landless Peoples were required so the confiscated land would be effectively redistributed. Kwayana thundered that these were

the only organizations in the country which are truly inter-racial, truly representative of the have-nots and in which there is no power politics, no attempt at power politics and which can defeat attempts at inter-racial conflict and maintain revolutionary peace against the enemy, the exploiter. In the People's Committees, the Indian and African comrades discuss things frankly and have no fear of one another.[27]

As elections appeared imminent, Llewellyn John suddenly decided to return to the arena. As the PNC's minister of home affairs in 1968, he surely knew if there had been fraud during that election. Having severed his ties with Burnham when the government veered leftward, John announced in March 1973 the formation of a new party, the People's Democratic Movement. Growing concern about the loss of basic civil liberties and PNC talk advocating a one-party state had also led to the formation of several citizen groups: the Fundamental Rights Action Committee (FRAC), the Guyana Anti-Discrimination Movement (GADM), and the Civil Liberties Action Council (CLAC), among others. Father Harold Wong, Jesuit editor of the Catholic Standard, became a more vigorous critic of the government, along with other church leaders from all denominations.[28]

A significant part of Guyana's nonpartisan middle class had become deeply distressed by the dictatorial tendencies of Forbes Burnham. They were patriotic citizens, favorable to free enterprise and opposed to Jagan's extremism, who now recognized there was a new problem to confront. Prepared to accept some of Burnham's moderate socialist proposals if they would build a better Guyana for everyone, these citizens saw, instead, corruption and incompetence with no chance for a constitutional change if elections were permanently rigged.

By April 1973, Cheddi Jagan had decided to participate in the expected election, despite the cheating of 1968 and over the objection of a small group of revolutionary enthusiasts who yearned for street fighting in Georgetown. He was retreating from the more extreme statements he had uttered in Moscow in June 1969. Representing the PPP at the World Conference of Communist and Workers Parties, Jagan had ended all doubt about his loyalties. The PPP was now openly enrolled as a Marxist-Leninist party. This affiliation could only make it more difficult for the PPP to win moderate support if free elections were held in Guyana. So far as the United States government was concerned, it could now feel justified for having worked to remove Jagan when he was in office.[29]

The nation was not surprised when the prime minister announced in late May that elections would take place on Monday, 16 July. Burnham indicated that an entirely new register of voters would be prepared, including the overseas register of voters. He refused to abolish proxy voting as demanded by the opposition parties, but it would be limited to certain occupations. One individual would now be able to cast only two rather than three proxy votes. Postal voting could be used if necessary. He also proposed lowering the voting age to eighteen.

Earlier in the month Jagan had met with Burnham to discuss PPP demands for a fair election. Jagan demanded an impartial Elections Commission and the drawing up of a new and correct voters list. Overseas voting and proxy voting must cease. Also, all ballots must be tabulated at the respective polling stations and voting should be granted to eighteen-year-olds.[30]

The prime minister's election announcement made no concessions to the PPP with the exception of the eighteen-year-old vote. He no doubt threw this bone to Jagan expecting it to be refused. This refusal would enable Burnham to embarrass Jagan by pointing to the PPP's traditional support for the eighteen-year-old vote. Jagan responded as anticipated; he denounced what he had previously supported, for he feared that allowing the eighteen- to twenty-one-year olds to vote would only mean more padding of the electoral lists by the PNC. As this change was a constitutional matter requiring a two-thirds vote of the Legislative Assembly, the PPP prevented passage when the measure was introduced a short time later.

The announcement of the election brought a wave of excitement and fear to Guyana. Would there, once again, be fraud and racial violence? In early June, Feilden Singh, leader of the UF, declared his party would join with a new party, the Liberator party, for the election. The Liberator party was really a transformed Guyana Anti-Discrimination Movement. It was led by Dr. Makepeace Richmond and Dr. Ganraj Kumar. The East Indian bourgeoisie was making another attempt to reorganize. Their party's hope was to restore civil rights and to encourage foreign investment.

A government decree that all votes would be counted at three centers, rather than at the polling places, further angered the opposition parties. Attempts to have the courts rule against the government's electoral tactics were unsuccessful; the judges had no intention of irritating Burnham and the PNC.[31]

Burnham toured the country, chanting a tune of PNC achievements over the past nine years.[32] The new 1972 to 1976 Development Plan would continue its already successful efforts in education, health, forestry, mining, agriculture, manufacturing, and housing. If the PNC was victorious, Burnham promised to open talks with Reynolds about their Kwakwani holdings. But, Burnham argued, the PNC needed a massive victory--two-thirds of the seats would be perfect. Then they could alter the entrenched constitutional clauses without having to worry about the PPP.

Election officials carefully guarded the electoral registers, making it difficult for the opposition parties to see them. The register for Guyana had increased by a total of 75,000 voters since 1968 even though the total Guyanese population had only gone up by about that number. The overseas register dropped from 68,588 to 33,546, or more than 50 percent. Here the government was conceding that its 1968 statistics were outrageously inflated and that it did not wish to be embarrassed again in this particular area.[33] In preparing the list of PNC candidates, Burnham was delighted to include four former parliamentarians elected on the PPP list in 1968. For a variety of reasons, they had defected and were now PNC enthusiasts.

Meetings of the three opposition parties were disrupted by Georgetown hooligans. The police provided inadequate assistance. Concern grew over violence in the countryside as black youths from Georgetown broke up PPP meetings in the sugar regions. In an atmosphere of fear and suspicion, the Guyanese voted on 16 July. Once again the poll watchers from the opposition parties were harassed. Some panic did develop in the government camp as normally solid PNC strongholds in Georgetown were marked by very small voter turnout. Disenchanted with the PNC, but unwilling to vote for the PPP, many PNC supporters simply stayed at home.

Poll watchers for the opposition parties were prevented from travelling with the ballot boxes to the
three places designated for the counting. Many of the
ballot boxes were brought to the Guyana Defense Force
Headquarters at Thomas Lands, Georgetown, where there is
evidence that locks were broken and ballots destroyed or
changed. What frightened the PNC and necessitated far
more tampering than they had anticipated were the early
returns from the capital. Expecting a massive sweep in
their strongholds, the PNC permitted a fair count of the
votes in several Georgetown constituencies, with poll
watchers from the opposition present. But when the PNC,
horrified, viewed the Georgetown slump, its leaders knew
an honest tally of the votes could not be permitted.
Poll watchers were ejected and the GDF, for all practical purposes, was given control of the ballots.[34]

Throughout Tuesday the counting, if such it can be
called, continued. The results were slowly dribbled to
the public; clearly the PNC was awarding itself a splendid victory. The PNC obtained more than 90 percent of
the postal, proxy, and overseas votes. For example, the
party won 29,031 of the 29,643 overseas votes cast. The
final total struck most of the nation as unbelievable.
The PNC gave itself 244,403 votes, or 70.15 percent of
the 350,181 votes cast. The PPP was awarded only 92,368
votes or 25.51 percent. In addition, the PNC had
achieved its goal of winning two-thirds of the seats in
the Legislative Assembly. It acquired thirty-seven
seats, whereas the PPP won fourteen, the Liberator party
won two, and the PDM failed to win any seats.

The editor of The Sunday Graphic, Ric Mentus, observed on 22 July that "the nature and scope of the irregularities reported are serious enough to demand an
important inquiry into the entire electoral process."
He wondered just "what kind of nation-building are we
going to move into from a beginning as suspect and tense
as this?" Under the heading, "Fairy Tale Elections,"
the Catholic Standard commented that the election results "put a severe strain on one's credibility. No one
seriously believes it. That this is so must be laid
firmly at the door of the government." In a statement
on 21 July, the opposition parties denounced the election and argued that the army and police had intervened
"to enable the PNC to usurp powers by fraud." The government was accused of "massive irregularities, including the seizure, impounding and tampering with ballot
boxes, all of which were calculated to ensure that elections were neither free nor fair."[35]

Disguised as a United States film team, Granada
television had decided upon a follow-up to its disclo-
sures of 1968. Granada's "World in Action" unit managed
on-the-spot coverage of the election. It was a difficult moment for Llewellyn John; as home secretary in

1968 he had played a major role in rigging the elections.
Now he was a victim of the tactics he had employed in
1968. While John delicately noted that "any system of
election is subject to manipulation," the "World in Action" commentator observed: "The ultimate insult for Mr.
John was the appearance of his own parents as postal
voters. They had both died two years previously."[36]
    "World in Action" found numerous faked names on the
overseas register in London and Birmingham. Undoubtedly,
the election was characterized by dishonesty and fraud.
Flexing its muscles in response to Jagan's criticism,
the government arrested the PPP leader a few days after
the election for allegedly not having a license for a
firearm in his possession. When Jagan showed his permit,
he was released.
    Jagan urged John, Kumar, and Feilden Singh to join
him in a boycott of Parliament. He also called for a
campaign of civil disobedience and non-cooperation.
John and Kumar agreed with Jagan, but Feilden Singh decided, as deputy leader of the Liberator party and former chief of the UF, to enter the Legislative Assembly
and to appoint Elinor da Silva to the other seat assigned
to the Liberator party. When Singh was challenged in
court by those members of the Liberator party who favored abstention from the Legislative Assembly, the chief
justice ruled that Feilden Singh acted legally. The PPP
did not finally attend Parliament until 24 May 1976.
But the civil disobedience campaign was a failure; once
again Jagan talked action, but little happened. The
East Indian middle class continued to emigrate while the
East Indian sugar workers grumbled and growled about a
government that failed to look out for their interests.
    With a two-thirds majority in the Legislative As-
sembly, Burnham could do just as he wished, with the exception of tampering with those entrenched clauses of
the constitution requiring not only a two-thirds vote of
Parliament, but a referendum as well. Within a month he
removed the British Privy Council from the constitution.
No longer could there be an appeal from the Guyana
courts to the Judicial Committee of the Privy Council.
There had been discussion about the need for a Caribbean
Court of Appeal, but none had been established; therefore, charges of electoral fraud could not be pursued
beyond Guyana's own courts.[37]
    Unable to attract much foreign investment, fearful
of the rapid increase in oil prices after the Arab oil
boycott of late 1973, and hoping to maintain his position as a leader of the non-aligned world, Burnham embarked on a new program of nationalization. Three years
after nationalizing DEMBA, the PNC chief opened negotiations with the Reynolds Bauxite Company of Guyana, a
subsidiary of the United States-owned Reynolds Metals
Company. Reynolds began its operation in Guyana in 1954
but had not declared any profits until 1963; therefore,

it had not, during that period, paid taxes. Burnham reached an agreement with Reynolds shortly after he came to power in 1964 in which Reynolds consented to an increase in production. In turn, the government promised to hold taxes at $250,000 a year for twenty-five years. But the price of aluminum was soaring upward in 1973, and Burnham saw an opportunity to obtain needed funds.

Talks with Reynolds for majority participation broke down, as they had with DEMBA. Angered, Burnham passed legislation imposing a $6 million fine on the company. Half of this sum was to be paid within two weeks. The company balked, went to court, and was defeated. Continuing its tough stance, Reynolds began to bring its workers home. Unwilling to be humiliated, the PNC retaliated; Reynolds was nationalized.[38]

Fearing reprisals from the United States because of the Reynolds nationalization, Burnham turned even more decisively to the left. The People's Republic of China had been recognized and an embassy established in Georgetown in 1972. Diplomatic relations had been arranged with Cuba in 1972 and in September 1973, when Fidel Castro was flying to a meeting of the non-aligned states in Algiers, he stopped in Guyana for a twenty-four-hour hero's welcome. Burnham, the same man who had denounced Jagan's pro-Castro policies in the early 1960s, introduced his guest to a cheering crowd of more than 2,000 people at the prime minister's home. Visiting Cuba in 1975, Burnham was presented with Cuba's José Martí award.[39]

To Jagan's irritation, the PNC even began to refer to itself as a Marxist-Leninist party, although it did not formally affiliate with the international communist movement. Tanzania's Julius Nyerere and Sri Lanka's Mrs. Sirimavo Bandaranaike, distinguished third-world socialist leaders, paid friendly visits to Guyana; it was difficult for Jagan to argue that he was the only anti-imperialist and only true socialist in Guyana. Burnham was running skillfully with the non-aligned world and had successfully adopted a number of Jagan's policies. But Burnham still needed the willing support of Guyana's sugar workers. The industry continued to be plagued with strikes, which had not been too damaging until prices plummeted in 1975. The seeds of a reconciliation, however, had been planted; Burnham wanted a happier sugar industry, while Jagan hoped to end his isolation.

Addressing the annual Conference of the PPP in August 1975, Jagan argued that imperialism must be destroyed before socialism could be attained. "And whoever helps must be praised." They must continue to pressure the PNC but a "more flexible approach" was required. The PPP had no "monopoly on socialism" and was "prepared regardless of ideological and tactical differences to work with others if they are interested in building socialism in Guyana. And this includes the PNC. Our political line should be changed from non-cooperation and civil resistance to critical support."[40]

Jagan was also responding to his life-long ambition to nationalize the sugar industry. Two large British concerns, Jessel Securities Ltd. and the Booker McConnell Co., owned all the important sugar estates in Guyana. In February 1975, the government nationalized Jessel and agreed to pay $7 million in compensation. Jessel, with some 2,500 employees, also owned a large retail-wholesale outlet, interests in the liquor industry, and a sugar terminal.[41]

As a further concession to Jagan, Burnham finally allowed a free collective bargaining vote by the sugar workers in December 1975. They voted overwhelmingly (97.9 percent) for representation by the PPP's GAWU rather than the discredited MPCA. GAWU received 21,487 votes, compared to 376 for the MPCA.[42] Burnham's gesture to Jagan was linked to his fears about United States attempts to destabilize the Guyanese government because of the prime minister's march to the left. The reactionary Brazilian generals were distressed with his policies and the Venezuelans were less than enthusiastic. A unified nation would present a united front to Guyana's hostile neighbors and might also mean an increase in sugar production.[43]

With Jagan's support Burnham now moved to nationalize Booker McConnell, the dominant economic interest in Guyana, and the symbol of foreign control. While the company had pursued socially just policies under the wise leadership of Lord Campbell of Eskan, the Guyanese, understandably, wished to control their own economy. Bookers had prepared for nationalization in Guyana. It had become a massive multinational concern, only a part of whose operation depended upon its investments in Guyana. Along with the nine sugar estates it wholly or partially owned, Bookers was also involved in the retail trade, shipbuilding, rum, and rubber. The company produced 85 percent of Guyana's sugar and was responsible for about 40 percent of Guyana's exports. It employed 23,000 people, and many others indirectly earned their livelihood from the activities of Bookers.

Although Jagan opposed compensation, arguing that Bookers' massive profits over the years were more than enough, Burnham agreed to pay G$102.5 million over twenty years. A good start had already been made on these payments because of a special government levy imposed on the sugar industry two years before when sugar prices were high. Jagan brought the PPP back into Legislative Assembly for the formal takeover of Bookers in May 1976, the tenth anniversary of independence.[44] Shortly before, he had participated in a May Day rally with Burnham. It seemed to some that despite a few ominous signs, Burnham and Jagan were moving together. There was even talk of a coalition government. Perhaps, black and East Indian might be reconciled and a Guyanese nation forged in national unity. Only through equal sacrifice and national reconciliation would it be possible to feed, clothe, and house the Guyanese nation and end the high rate of unemployment, underemployment, and crime.[45]

But Forbes Linden Sampson Burnham had become King Forbes I in 1968 when rigged elections had been required to keep him in power. If the king is wise, benevolent, and philosophically inclined, there may be some justification for arbitrary and dictatorial power at critical moments in a nation's history. But if the king lacks wisdom and fails to govern in a generous, just manner, he must be prepared to confront the consequences of his deficiencies, especially if he has demonstrated that he will not permit himself to be peacefully ousted. For when one has great power and promises many things, much is expected. If the expectations are not fulfilled, political crisis is certain to develop. By the mid-1970s, Burnham must have given some thought on dark evenings to the events surrounding the reigns of Charles I, Louis XVI, Nicholas II, and the "Emperor Jones."

NOTES

1. Nascimento and Burrowes, eds., A Destiny to Mould, pp. 59-64.

2. Ridgwell, The Forgotten Tribes of Guyana, pp. 221-40; Nath, A History of Guyana, vol. 3, pp. 185-93; and The Economist, 11 January 1969, pp. 32, 34.

3. Nascimento and Burrowes, eds., A Destiny to Mould, pp. 163-70. For criticism of Burnham, see H. J. M. Hubbard, The Venezuelan Border Issue: A Sell-Out by the Coalition Government in Guyana (Georgetown, Guyana, 1966); and Jagan, The West on Trial, pp. 394-98.

4. Nascimento and Burrowes, eds., A Destiny to Mould, pp. 171-76.

5. Robert H. Manley, Guyana Emergent: The Post-Independence Struggle for Nondependent Development (Boston, 1979), pp. 49-53. See also Della Walker, "Problems in Amerindian Acculturation," in Brian Irving, ed., Guyana: A Composite Monograph (Hato Rey, Puerto Rico, 1972), pp. 62-65.

6. Nascimento and Burrowes, eds., A Destiny to Mould, pp. 136-45.

7. Ibid., pp. 152-60.

8. See Andrew Salkey, Georgetown Journal: A Caribbean Writer's Journey from London via Port of Spain to Georgetown, Guyana, 1970 (London, 1972). Salkey, a Jamaican, was in Guyana for the establishment of the Cooperative Republic. He had lengthy interviews with both Burnham and Jagan. For an evaluation of East Indian-African relations in Trinidad and the "black power" violence of February-April 1970, see David Nichols, "East Indians and Black

Power in Trinidad," Race, 12 (1971), pp. 443-59.

9. Embert Hendrickson, "New Directions for Republican Guyana," The World Today (January 1971), pp. 33-39. There are a number of useful articles in the government publication, L. Searwar, ed., Co-operative Republic: Guyana 1970 (Georgetown, 1970). See also Ved. P. Duggal, "Economic Development Since Independence," in Irving, ed., Guyana: A Composite Monograph, pp. 48-61.

10. Nascimento and Burrowes, eds., A Destiny to Mould, pp. 146-51. See also K. F. S. King, Land and People in Guyana (Commonwealth Forestry Institute Paper No. 39, Oxford, 1968).

11. Policy for the New Co-op Republic (Georgetown, Guyana, 1970). This is the report of the 13th Annual Conference of the People's National Congress which took place in Georgetown in April 1970.

12. See the excellent discussion in Robert Chodos, The Caribbean Connection (Toronto, 1977), pp. 131-50.

13. Cedric Grant, Company Towns in the Caribbean: A Preliminary Analysis of Christianburg-Wismar-Mackenzie (Waterloo, Canada, 1970).

14. There is a fine analysis in Ralph R. Premdas, "Guyana: Socialist Reconstruction or Political Opportunism?" Journal of Interamerican Studies and World Affairs, 20 (May 1978), pp. 133-64.

15. Nath, A History of Guyana, vol. 3, pp. 204-7.

16. See Forbes Burnham's summary of the way in which DEMBA was nationalized in To Own Guyana (Georgetown, Guyana, 1971). This is the published version of Burnham's address to the 14th Annual Delegates' Congress of the People's National Congress.

17. The Sunday Graphic, 3 November 1974, p. 4, and 10 November 1974, p. 4.

18. See the articles by Harold A. Lutchman and Brian Wearing in Irving, ed., Guyana: A Composite Monograph, pp. 13-39. See also the special report about Guyana in The Times of 26 May 1971.

19. See J. E. Greene, "The Politics of Economic Planning in Guyana," Social and Economic Studies, 23 (June 1974), pp. 186-203.

20. Forbes Burnham, Perform Now Comrades: The National Revolution in Guyana (Georgetown, Guyana, 1972). This is the printed text of Burnham's address to the 15th Annual Delegates' Congress of the PNC. See the articles about Guyana's economy in New Commonwealth and World Development, No. 2, 1971; and Ethlyn A. Prince, "The Development of Public Enterprise in Guyana," Social and Economic Studies, 23 (June 1974), pp. 204-15.

21. Forbes Burnham, Address on the Occasion of the Opening of the Conference of Foreign Ministers of Non-Aligned Countries (Georgetown, Guyana, 1972).

22. Forbes Burnham, Our World of the Caribbean (Georgetown, Guyana, 1972).

23. Cheddi Jagan, The Caribbean Revolution: Tasks and Perspectives (Georgetown, Guyana, 1972).

24. The Sunday Graphic, 12 November 1972, p. 5. See Ralph R. Premdas, "Elections and Political Campaigns in a Racially Bifurcated State: Guyana," Journal of Interamerican Studies, 14 (August 1972), pp. 271-96.

25. The Sunday Graphic, 26 November 1972, p. 5.

26. The Sunday Graphic, 7 January 1973, p. 5.

152

27. The Sunday Graphic, 28 January 1973, p. 5, and 25 February 1973, pp. 4-5. See Perry Mars, Structural Inequalities and Political Violence in a Multi-Racial State: The Guyana Example (Georgetown, Guyana, 1973).

28. The Sunday Graphic, 29 April 1973, p. 5.

29. See Cheddi Jagan's reflective article in The Sunday Graphic, 31 December 1972, p. 4.

30. The account of the election campaign and the July election is drawn from The Guyana Graphic and The Sunday Graphic (independent), the Catholic Standard (independent), The Chronicle (pro-PNC), The Mirror (pro-PPP), The New Nation (theoretical organ of the PNC), and Thunder (theoretical organ of the PPP).

31. See Rickey Singh's analysis of the unwillingness of Sir Donald Jackson, chairman of the Elections Commission, to faithfully discharge his constitutional obligations in The Sunday Graphic, 24 June 1973, p. 5.

32. See Kempe R. Hope and Wilfred L. David, "Planning for Development in Guyana: The Experience from 1945 to 1973," Inter-American Economic Affairs, 27 (Spring 1974), pp. 27-46. The authors observe (p. 45):

> The rather disappointing experience with planning in Guyana during 1945-1972 reflected the fact that the Planners were more concerned with constructing a Plan for publication. As a result, the Plans have been statements of aspiration rather then what could reasonably be expected from the economy.

33. The Trinidad Guardian, 9 July 1973, p. 6.

34. There is a devastating evaluation of the election in Janet Jagan, Army Intervention in the 1973 Elections in Guyana (Georgetown, Guyana, 1973).

35. See the editorials by Ric Mentus and the articles by Rickey Singh in The Sunday Graphic of 22 July 1973 and 29 July 1973.

36. Thanks again to Granada television and Miss Julie Sinclair for arranging a showing of this television documentary.

37. For a perceptive and well-written essay about Guyana at this time, see Jane Kramer, "Letter from Guyana," The New Yorker, 16 September 1974, pp. 100-28.

38. Premdas, "Guyana: Socialist Reconstruction or Political Opportunism?" pp. 146-48. See also The Sunday Graphic, 12 January 1975, pp. 1, 4.

39. The Sunday Graphic, 13 April 1975, p. 1. At their sale by the Thomson organization to the government in 1974 and the departure of Ric Mentus and Rickey Singh, The Guyana Graphic and The Sunday Graphic rapidly became yet another mouthpiece of the Burnham government. Fortunately, Rickey Singh became editor of Caribbean Contact in 1974. This is a monthly publication of the independent-minded Caribbean Conference of Churches and an excellent source of information about the entire Caribbean region.

40. Caribbean Contact, September 1975, pp. 10-11. See also the PPP publication This Is Guyana (Georgetown, Guyana, 1976).

41. Premdas, "Guyana: Socialist Reconstruction or Political Opportunism?" pp. 151-53.

42. Caribbean Contact, January 1976, p. 8; and This Is Guyana, p. 24.

43. Manley, Guyana Emergent, pp. 55-71.
44. Caribbean Contact, March 1976, p. 10, and June 1976, p. 5.
45. Caribbean Contact, April 1976, p. 7.

9
Jonestown and the House-Mouse Referendum

Ain't I de Emperor? De laws don't go for him. You heah what I tells you, Smithers. Dere's little stealin' like you does, and dere's big stealin' like I does. For de little stealin' dey gets you in jail soon or late. For de big stealin' dey makes you Emperor and puts you in de Hall o' Fame when you croaks.

Eugene O'Neill,
The Emperor Jones

Although Burnham wanted Jagan's assistance if it would mean a less dissatisfied East Indian population, he had no real intention of sharing power with his old adversary. He knew his militants objected to rapprochement with the PPP; it would mean fewer jobs for the faithful, most of whom detested the East Indians. His decision, reached by the summer of 1977, to reject Jagan's proposals for a PNC-PPP coalition closed one major approach to a new start for Guyana.

Burnham confronted an even more perplexing problem, linked to Guyana's slow rate of economic growth and the failure to achieve any real social development. As time passed, and even though he had moved to the left, Burnham was increasingly dismayed to find more and more of his traditional black followers defecting. The black bourgeoisie had never wanted socialism in the first place and was outraged by governmental corruption and the high crime rate. In addition, the black working class found its standard of living declining due to inflation. Trade union leaders were appalled by the high levels of unemployment and underemployment. Waiting to provide leadership for some of the discontented was the black ascetic socialist, Eusi Kwayana, now also linked to the East Indian masses through the recently formed

Working People's Alliance. Burnham's unwillingness to
broaden the base of his support between 1974 and 1977
(except on his own terms) and his final decision after
three years of hesitation to harass and ignore the opposition, brought about the most critical phase of Guyanese history since the events of 1953 and 1961 to 1964.

After the massive fraud of the 1973 election, the
PNC set out to enhance its position throughout the nation. What it had failed to win at the elections, it
hoped to achieve through a sophisticated propaganda campaign. At a special Congress at Sophia in Georgetown,
on 14-15 December 1974, the party again pledged itself
to building cooperative socialism. A new constitution
gave greater power to the party leader, and, in an attempt to disarm critics of governmental corruption, provided for a higher standard of conduct for all PNC members. Disciplinary action was promised for all offend-
ers.[1]

The proposals, designed to raise the level of morality, accomplished little, but the new constitution did
give far more authority to the party at every level of
society. PNC enthusiasts now stressed the doctrine of
"Party Paramountcy." Opponents of the PNC wondered if a
one-party state was next on the agenda. Criticism of
the government was rarely heard on the radio, for Guyana
Broadcasting Service was owned by the government. Radio
Demerara, still in the hands of a large English company,
was not taken over until the late 1970s, but it decided
to swim with the tide.[2]

The purchase of the Graphic (both daily and Sunday)
in 1974 from Lord Thomson's publishing chain eliminated
one more honest voice of intelligent criticism. Rickey
Singh, its chief investigative reporter, had already
been forced to leave the country and Ric Mentus, its
editor, soon followed. Fortunately, Singh would become
editor of Caribbean Contact in 1974, the independent
monthly publication of the Caribbean Conference of
Churches. Only The Mirror and the Catholic Standard remained independent, but The Mirror often had difficulty
obtaining newsprint as a consequence of governmental import regulations. When critical articles appeared,
thin-skinned ministers rushed to friendly courts to introduce libel suits.

The always suspicious and truculent PNC leadership
was surprised in November 1974 when a number of its
left-wing opponents managed to form the Working People's
Alliance (WPA). Ever since his departure from the PNC
in 1971 and his campaign for the landless in 1973, Eusi
Kwayana had been searching for ways to lead ASCRIA into
an alliance with East Indian working class groups.[3] After two years of discussions, agreement was finally
reached between ASCRIA, the Indian Political Revolutionary Associates (IPRA), Ratoon, and the Working People's
Vanguard party (WPVP). IPRA was led by the East Indian

lawyer, Moses Bhagwan, a former PPP enthusiast expelled by Jagan for excessive revolutionary zeal.[4] Ratoon, a small group of intellectuals centered at the University of Guyana, included the noted economist, Clive Thomas. Brindley Benn, another former Jagan aide who had been eased out for his left-wing proposals, presided over the WPVP. Several years later, however, Benn became disenchanted with the WPA and withdrew his organization.[5]

The WPA issued its first press release on 30 November 1974. Bitterly critical of the government, it concluded that "racial solidarity is proclaimed while, in fact, racial insecurity is promoted as the foundation of dictatorship." The WPA committed itself to the unity of all working people. Every citizen should be guaranteed employment. Most important, the WPA wished to bring together the East Indian and black working people behind a program of justice through democratic socialism.

Walter Rodney had just become a new and valuable addition to the ranks of the WPA. A native Guyanese, Rodney had received a Ph.D. in history from the University of London in 1966. His growing commitment to socialism led to banishment from a teaching post at the University of the West Indies in Jamaica in 1968. He then taught in Tanzania before being offered a post in the Department of History at the University of Guyana in 1974.[6] Although Rodney was black, the Burnham government wanted no part of this independent-minded young man. The government stepped in and vetoed Rodney's appointment at the University.[7]

Worried now about the disaffection of both black and East Indian young people, the government decided upon a system of national service. The prime minister announced this proposal to the public when he opened the Faculty of Education building at the University of Guyana on 17 October 1973. Burnham proposed that all students wishing to attend the university should first perform twelve to fourteen months of national service, "so they could understand how the farmer thinks, so they could enjoy the beauties of Guyana."[8]

Much of the country was indignant. Many conceded that, in theory, the idea of national service was sound, but it appeared that Burnham simply wished to indoctrinate all Guyanese eighteen-year-olds desiring higher education in the principles of PNC cooperative socialism. Burnham had linked his suggestions to opening the interior, but it was argued that this project required settlers committed to permanent residence rather than students who would depart after one year.

The East Indian community was especially irritated, for Burnham had indicated that young women must also participate. Tradition among the East Indians required that all unmarried women live at home. By 1974, when the National Service Act became law, the government had retreated from its original proposals. Service would be

voluntary unless one attended the University of Guyana;
then it would be mandatory for obtaining a degree.

Although national service provided some training
for some of the young Georgetown unemployed, it became a
very divisive factor at the University of Guyana. Ex-
emptions have been made for those with influence. For
example, in 1976, 63 students at the university were
listed for compulsory induction; 53 were East Indians.
Of the 25 women among the 63, about 90 percent were East
Indians. Some of the students resigned from the university to avoid induction, while others were suspended for
refusing to serve.[9]

Middle class opinion was further outraged when the
government announced in 1975 that the dual control of
education must end. The churches administered more than
90 percent of Guyana's primary schools, mostly Christian
though a few were Hindu or Moslem. Parents with sufficient funds sent their children to the church schools,
considered superior to the state schools. Many East Indians had always been resentful because they feared
Christian indoctrination of their children, and the PPP
had always advocated secular education.[10]

It will be recalled that one of the original, unfulfilled aims of the PPP government in 1953 had been to
secularize the church schools. Both Jagan and Burnham
agreed that church schools were a divisive force. But
when Jagan introduced legislation to seize fifty-one,
Christian-controlled schools in 1960, Burnham, by then
head of the PNC and thrashing about for middle class
support, reversed his course. "In 1953 I did say that I
proposed to abolish dual control of schools by legislation. I am not afraid to admit that, after careful
thought, I have decided to change my approach to this
question."

Fifteen years later, Burnham twisted about to his
1953 views. The PPP could do little in 1976 but join
with Burnham in approving government control of all
schools. It did, however, regret that Christian prayers
would continue to be used in many schools, and it lamented the lack of a good required course in Marxism-
Leninism.[11] Only the United Force opposed the take-over
legislation. To facilitate the seizure without compensation, the government hastily modified a fundamental
rights section of the constitution. Jagan ought to have
paused before supporting constitutional changes that
would diminish the rights of Guyanese citizens.

Although the Guyanese were bitterly divided on the
schools issue, there was outrage throughout the nation
on 6 October 1976 when a Cuban Airlines plane blew up on
departure from Barbados. All seventy-three passengers
and crew were killed, including eleven Guyanese. Anti-
Castro Cubans, now naturalized Venezuelan citizens, were
accused of the crime, but many Guyanese suspected CIA
involvement. It was believed the CIA had become more

actively involved in destabilizing the Castro regime because of its growing alarm, not only over Castro, but
also over the sharp swing to the left in Guyana and in
Michael Manley's Jamaica.[12]

Guyanese remembered Washington's indignation earlier in the year when Prime Minister Burnham declined to
formally declare that Guyana would not refuel Cuban
planes carrying troops to Angola. Brazil and Venezuela
had also criticized Burnham, and speculation grew that
Washington might use Brazil's military dictatorship to
foment trouble in Guyana. Burnham knew, however, that
so long as Jagan remained the primary alternative to the
PNC, Washington was not likely to act. On the other
hand, Burnham's drive to the left had enabled him to win
"critical support" from Jagan.[13]

By late 1976, it was obvious that the nationalization of most industries had not promoted economic development. Presenting the 1977 budget to the National Assembly on 30 December 1976, Finance Minister Frank Hope
painted a gloomy picture of prolonged austerity measures.
Falling sugar prices since early 1975 had produced catastrophe, especially when linked to the increasing price
of oil. Sugar had fallen from £650 per ton in late 1974
to just under £300 per ton in 1976.

The finance minister anticipated a large budget deficit. Loans would be required, most likely from the
International Monetary Fund and the western capitalist
states. Sugar and rice production had failed to reach
anticipated levels, and exports were not paying for
needed imports. Economy measures were required to service the national debt. Funds for housing and health
care would be cut and subsidies withdrawn from flour and
electricity. Nonessential imports would have to be limited. All these measures meant a decrease in the standard of living for Guyana's working people.[14]

By 1977, it had become clear that the great dreams
for the Caribbean Common Market (CARICOM) were not being
realized. The failure of the West Indies Federation in
1962 led many to hope that while political unity was
dead for the moment, it might be possible to achieve
economic cooperation throughout the English-speaking
Caribbean.

It will be recalled that Jagan had to move carefully on Caribbean unity because of East Indian fears of
being swallowed up by the blacks in the region. But
Burnham and the PNC were ardent advocates of Caribbean
integration. In 1965, Guyana, Barbados, and Antigua established the basis for a Caribbean Free Trade Association (CARIFTA). By 1971, the three founding states had
been joined by the great majority of English-speaking
islands and territories in the region, including Jamaica
and Trinidad which, along with Guyana and Barbados, were
more developed than smaller territories such as Dominica,
Grenada, St. Kitts-Nevis, St. Lucia, St. Vincent, Mont-

serrat, and Belize.[15]

At CARIFTA's beginning, enthusiasm swept the entire Caribbean community and economic development moved ahead. CARIFTA's aim was to increase trade within the region and to construct a Common External Tariff. A Caribbean Development Bank was set up to equalize the distribution of benefits among the twelve member states and to prevent the "Big-Four" from profiting at the expense of the smaller territories. A proud Georgetown became headquarters for the Commonwealth Caribbean Regional Secretariat.[16]

Pushing bravely ahead, CARIFTA was transformed into the Caribbean Common Market (CARICOM) in 1973. A common external tariff was hammered into shape, and there was some coordination in trade, foreign affairs, and the location of new industry. A Caribbean Investment Bank was also established. Euphoria was everywhere; however, within a few years, the community was near collapse. The eight less-developed states felt exploited by the "Big-Four"; and, the "Big-Four" were split between the moderate tactics of Eric Williams and Tom Adams in Trinidad and Barbados, respectively (Adams succeeded Errol Barrow in 1976), and the socialist policies of Forbes Burnham in Guyana and Michael Manley in Jamaica. Oil-rich Trinidad had no intention of permitting its wealth to disappear into the other states of the Caribbean.[17] By 1975-1976, the entire Caribbean was reeling under the impact of staggering oil costs and the generally high prices of essential imports, while prices for exports of sugar, rice, bauxite, and tropical fruits were much too low. Unemployment and underemployment increased, and economic development ground to a halt.

At this critical juncture in 1976-1977, Forbes Burnham missed a great chance, perhaps the last, for reconciliation with Cheddi Jagan and the East Indian community. Jagan, reaching out desperately for some form of coalition as the years slipped away, took the initiative several months before the second PNC biennial Congress, scheduled to start in Georgetown on 12 August 1977. Interviewed by Caribbean Contact in May 1977, Jagan conceded that "critical support" had not dramatically altered the political and economic climate. Conversations with Burnham the previous November had been fruitless. He remained convinced, however, that "Mr. Burnham is the PNC. From the way the party was formed and the way it is run, we feel he determines the tendency." Jagan had no doubt that there must be "cooperation between the masses of the people in both parties." Unfortunately, "the new shirt-jac elite" of the PNC was determined to monopolize every governmental job. A restoration of democracy in Guyana would "mean a lot of people will lose positions."[18]

When asked if he preferred a "shared Government between the PNC and the PPP as a spur to racial harmony,

maximum production and accelerating the thrust to socialism," Jagan responded:

> I am saying that the ideal is a political solution, not
> just a sharing of government. The important things are
> what the country is going to do, what are going to be
> the policies and programmes of government. Those matter
> more to us than sharing Government. We are not concerned
> just to go into the government. (Caribbean Contact May 1977: 12-13)

A few months later, shortly before the PNC Congress,
the PPP leader became more precise. At a press conference on 9 August 1977, Jagan demanded "the establishment
of a National Patriotic Front Government, including all
parties and groups which are progressive, anti-imperial-
istic and who do wish to see Guyana take a socialist-
oriented path of development." National disaster beck-
oned, Jagan argued, unless immediate steps were taken to
resolve the financial crisis, put people to work, and
cut down on crimes of violence.[19]
    According to Jagan, free elections were a first
priority. After elections, there could be a sharing of
power between the two major parties and other progressive groups. He advocated one new political position,
an executive president. The prime minister would still
be the leader of the largest party, and the second largest party would designate the executive president. The
cabinet, presided over by the prime minister, would be
drawn from each party that accepted the socialist basis
of the patriotic front, in proportion to its representation in the National Assembly. The executive president
could send proposals to the National Assembly, address
that body when he wished, and veto its measures, but a
two-thirds vote of the National Assembly could override
the veto.
    Jagan went on to propose a program for the national
front. Nationalization of the major components of the
economy should continue; banks and insurance companies
were next on his list. Participation of all the people
was required in every aspect of development. Wage inequities must be rectified and all forms of discrimination and corruption cease. The fundamental human rights
listed in the constitution must be respected.
    Behind all these proposals was Jagan's knowledge
that free elections would bring a victory for the PPP.
Cheddi Jagan would become prime minister while Forbes
Burnham would be relegated to the less prestigious post
of executive president. The moment of final decision
had arrived for Forbes Burnham. Jagan's proposals were
statesmanlike, reasonable, and sensible. It might still
be possible for the two aging leaders to bridge the ethnic hostility separating East Indian and black, but it
would require Burnham to accept a lesser position than
Jagan. It would also mean a loss of jobs for some of

the party faithful.

The eyes of the PNC militants swiftly focussed on their beloved "Comrade Leader." He did not fail them. Retreating from statesmanship, he rejected Jagan's proposals and reaffirmed the paramountcy of the PNC. To the cheers of his disciples, at the conclusion of the second biennial Congress of the PNC on 21 August 1977, he affirmed that only the PNC could resolve Guyana's problems by increasing productivity and dissolving racial tension. An alliance of leaders was no solution, for it was the PNC that had unified the Guyanese nation. No doubt amused by the analogy, Burnham reminded Jagan that the Bolsheviks had not compromised with the Mensheviks. Even more disturbing to many observers was the new loyalty pledge to the PNC now required from members of the Guyana Defense Force, the police, the People's Militia, the Fire Service, and the National Service.[20] Was loyalty now being given to the paramount party rather than to the nation and the principles upon which it had been established?

In retrospect, Burnham's refusal to compromise with Jagan may have been his most fundamental decision since accepting CIA aid in destroying Jagan's government in the early 1960s. Fearing rebellion from the militant rowdies who had cleared his path to power, Burnham opted to maintain PNC minority rule over the majority of Guyanese people. Having rejected free and fair elections, Burnham had no alternative but to neutralize or destroy his opponents, or else be destroyed by them. The issue was clearly drawn. No chance for such a fine compromise was likely to appear ever again. Only the guns of his armed supporters propped him up, for a majority of the population detested the PNC. Between 1973 and 1976, expenditure on Guyanese security services more than doubled, and has continued to increase. In 1964, there had been just over 2,000 policemen and soldiers. Now there were more than 20,000, with some observers expecting the total to reach 30,000 by 1980. Estimates indicated that the top ranks in the Guyana Defense Force and the police were almost entirely black, while more than 90 percent of total membership in both bodies was black.

Jagan, ever the romantic revolutionary, always prepared with the first step without considering the second, picked up the challenge and called out GAWU on strike four days later. The sugar workers were restless; profit-sharing revenues they had expected for two years had never materialized.[21] All talk of political coalition vanished. The government regarded the strike a political challenge and reacted with tough measures. The strike was, indeed, a half-hearted attempt to upset the government, although the sugar workers did have legitimate grievances. Burnham and the PNC decided to break the PPP's main base of support, and the recruitment of scabs from among Georgetown's unemployed started immediately. Government supporters were urged to spend a few hours each day cutting cane.[22]

This scabbing was a challenge to the entire trade union movement. Though Guyana's TUC was normally sub-servient to the PNC, its secretary general, Joseph Polly-dore, regretted the failure of Burnham and Jagan to form a coalition. Militant trade unionists were disturbed by the government's strike-breaking tactics and managed to push through proposals at the TUC's annual conference in late September calling for "no victimisation by either side." The proposals asked that all workers on the pick-et line be rehired when the strike terminated; no one hired for a striker's job should be retained when peace returned to the sugar industry. Three unions were espe-cially active in aiding the sugar workers: the Clerical and Commercial Workers Union (CCWU), the National Asso-ciation of Agricultural, Commercial, and Industrial Em-ployees (NAACIE), and the University of Guyana Staff As-sociation (UGSA). The CCWU and NAACIE were composed primarily of black trade unionists with only a sprink-ling of East Indians, but both organizations insisted that trade union principles must come first; justice for the sugar workers would be a victory for all trade union-ists. Just a few years before, the CCWU had been quite close to the government. NAACIE, however, was rather different since Ashton Chase had always been a key lead-er of the union. Support also came in from the dissi-dent bauxite workers in Linden, banded together as the Organization of Working People (OWP). Guyanese church leaders also endorsed the compromise proposals of the TUC. Meeting in Georgetown in November, the Caribbean Conference of Churches supported the sugar workers and urged the government to accept the TUC proposals, al-ready ratified by GAWU.

Burnham, angered by the number of his opponents, decided to fight to the end, even though it meant more division in the nation and a serious shortage in the sugar crop. The police and the Guyana Defense Force were ever present to enforce the will of the government and to protect the strike breakers. Finally, after a 135-day strike, the sugar workers surrendered on 5 Janu-ary 1978. The sugar workers were denied a share in profits, and many failed to obtain their old jobs as numerous strike breakers were retained.

GAWU was bruised by the defeat, but the three mili-tant unions, CCWU, NAACIE, and UGSA, refused to give up the struggle. They denounced the antidemocratic and antitrade union activities of the government and its mo-nopoly state enterprise, the Guyana Sugar Corporation (GUYSUCO).

> The methods used to bust the strike--arrest and prosecu-tion of union organisers, excessive bail, the banning of public meetings, the seizure of strike relief, the use

of military and para-military forces, as well as public
servants, to do the work of the strikers and the mass recruitment and use of scab labour, including child labour,
from the ranks of the unemployed--recall the worst anti-
labour practice of the capitalist bosses.

They must be seen as resulting from a deep-seated
fear of the working class on the part of an anti-people's
government. When to all of these is added the threat of
detention without trial and of curfew under Part Two of
the National Security Act, it is clear that we must fight
against a type of neo-colonial barbarism.[23]

GAWU had been beaten, but Guyana would never be the
same again. Burnham retained the guns, but the base of
his support was slowly eroding. A significant portion
of the black working class had joined the other side.
Only Jagan's Marxism-Leninism prevented the formation of
a united opposition. More people than ever before began
to look favorably upon the activities of the militants
and idealists who marched behind the banner of the Working People's Alliance. They also admired the middle
class opponents of the regime. But would it ever be
possible to bring together the PPP, the WPA, bourgeois
moderates, and religious activists?[24]

Many Guyanese now wondered what Burnham would do
about the parliamentary elections required by the fall
of 1978. Deciding against a replay of 1968 and 1973,
the PNC magicians conjured up a referendum for 10 July
1978. The referendum would ask the Guyanese people to
decisively alter the constitution. Article 73 of the
constitution provided that certain entrenched clauses
could only be altered after the changes were first approved by the National Assembly and then submitted to
the population in a referendum. The entrenched clauses
included such fundamental matters as the electoral system itself and the composition and dissolution of Parliament. This procedure was designed to protect the basic rights of the Guyanese people. Other parts of the
constitution could simply be changed by a two-thirds
vote of the National Assembly; no referendum was required. The PNC now proposed that the 10 July referendum be final. If they won, a two-thirds Parliamentary
majority could do as it wished--even write a new constitution.[25]

Since the existing Parliament legally terminated on
25 July, with elections due not later than 25 October,
Burnham's plot was obvious. He would win the referendum
on 10 July, postpone elections for the National Assembly,
write a new constitution giving even greater power to
himself and the PNC, and then have it approved by the
PNC-controlled National Assembly, without bothering to
consult the people in a referendum.

The PNC introduced the Referendum Bill in haste on
1 April and pushed it through within ten days, at a time

when most of Georgetown's attention was centered on a
breakdown of electricity and water supply. Once again
the PNC prepared to win an election through massive
fraud. The padded lists of voters, the fake proxies,
and the bogus absentee ballots were again made ready.
Many were indignant, but Burnham controlled Georgetown
and he had the guns.[26]

On 11 April 1978, shortly after announcing the referendum, Burnham departed for a twenty-four-day trip to
North Korea, the Soviet Union, East Germany, and the
United Kingdom. He received little economic aid from
the communist states, though he probably wished to reaf-
firm his friendly ties with Moscow now that he had, once
again, turned against Cheddi Jagan. Jagan must have
raged inwardly as his ideological allies wined and dined
his enemy.[27] Burnham was embarrassed, however, several
weeks after his return to Guyana when it was reported
that his entourage of more than thirty people, including
two physicians, had cost more than $200,000.[28]

Informed political analysts estimated that three-
fourths of the nation rallied behind the anti-Burnham
banner. A Committee in Defense of Democracy (CDD) was
quickly organized, eventually including, among others,
the People's Progressive party, the Liberator party, the
Working People's Alliance, the People's Democratic Movement, GAWU, the Civil Liberties Action Council, the Guyana Peace Council, the Rice Producers Association, and
the Organization of Working People. A number of professional and civil bodies formed a Concerned Citizens'
Committee to oppose the referendum. Among the groups
joining were the Lawyers' Committee, the Architects'
Committee, the Committee of Medical Practitioners, the
Committee of Concerned Educators, the University of Guyana Staff Association, the Clerical and Commercial Workers Union, and NAACIE. The Guyana Council of Churches
had an observer on the Concerned Citizens' Committee.
More and more of the informed, articulate middle class
was abandoning neutrality and joining the anti-Burnham-
ites.[29]

Hooligans began to break up opposition meetings.
Newsprint became difficult to find, and government newspapers refused to carry advertisements critical of the
referendum. Opposition attempts to use the courts were
unsuccessful. Participating in a protest march against
the referendum on 17 May, Martin Carter, Guyana's finest
poet and a former PNC supporter, was beaten by pro-
Burnham agitators. Several other antireferendum demonstrators were injured at the same time.

The Lawyers' Committee noted that "the referendum
seeks to deprive the people of their right to approve or
disapprove any new Constitution" and would put "absolute
power to alter the Constitution in the two-thirds majority in Parliament." The future of the nation would be
placed "in the hands of a dying Parliament." The Guyana

Council of Churches observed that, "the Bill places too
much power in the hands of any parliament and too great
a temptation for this, or future parliaments, to assume
more power than is just."

The referendum became even more ludicrous when the
government unilaterally decided that a "house" would be
the symbol for a "yes" vote while a "mouse" would signi-
fy a "no" vote. Confident that the government would be
defeated if an honest referendum were conducted, the
Concerned Citizens' Committee and the Committee in Defense of Democracy contacted the minister of home affairs to work out the details for a fair election. The
minister refused to meet with the committees. After the
minister's refusal to discuss the procedures for the
referendum and for counting the votes, the CCC and the
CDD decided, at the beginning of July, upon a boycott.
The United Force agreed to the decision. They would hu-
miliate the prime minister by keeping the majority of
the nation at home.

The government even refused to release the loca-
tions of polling places until two days before the vote
since the opposition indicated it would monitor the voting. As election day dawned, there was an ominous military presence in Georgetown; armed patrols moved about
the city and throughout the countryside.

Although the opposition failed to have observers at
all the polling stations, it concluded that only about
15 percent of eligible voters had participated. Even if
this figure is too low, clearly the nation was saying
"no" to the Burnham government. The opposition monitors
reported that many government supporters voted more than
once, people were voting outside their own electoral
district, government vehicles were carrying voters to
the polling stations, young people under eighteen were
voting, opposition election agents were chased from the
polling stations, and armed soldiers often collected the
ballot boxes. The report of the Committee of Concerned
Citizens concluded that the announced results of the
referendum were "massively fraudulent."

The PNC ridiculed its opponents, ignored the boycott, and proudly announced that 71.45 percent of the
eligible voters had participated. It claimed an electoral list of 609,225 local and overseas voters. From
these eligible voters, the government stated that 431,120
votes were cast. The "yes" votes amounted to 419,936 or
97.4 percent of the total; there were only 8,956 "no"
votes, or 2.1 percent of the total. The remaining votes
had been ruined.

The solidarity of the opposition astonished the PNC.
Middle class opinion, which had accepted Burnham because
it feared Jagan, was now solidly against the PNC. All
the important church leaders, including Bishop Benedict
Singh of the Roman Catholic Church and Bishop Randolph
George of the Anglican Church, had joined the opposition.

Burnham's retention of office through fraud and violence
had become intolerable.[30]

Writing in the London Times on 11 August 1978,
Peter Strafford concluded that "the referendum was merely the latest step in a process by which the PNC has
virtually turned Guyana into a one-party state." The
boycott had been remarkably successful, "though the PNC
made up for this by taking busloads of supporters from
one polling place to another." Strafford observed that
if Guyana were efficiently administered, it would have
"a reasonably successful economy based on sugar, aluminum, and rice. But today, it is run down and repressive,
and bedevilled by racial tensions that are not far be-
neath the surface. Middle class people from the major
racial groups are emigrating."

Having found little monetary comfort during his
trip to the communist countries in April, Burnham decided to try Washington and the International Monetary
Fund. Aid was imperative for a faltering economy and
for a start to what had become Burnham's panacea, a massive hydroelectric project on the Upper Mazaruni River.
This project would provide the energy Guyana required to
construct her own aluminum smelters.[31]

By early August the prime minister had agreed to
the terms of a very demanding International Monetary
Fund. Guyana would receive an additional G$46 million
in aid; but, the IMF insisted upon a 5 percent rate of
economic growth, upon cutting the balance of payments
deficit, upon reducing imports by 10 percent, and upon
lowering the foreign commercial debt. In a country already suffering from shortages, these requirements would
mean further belt-tightening for the population.[32] Writing in the Catholic Standard on 13 August 1978, its editor, Father Andrew Morrison, observed:

> Productivity results, in part from motivated people and
> in part from technical efficiency. For people to be mo-
> tivated to accept sacrifice they must feel they have a
> stake in the benefits which the sacrifice will bring. It
> is precisely at this juncture that the IMF policy seems
> to hold out little hope of producing the improvements the
> economy so badly needs; politically the referendum gave
> the present ruling party the power to distribute those
> benefits as it alone sees fit, and economically, it en-
> sures that whatever benefits may be will not reach the
> working man and his family.

Also commenting upon the IMF agreement was Dr. Maurice Odle, head of the Institute of Development Studies
at the University of Guyana. Pointing to the negative
economic growth of the past two years and the way in
which the withdrawal of government subsidies for many
essential goods and services had forced the cost of living upward, Odle noted in the Caribbean Contact of

October 1978:

> The foreign exchange problems in Guyana, where 80 percent
> of the productive sector is owned by the State, are only
> partly a product of the crisis of the international cap-
> italist economy and the failure of the state capitalists
> to disengage from the previous colonial pattern of trade.
> Probably more important are the failure to plan effective-
> ly; to motivate the mass of workers; to reduce wasteful
> expenditures and to solve the country's political prob-
> lems. The balance of payments crisis, therefore, has lit-
> tle or nothing to do with the so-called "birth pangs" of
> socialism.

Especially striking was the increase of government spending for the state bureaucracy and for the military and
paramilitary forces, the essential props for the regime
itself.

After the referendum results were announced, the
National Assembly voted to suspend parliamentary elections for fifteen months. The two-thirds PNC majority
then turned the National Assembly into a Constituent Assembly to draw up a new constitution for Guyana. Despite mounting opposition, Burnham retained the driver's
seat; civil servants, army, police, and Georgetown rowdies remained in his pocket. He also owned the best of
both worlds in international affairs. Guyana had friendly relations with Cuba, the Soviet Union, the People's
Republic of China, and the United States. The United
States, unhappy over his swing to the left and to non-
alignment, would never destabilize his regime so long as
Jagan remained a likely alternative. Although Guyana's
economy was passing through difficult times, Forbes
Burnham and the faithful were prosperous, contented, and
arrogant.

Then, unexpectedly, a catastrophe occurred and the
world's eyes turned toward Guyana. Revivalist and mil-
lenarian evangelists had always been active among Guyana's population, especially the black Protestants. It
was not uncommon for United States ministers to undertake short religious crusades in Guyana. The Reverend
Jim Jones seemed an even more remarkable catch for the
Guyana government. Arriving with impeccable credentials,
vast sums of money, and a large multiracial following,
he proposed to establish a farming community in a remote
area, near Port Kaituma, not too far from the Venezuelan
border.

Jones appeared perfect. Jonestown would serve as a
fine example for the Guyanese, who perhaps would be encouraged to leave the coastal belt for the interior. The
town would represent cooperative socialism at its best
and would install a fair number of people into the area
claimed by Venezuela. Government officials were especially pleased by the willingness of Jones and his asso-

ciates to pay for special favors.

Criticism of his People's Temple in California brought Jones and most of his followers to the Jonestown commune by the end of 1977; the preliminary clearing of land had started a few years before. Friends in high places enabled Jones to ignore Guyana's immigration, customs, and firearms laws. Earlier, in 1975, concern had been expressed over some faith-healing activities on the part of Jones in Georgetown,[33] but the government now enthusiastically endorsed the Jonestown experiment in cooperative socialism.

Back in California, criticism intensified. Relatives of those living at Jonestown and former members of the People's Temple complained about abusive treatment, and they demanded an inquiry. Congressman Leo Ryan of California decided to investigate when he became convinced the United States embassy in Georgetown had been negligent. While probing conditions at Jonestown in November 1978, Ryan was murdered along with some members of his party. Jones, knowing he was about to be exposed, called upon his followers to take their lives in a mass suicide. More than nine hundred people, most from loyal dedication, others because of force, died at Jonestown on Saturday, 18 November 1978.[34]

From being a rather hot, run-down, tropical capital, Georgetown suddenly became the center of the world's attention. Newspaper reporters and television crews descended on the city; taxi drivers and hotel managers were overjoyed. But the government was horrified. Its links with Jones must be pushed under the rug. Forbes Burnham, normally a lover of floodlights, was not to be found. Other members of the government, especially the deputy prime minister, Ptolemy Reid, were assigned the task of discussing Jonestown. All opposition groups joined together to demand a proper investigation of Jim Jones, the People's Temple, and Jonestown. To this day the government has continued to procrastinate. More than five years after the catastrophe, the government insists that Judge Victor Crane has been designated to conduct a one-man inquiry. This task would seem awesome for one man, especially when Judge Crane insists he has received no letter of appointment. In an interview with a New York Times reporter on 3 December 1978, Burnham dispensed with the whole affair: "We could have done without these problems but essentially it's an American problem. We're just unfortunate that they came."

After Jonestown, public attention turned to United States fugitive David Hill, another recipient of special protection from the Burnham regime. Self-baptized as Rabbi Edward Emmanuel Washington, he presides over a Georgetown cult, the House of Israel. Preaching a mesmerizing doctrine calling black people the true children of Israel, the rabbi found eager supporters among Georgetown's black unemployed. He claimed eight thousand followers throughout the country and dressed them in black, red, and green uniforms, the same colors used in PNC emblems. His acolytes could usually be found breaking up opposition meetings and wildly cheering for government speakers. The government's reply to Washington's critics was that the rabbi had broken no laws in Guyana.[35]

Most opposition groups, including the Guyana Council of Churches, did not bother to participate in rewriting the constitution, for the government paid little attention to those groups which presented proposals. The economy continued to deteriorate. In March 1979, Desmond Hoyte's budget speech announced that the government intended to renege on its pledges to introduce a G$14 daily minimum wage for all government workers. There was simply not enough money. The trade union movement thundered its disapproval. One-third of government spending now went to servicing foreign debts and paying for the nationalized industries.

CARICOM was in disarray; Eric Williams still refused to use his oil income to aid the unstable economies of Guyana and Jamaica. The great dreams of 1973 were a shambles. There was no real common market, few common services, and no common foreign policy. Each member of CARICOM was desperately struggling to survive, and there was little thought of helping one's neighbors.

In February 1979, the various opposition groups organized a Council of National Safety, with Eusi Kwayana as secretary, to force the government to investigate Jonestown. More and more of Guyana's working people were turning toward the increasingly active Working People's Alliance. Moses Bhagwan, Walter Rodney, Eusi Kwayana, and Clive Thomas seemed absolutely dedicated to building a new Guyana based upon free elections, national unity, and social justice.[36] The Council of National Safety soon broadened its activities to insist upon a return to constitutional government. There was much excitement in the Caribbean when the repressive government of Eric Gairy in Grenada was toppled by Maurice Bishop's socialist-leaning New Jewel Movement in March 1979. This takeover was the first revolutionary seizure of power in the British Caribbean. Guyanese wondered if this method might be the only way to remove Forbes Burnham and the PNC.

Concern mounted over the emigration of the well-to-do and talented Guyanese middle class--they were voting with their feet. More than 7,500 left in 1975; in 1978, 13,000 departed.[37] Many left reluctantly, not because they were seduced by higher salaries in wealthier countries, but because they had lost all hope. By April 1979, fifteen concerned, moderate Guyanese established COMPASS, a body designed to discuss the problem of national "unity." This group insisted there was no substitute for "a political and constitutional framework" that would "command a general, national consensus."

Among the members of COMPASS were Joseph Pollydore, general secretary of the TUC, Gordon Todd, president of the CCWU, Pat Thompson from GUYBAU, Brenda Do Harris, an activist high school teacher, Bishop Randolph George of the Anglican Church, Father Andrew Morrison, editor of the _Catholic Standard_, Mike James, assistant editor of the _Catholic Standard_, and lawyers Miles Fitzpatrick and David de Caires.[38]

The government again postponed local government elections; none had taken place since 1970. Then the PNC endorsed greater authority for magistrates and judges so that jury trials would not always be necessary. A group of Guyanese lawyers immediately protested this further government invasion of basic rights.[39] Attempts by the PPP and the Working People's Alliance to participate in the May Day celebrations of 1979 in Georgetown were howled down by government supporters and House of Israel activists.[40]

Meeting in late June at the headquarters of the Clerical and Commercial Workers Union, the CCWU, NAACIE, GAWU, UGSA, representatives from the Organization of Working People, and other discontented trade union groups established a permanent committee to further the interests of Guyana's working people and to democratize the structure of the TUC to make it more representative of the working people. Many small unions supporting Burnham had been granted excessive power within the TUC. GAWU had 32 percent of the total union membership enrolled with the TUC, but the pro-Burnham bureaucracy in the TUC only awarded GAWU 16 percent of the total votes permitted to be cast at the annual congress of the TUC.[41]

The Council of National Safety, which now included the Working People's Alliance (recently transformed into a political party), Makepeace Richmond's and Ganraj Kumar's Liberator party, Llewellyn John's People's Democratic Movement, and Brindley Benn's Working People's Vanguard party, decided upon a week of remembrance to commemorate the passage of one deplorable year since the "House-Mouse" referendum. Demonstrations had scarcely started when Georgetown awakened on the morning of Wednesday, 11 July 1979, to find the building on Camp Street, which housed the Ministry of National Development and the office of the general secretary of the PNC, in flames.[42]

The police and the government instantly accused the opposition groups of arson. Three WPA activists were promptly arrested. Charged with setting the fire were Dr. Walter Rodney and two other University of Guyana teachers, Dr. Rupert Roopnaraine and Dr. Omawale. When they were brought to Magistrate's Court three days later to be charged and then released on bail, their supporters demonstrated in the street below to show their solidarity. Public opinion was confused. Had the opposition groups been responsible for the fire or had the government set the fire itself as a pretext for punishing the opposition?

While the pro-WPA demonstration continued, government activists and House of Israel supporters arrived on the scene. Scuffling developed, and Mike James, assistant editor of the Catholic Standard, found himself being manhandled. At that moment, a Jesuit priest, Father Bernard Darke, teacher at St. Stanislaus College and a professional photographer, arrived on the scene to record the events. Eyewitnesses claimed that a House of Israel activist struck Father Darke with a knife. The incident took place in Brickdam, very close to the police station, where many policemen lounged about but failed to intervene.[43]

Rushed to the hospital, Father Darke died six hours later. The murder of a gentle, kindly priest was a vivid reminder of the depths to which Guyanese life had sunk. The arson charges were temporarily forgotten. Would anything be done to arrest the assassin or to restrain the other thugs who had beaten peaceful demonstrators? Many wondered if the killer had been influenced by the violent language employed in recent PNC publications. More than three years would elapse before the accused assassin was brought to trial, even though he had been quickly apprehended and photographs of the knifing were available.

Overly optimistic, the PPP and the WPA thought they had found an issue to topple the government. Speaking to some two thousand people on 20 July, WPA leaders Rodney and Kwayana demanded industrial action be taken to drive Burnham from office. But they underestimated the support he still retained--the unemployed bullies of Georgetown, the black-controlled civil service, and, most important, the police and the army. The opposition was fragmented, divided, and not quite sure what to do next.

All was not well, however, in one of the regime's essential props--discontent had surfaced in the GDF. Most GDF members were only dissatisfied with salaries, but a few genuine professionals were distressed over the special oath of loyalty to the PNC rather than to the nation. Brigadier Clarence Price, the chief of staff, was replaced by Norman McLean, a former policeman who had been running the Guyana National Service. Some key officers muttered their distaste for the McLean appointment.[44] The government did not retreat from its tough policy. Newsprint was denied The Mirror, opposition views were kept off the two, state-controlled radio stations, and NAACIE's offices were raided and some duplicating equipment removed. The Catholic Standard also dissented, and the government responded by beating its delivery people.

Moses Bhagwan's wife was fired from her post at Guyana Pharmaceutical Corporation and Bhagwan was beaten by the police on 22 August. The bauxite workers had already struck for higher wages during that frantic July. Their strike dragged on into August, with NAACIE, CCWU, and GAWU undertaking sympathetic demonstrations. The government decided to make an example of CCWU and its president, Gordon Todd, when he called out his union followers at Guyana Stores. Todd was detained by police as he organized the picket line, and a Burnham spokesman announced that all eighty-two striking workers would be replaced. By the end of August the government made some concessions and the bauxite workers returned to work. Merit pay increases were approved, even though the IMF might frown. The eighty-two CCWU members, however, were not rehired.[45]

When Burnham spoke to the biennial Conference of the PNC on 26 August he denounced his opponents. The right to strike was inalienable, but political strikes would be met with political sanctions which were also legitimate. He would not "sit idly by and permit reactionary and political zealots to ruin the economy and jeopardise the well-being of the workers and the nation. . . . We shall match steel with more highly-tempered steel. What is at stake is the revolution itself."[46]

Fearing a collapse into either absolute despotism or revolutionary violence, some fifty of Guyana's most important businessmen and professionals urged the formation of a broad-based government of national reconstruction. The present political and economic crisis had been brought about partly by the "erosion of the legal and constitutional rights of Guyanese citizens." All political parties and interest groups must join a unity administration with no one party or group dominating. This regime would only hold power long enough to restore stability and democracy. Then elections would be held under international supervision.

In early September, Martin Carter, Guyana's poet laureate, addressed an open letter to the nation in which he denounced the PNC for degrading the people. Its "main pre-occupation is self-perpetuation." The government's purge of its enemies, however, continued. Dr. Aubrey Armstrong, United States-trained director of Guyana Management Development Training Center and management consultant to the government, objected to firing one of his secretaries for "security reasons," and he promptly resigned. His conscience balked at ousting someone merely because of accusations that she belonged to the WPA.

Lack of newsprint forced The Mirror to close again in early September. The government also began reassigning teachers critical of the government, moving a number to remote posts in the interior. Bonita Bone-Harris, executive member of the WPA and a teacher at Queen's College, refused a transfer to the Port Kaituma Community School. In an open letter she listed the criminal

activities of the PNC and concluded: "Finally, I refuse
to go because the future of Guyana will be determined by
the capacity and will of the Guyanese people, of its
youth in particular, to resist this dictatorship."[47]

Increased criticism from staff and students at the
University of Guyana led to a delay in starting the academic year. Opening day was moved from September until
January 1980. The vice chancellor, Dr. Dennis Irvine,
asserted the postponement was caused by the university's
financial situation; however, most thought the government was demonstrating that it could close the university permanently if it so decided. More and more academics and students were now signing up with the WPA.

To add to the government's woes, an Inter-American
Development Bank report revealed that Guyana's bauxite
industry had shown no growth in eight of the nine years
since nationalization. Per capita production had declined so precipitously during the past five years it
would require an annual growth rate of 4 percent for the
next three years to bring the economy back to its 1974
levels. This poor economic performance left no funds at
home for investment; therefore, foreign loans were desperately needed. This borrowing, however, would mean
more foreign debts with the working class paying the
bill. The G$14 minimum daily wage had still not been
implemented. Further heavy cuts in education, health,
and transportation services were planned. The national
debt soared to more than G$2.5 billion.[48]

By early October of 1979, the WPA worked out its own
plans for a government of national unity and reconstruction. It considered itself the most important of the opposition groups. The WPA argued that the PNC must be removed, the rule of law be restored, trade union rights be
enlarged, the security forces made nonpartisan, and foun-
dations be prepared for a free and fair general election.
A Council of National Reconstruction should be set up composed of fifty persons. The WPA would designate nine, the
PPP would choose nine, the WPVP, PDM, and LP--now loosely
allied as the Vanguard for Liberation and Democracy--would
select nine, labor and peasant organizations would have
nine, and citizens organizations would choose fourteen.
Presiding over the nation during this transitional phase
would be an Executive Authority of fifteen persons reflecting the membership in the Council of National Reconstruction. The national government would then prepare
for elections within two years. Ironically, at that very
moment, the PNC again extended the life of Parliament.[49]

By mid-October, Mike James, assistant editor of the
Catholic Standard, acknowledged, contrary to the opposition's first reaction, that the Darke murder had not
been the incident that would start the collapse of Burnham and the PNC. Overthrowing the government would be
an arduous, dangerous task: "Realistic appraisal of the
difficulties ahead and a determination to organise to

achieve their goals are now being added to the spontane-
ous anger and frustration of the people. The real work,
perhaps, is only now about to begin." At the same time,
a Human Rights Association was set up under the presidency of three distinguished Guyanese, Bishop Randolph
George of the Anglican church, President Gordon Todd of
the CCWU, and the moderate University of Guyana professor, Harold Lutchman. The group planned to investigate
all accusations of human rights violations. Political
parties were banned from membership, but trade unions
and professional groups were welcome.

Suddenly, before the year was out, a new scandal
developed for the government. Vincent Teekah, a former
high-ranking member of the PPP who had defected to the
PNC a few years before and been quickly rewarded with
the Ministry of Education, was murdered in bizarre circumstances. An attractive, black, Jamaican-born woman
in her thirties, Dr. Oswaldene Walker, was with him when
he died. She had graduated with a dentistry degree from
Howard University in Washington, D.C., in 1972, become a
United States citizen, and established her residence in
Takoma Park, Maryland. Dr. Walker had been visiting
Guyana since April 1979 to provide dental services. She
was staying at the Pegasus Hotel and operated out of the
GDF health clinic.

Dr. Walker was in a car with Teekah when he was
shot, at close range, on Wednesday evening, 24 October
1979. The bullet burned his trousers, cutting both ar-
teries to his legs. Dr. Walker brought Teekah to St.
Joseph's Mercy Hospital just before midnight where he
was pronounced dead on arrival. She asserted that two
unknown men had shot Teekah in the Ruimveldt region of
Georgetown. Accompanied by a man she claimed was a
passerby assisting her, she then tried to telephone the
prime minister from the hospital. Failing to reach
Burnham, she drove off; Dr. Walker has not been seen
again in Guyana. The police quickly removed her belong-
ings from the Pegasus Hotel. Flown from the country on
a Pan American flight on Sunday morning, she has since
refused any comment.[50]

Rumors roared through Georgetown on Thursday morning. The car had apparently been parked in an area
where armed bandits were known to operate, but Teekah
had been shot at close range from within the car. Was
the motive sex, political, or both? On Thursday evening
the prime minister spoke to the nation and blamed the
"assassin's bullet." The guilty people would be punished. On Friday the Home Affairs Ministry announced
that Teekah had been showing a visitor the recently completed Demerara Bridge before stopping near Thirst Park.
The police suspected a political motive. Accidental
death was ruled out since Teekah's .25 caliber gun was
found on the seat of his car, and he had been killed by
a .32 caliber bullet. People near the murder site re-

ported the sound of two shots between 11:30 P.M. and midnight, just before a parked car started up in great haste.

The various opposition parties, the four independent-minded trade unions, and the civil rights and professional groups met hastily on Friday and demanded that the best Caribbean newspapers send investigative reporters. Some kind of independent, fact-finding body must be created, they argued. They doubted government innuendos that Teekah was the victim of a "political assassination." More likely, Burnham and the PNC were "setting the stage to deceive Caribbean public opinion, in order to continue acts of aggression against the political rights of the Guyanese people."

Teekah had called Rickey Singh, editor of Caribbean Contact, on 27 September urging him to be more generous to Forbes Burnham. Hoping to arrange a Singh-Burnham meeting, Teekah argued that the Guyanese prime minister was being blamed for things done "by certain elements around him." Caribbean Contact spoke with Teekah's grieving widow on 20 November; she could add nothing for she had no information of "what the government is doing." Asked for an explanation of her husband's death, Mrs. Teekah replied: "You know how things are." More than four years later, there has still been no proper investigation and no adequate explanation.

The killings in 1979 were not yet over. On Sunday, 18 November, shortly after 5:15 P.M., the Guyanese police killed WPA activist Ohene Koana. The police charged the dead man with raising a rifle to resist arrest when they stopped to query him about a bag being placed in the trunk of his car. According to the police, Koana had two stolen GDF rifles in his possession. The WPA and some onlookers claimed that Koana was without weapons and had been ambushed by the police.[51]

The year 1979 had surely been dreadful for the PNC. The condition of the economy was worse than ever. Haslyn Parris, chairman and chief executive officer of the Guyana Mining Corporation (GUYMINE), complained that industrial relations in the industry were "bloody awful," production had been "miserable," and profitability was "less than commendable." Parris concluded that "the reputation of Guyana as a reliable source of bauxite products has been tarnished, and 1980 will be the year of the final test." Rice production dropped 30 percent below target, with 45,000 tons less than in 1978. Drainage and irrigation schemes had been neglected and available machinery had been poorly allocated. Sugar was 25,000 tons short of its goal. It seemed almost impossible that the morale of the nation could sink any lower.[52]

Reacting like a wounded animal, the PNC intensified its campaign against a growing opposition. The brief flash of sympathy felt for the PNC when its buildings

were destroyed in July had evaporated with the murder of
Father Darke, the strange death of Vincent Teekah, and
the harassment of all opposition groups. Tear gas was
now being employed not only against striking bauxite
workers, but also upon angry housewives in a food line.

Even though the government was in disarray, the opposition groups could point to few positive achievements.
Burnham was still dug in behind the loyal guns of the
GDF and the police. The civil servants and the bully-
boys of Georgetown remained in the trenches with the
battered, but unyielding, prime minister. While his
enemies agreed that Burnham must go, they differed as to
who, or what, should replace him. For the opposition,
it was, "the best of times, and the worst of times."
One could visualize a "season of Light" in the future,
but it still remained a "season of Darkness."[53]

NOTES

1. Forbes Burnham, Declaration of Sophia (Georgetown, Guyana,
1974). This is the published copy of Burnham's address to a Special Congress of the PNC to mark the tenth anniversary of his accession to power. See also the PNC publications, Party Constitution and Meeting Companion (Georgetown, Guyana, 1974); and A Supplement to the Declaration of Sophia (Exercises and Activities)
(Georgetown, Guyana, 1975). See also the December 1974 issues of
The Sunday Graphic. For criticism of the "code of conduct," see
the interview with Eusi Kwayana of the WPA in Caribbean Contact,
March 1976, pp. 11, 15.
2. Ron Sanders, Broadcasting in Guyana (London, 1978). The
Guyana government's position on limiting press freedom was clari-
fied by Minister of State Kit Nascimento in Caribbean Contact, December 1974, p. 14. He is answered by Guyanese journalist, Hubert
Williams, in the same issue.
3. The Sunday Graphic, 19 August 1973, p. 1.
4. The Sunday Graphic, 23 September 1973, p. 1.
5. See the collection of articles and statements prepared by
the Working People's Alliance and published under the title, The
Crisis and the Working People (Georgetown, Guyana, 1977).
6. Among the more important of Rodney's publications to this
date were A History of the Upper Guinea Coast, 1545-1800 (Oxford,
1970); How Europe Underdeveloped Africa (London, 1972); and the in-
fluential "black power" tract, The Groundings with my Brothers
(London, 1969).
7. Caribbean Contact, December 1974, p. 7.
8. The Sunday Graphic, 25 November 1973, p. 1; 13 January
1974, p. 1; and 18 May 1975, p. 1.
9. See the incisive analysis in Janet Jagan, An Examination
of National Service (Georgetown, Guyana, 1977). See also Caribbean
Contact, January 1977, p. 15.
10. Hubert Williams discusses the controversy in Caribbean

178

Contact, October 1976, pp. 8-9.

11. The PPP interpretation of events is in *Thunder*, 8 (October-December 1976), pp. 3-15.

12. *Caribbean Contact*, November 1976, pp. 1, 6-7.

13. See James Nelson Goodsell, "Guyana Blasts Cuban Troop Rumors," *The Christian Science Monitor*, 11 March 1976; Jonathan Kandell, "A Marxist Guyana Bucks Trend in South America," *The New York Times*, 24 May 1976; Jonathan Kandell, "Always a Socialist, Says Guyana Prime Minister," *The New York Times*, 25 May 1976; and Peter Arnett, "Guyana Marxist Hotbed," *The Long Island Press*, 5 August 1976.

14. *Caribbean Contact*, January 1977, p. 5; and February 1977, p. 7. See the evaluation of Guyana's cooperatives in R. S. Milne, "Guyana's Co-operative Republic," *Parliamentary Affairs*, 28 (Autumn 1975), pp. 352-67. There is a sharp criticism of Burnham's cooperative socialism in Paul Singh, *Guyana: Socialism in a Plural Society* (London, Fabian Research Series 307, 1972). For a discussion of the troubled sugar industry at this time see "Sugar in for a Caning," *The Guardian*, 15 May 1978.

15. See the excellent summary in W. Andrew Axline, *Caribbean Integration: The Politics of Regionalism* (London, 1979).

16. The Caribbean Community Secretariat has published much useful information about the organization. See especially Alister McIntyre, *The Role of the Economic Integration Process in Regional Development: The Caribbean Experience* (Georgetown, Guyana, 1976). McIntyre was secretary-general of CARICOM at the time. See also Byron Blake, *The Development from a Free Trade Area to a Common Market: CARICOM and Its Effects on the Guyana Economy: Opportunities and Challenges* (Georgetown, Guyana, 1976).

17. See Raoul Pantin's article, "Williams Socks it to CARICOM," *Caribbean Contact*, May 1977, p. 9.

18. *Caribbean Contact*, May 1977, pp. 12-13. See Ralph R. Premdas, "Guyana: Communal Conflict, Socialism and Political Reconciliation," *Inter-American Economic Affairs*, 30 (Spring 1977), pp. 63-83.

19. *Catholic Standard*, 14 August 1977, pp. 1, 7.

20. *Caribbean Contact*, September 1977, pp. 8, 24.

21. *Caribbean Contact*, October 1977, p. 9; and *Catholic Standard*, 11 September 1977, p. 1.

22. This account of the sugar strike of 1977-1978 is based primarily upon reports in the *Catholic Standard* and *Caribbean Contact*.

23. *Caribbean Contact*, February 1978, p. 8.

24. See E. E. Mahant, "The Strange Fate of a Liberal Democracy: Political Opposition and Civil Liberties in Guyana," *The Round Table*, January 1977, pp. 77-89.

25. *Caribbean Contact*, April 1978, p. 7; and May 1978, pp. 5-6. Greg Chamberlain, "Guyana Opposition Fears a Swing to Dictatorship," *The Guardian*, 17 April 1978.

26. See *Catholic Standard*, 14 May 1978; and 21 May 1978. See also Peter Strafford, "Guyana's Referendum to Do Away with Referenda," *The Times*, 21 June 1978.

27. David A. Jessop, "Can Guyana Remain Non-aligned," *West Indies Chronicle*, 93 (April/May 1978), p. 4; and Edmund Stevens,

"Russia Pins Its Hopes on Guyana," The Times, 17 April 1978.

28. Caribbean Contact, July 1978, p. 5.

29. For an excellent analysis of the referendum, see the booklet prepared by the Committee of Concerned Citizens, A Report on the Referendum Held in Guyana July 10th 1978 (Georgetown, 1978). This account of the referendum is based primarily on the report just mentioned and the coverage provided by Caribbean Contact and the Catholic Standard. Polemical literature prepared by the various political parties and groups was also consulted.

30. See especially Caribbean Contact, August 1978, p. 7.

31. The Economist, 18 March 1978, pp. 80-81. Excellent material on Guyana's economy can be found in the Quarterly Economic Reviews and the Annual Supplements prepared by the Economist Intelligence Unit.

32. Caribbean Contact, September 1978, p. 7.

33. The Sunday Graphic, 5 January 1975, p. 1; and 12 January 1975, pp. 1, 4.

34. Much has been written about the Jonestown catastrophe. The initial reporting is best followed in The New York Times, Caribbean Contact, and the Catholic Standard. Two eyewitness commentaries of value are Charles Krause, Guyana Massacre (New York, 1978); and Marshall Kilduff and Ron Javers, Suicide Cult (New York, 1978). Among the better of the more reflective books about the event are Shiva Naipaul, Journey to Nowhere (New York, 1980); and James Reston, Jr., Our Father Who Art in Hell (New York, 1981). The most penetrating assessment is to be found in Gordon K. Lewis, "Gather With the Saints at the River"(Rio Piedras, Puerto Rico, 1979). See also Donald J. Waters, "Jungle Politics: Guyana, The Peoples Temple, and the Affairs of State," Caribbean Review, 9 (Spring 1980), pp. 8-13.

35. Caribbean Contact, May 1975, pp. 10-11; January 1979, p. 11; and February 1979, pp. 17-18.

36. Caribbean Contact, March 1979, p. 13; and the Catholic Standard, 15 April 1979, p. 4.

37. See the discussion on government plans to restrict emigration in the Catholic Standard of 28 January 1979. See also the Catholic Standard, 8 July 1979, pp. 5-6. This issue contains a summary of a COMPASS group report which estimated that Guyana had lost 50,000 emigrants between 1974 and 1979. There is an interesting Marxist view in Jim Sackey, "The Migration of High Level Personnel from Guyana: Towards an Alternative Analysis," Transition, 1 (1978), pp. 45-58.

38. Catholic Standard, 22 April 1979, pp. 1, 3.

39. Caribbean Contact, June 1979, p. 17.

40. See reports and commentary in the Catholic Standard of 6 May 1979, 13 May 1979, and 20 May 1979.

41. Catholic Standard, 1 July 1979, pp. 1, 3.

42. Catholic Standard and Caribbean Contact are the most reliable sources for the events which followed the burning of the government building on the evening of 10 July 1979.

43. See especially Caribbean Contact, August 1979, pp. 8-9; and September 1979, pp. 10-11; and the Catholic Standard, 15 July 1979, 22 July 1979, and 29 July 1979.

44. See the analysis of Guyana's military and police in

180

George K. Danns, "Militarization and Development: An Experiment in Nation-Building," _Transition_, 1 (1978), pp. 23-44. See also the response to Danns by Jay Mandle in _Transition_, 2 (1979), pp. 69-70.

45. _Catholic Standard_, 26 August 1979; and 2 September 1979.

46. _Caribbean Contact_, September 1971, p. 1.

47. _Catholic Standard_, 16 September 1979, p. 5; and _Caribbean Contact_, October 1979, p. 15.

48. _Caribbean Contact_, November 1979, p. 7.

49. _Catholic Standard_, 14 October 1979, p. 2; and 21 October 1979, p. 2.

50. _Caribbean Contact_, December 1979, p. 11; and January 1980, pp. 7, 10. See also the _Catholic Standard_ of 28 October 1979, 4 November 1979, and 11 November 1979.

51. _Catholic Standard_, 25 November 1979, pp. 1-2.

52. _Catholic Standard_, 6 January 1980, pp. 1, 3-4.

53. Charles Dickens, _A Tale of Two Cities_ (London, 1891), p. 1. See Percy C. Hintzen and Ralph R. Premdas, "Guyana: Coercion and Control in Political Change," _Journal of Interamerican Studies and World Affairs_, 24 (August 1982), pp. 337-54.

10
What Happens to a Dream Deferred?

The 1980s started with the police descending upon
the home of Dr. Frank Williams, personal physician to
the prime minister. His daughter, Andaiye, however, belonged to the Working People's Alliance. Police claimed
she had been observed moving ammunition into the house.
None was found.[1] Determined to spread fear among its
opponents, security units invaded the houses and apart-
ments of other WPA members at the same time. The University of Guyana reopened in January amidst turmoil and
political strife. An antigovernment majority squared
off against a minority of militant Burnhamites. Students also complained about shortages of books and equipment.[2]

The government reorganized its information and newspaper services to improve Guyana's image. In response
to the Soviet invasion of Afghanistan, the PNC supported
the United States by demanding the immediate withdrawal
of Russian troops, while the PPP concluded that a kindly
President Brezhnev was helping "to beat off the imperi-
alist-hatched and well orchestrated external threat
against the young Afghan revolution." The PPP position
could not help but disturb the middle class opponents of
Burnham. The United Nations General Assembly voted 114
to 18 to call for the removal of Soviet troops.

Guyanese eyes watched intently as the long-awaited
arson trial of Drs. Rodney, Roopnaraine, and Omawale
slowly moved through the courts. In late October of
1979, Principal Magistrate Owen Fung-Kee-Fung refused
the defendants' request for trial by jury and agreed to
the prosecution's application for a summary judgment.
Co-prosecutor Rex McKay's argument was highly unusual.
Implying arson was not that grave a crime and reflecting
upon the good character of the academics concerned, he
would be content with the three-year, maximum sentence a
summary court, a judge sitting without a jury, could
award.

Defense attorneys stressed the gravity of the charge
and demanded a jury trial. Without the recently passed

Administration of Justice Bill, this case would automatically have been tried before a jury. The defense noted that Burnham had already denounced the WPA and had clearly stated that he instructed magistrates about their work. Regrettably, the attorneys continued, no member of the judiciary had formally repudiated the PNC's views about party paramountcy. Despite the overwhelming case for a jury trial, Magistrate Fung-Kee-Fung assented to the government's presentation. Defense lawyers appealed to the High Court and the case was adjourned until the appeal could be decided.[3]

Fearful that the appeal for the arson case might be decided in favor of the WPA activists because the Administration of Justice Act of 1978 had been improperly drafted, the government rushed through an amending bill in four days, despite objections from Guyana's Bar Association. The government was not about to lose Rodney, Omawale, and Roopnaraine on a technicality. Making a mockery of Guyana's legal system, the new law decreed that certain parts of the earlier legislation should now be regarded as never having been enacted. Meeting in Barbados in May 1980, the Organisation of Commonwealth Caribbean Bar Associations condemned the Burnham government for "infringement of its citizens' rights to trial by jury" and for "the introduction of legislation calculated to have a retrospective effect on pending criminal proceedings."

Trying to divert attention from its many problems, the government prepared mass celebrations for the tenth anniversary of the Cooperative Republic at the end of February. Distressed when many young people and teachers refused to participate, the PNC promptly applied pressure. School time and money were wasted in glorifying a repudiated regime. The festivities brought out the party faithful but failed to hide a massive number of deserters.[4]

During the last week of January, the PNC presented its own draft constitution to the Constituent Assembly. It simply ignored TUC proposals about power sharing and a separate election for the post of executive president. Religious bodies were offended that references to God had been deleted. Opposition groups noted that their refusal to participate had been justified; the PNC had written the new constitution by itself. Even the prime minister must have been embarrassed, for Deputy Prime Minister Ptolemy Reid presented the finished document to the Assembly. What it all meant was that when the new constitution became law, Forbes Burnham would become executive president, with almost no limits on his power and without an election taking place.[5]

Father Andrew Morrison, editor of the Catholic Standard, was not displeased that references to God had been deleted from the constitution.

> The document that has been proposed to Parliament is, in
> essence, a denial of God. Its growth from rigged elec-
> tions and a fraudulent referendum through a charade of a
> consultative process that pretended to give all an oppor-
> tunity to speak, but listened to no one, all indicates a
> contempt for human rights, which is anything but godly.
>
> The proposed constitution itself has been designed
> to maintain the stranglehold of a small group on all ef-
> fective power in our community, despite the wishes of
> citizens. It is a constitution of injustice. And injus-
> tice is a denial of God in practice.[6]

The Roman Catholic church was further outraged by the
removal of several priests from the Amerindian region
deep in the Rupununi. Charging that Fathers John Bridges
and Patrick Connors were troublemakers and rabble rous-
ers, the Guyana Defense Force moved in, seized the two
priests, and returned them to Georgetown.[7]

The military seizure of power by sergeants and other noncommissioned officers in neighboring Surinam in
late February 1980 sent a tremor of alarm through PNC
breasts in Guyana.[8] It reminded Forbes Burnham that he
must emphasize the special oath of loyalty the military
and police had taken to the PNC as Guyana's paramount
party and to himself as the leader of that party. He
could still believe, however, that he had the best of
both worlds. He slept with the non-aligned, while United States Ambassador George Roberts reported that Guyana
received the highest per capita aid from Washington of
all countries in the world. Loans were on very favorable terms, usually at 2 to 3 percent and repayable for
twenty-five to forty years. The United States had helped
with roads, irrigation, health, and the modernization of
the police force.[9]

Inflation continued, however, at a staggering rate.
Much of the problem went back to 1973-1974 when sugar
prices had been high. Not realizing how short the period of high sugar prices was to be, the government embarked on too many ambitious schemes. During the boom
years, net foreign reserves had reached G$250 million.
By the end of 1979, net foreign reserves had sunk to
minus G$175 million. The national debt was G$267 million in 1970. It rose to G$673 million in 1974 and was
now G$1.8 billion. To meet its debts, the government
had simply printed money. The money supply, therefore,
doubled between 1974 and 1977. Grandiose schemes took
the place of maintaining necessary public utilities.
The electricity supply, water system, sewerage, and public transportation were close to collapse. Imported
equipment was rusting; no money was available for replacement parts. The road to Brazil became re-covered by
the jungle. Projects to grow local potatoes failed.
There was no longer even a national plan to replace the
unrealized draft Development Plan for 1972-1976, prepared

for the 1973 election. A State Planning Commission, established in 1979, did nothing. The government decided that the huge deficit in the balance of payments could only be lowered by cutting public services and lowering the standard of living of the workers.[10]

The IMF agreement of 1978 had intensified these public service cuts. It also provided for a decrease in the number of state employees plus a further reduction in imports. Unemployment was about 25 percent, with underemployment bringing the total to about 40 percent. Inflation had been over 18 percent in 1979 with the cost of living soaring upward by about 20 percent. Economic growth was negative. After a detailed investigation of "Socialism and Basic Needs in Guyana," Guy Standing of the International Labour Office in Geneva observed:

> Most cooperatives, on which so much faith and rhetorical commitment have been lavished, have been cooperative in little more than name, and in the context of a persistently dominant sugar industry and a centralized government, cooperatives have almost certainly reproduced inequality without making a substantial contribution to economic growth or indeed much expansion in working-class power over the allocation and distribution of economic resources.

Standing concluded that, "If the working class are not in a position to determine the pattern of production they are not likely to be prepared to make the material sacrifices and take the initiative and effort required to develop the economy."[11]

Conjuring up an organized plot against the nation, the government called several security alerts in Georgetown and throughout the country to frighten the opposition. In 1980, 10 percent of the budget was to be spent on the security forces; only 5 percent of the budget was designated for health needs. The government conceded that prices for sugar, rice, and bauxite had improved slightly in the world market but the failure to reach production levels had been catastrophic. New production goals were set for 1980, but the government failed to consult the hostile trade unions.[12]

In May, the government was comforted when the World Bank agreed to a proposed $1.5 billion hydroelectric and aluminum smelter project scheduled for completion in 1986. The World Bank would only grant a part of the money; Guyana would have to provide, or find, the rest. The hydropower scheme was to be built in the Mazaruni-Potaro region. It included a 750 megawatt power station, while the smelter would be capable of processing about 150,000 metric tons of alumina a year. Venezuela immediately protested because the dam would be constructed in the region it claimed.

No one knew where Guyana could find the foreign investment money needed. It was also feared that the smelter, due to a lack of experienced Guyanese, might be controlled, managed, or even owned by foreigners. What would this foreign intervention do to cooperative socialism? Foreign technicians at high salaries would be inevitable. The government was deeply embarrassed by its April budget, allotting 37 percent of total expenditure for debt payments, and 32 percent for salaries and allowances. This left only 31 percent for everything else.[13] While unemployment was still estimated at more than 30 percent, the government continued to provide exorbitant salaries for major political leaders, key bureaucrats, and senior officials of the GDF and the police to guarantee their loyalty.

In this atmosphere of fear, suspicion, despair, and rot, the government resumed the prosecution of Drs. Rodney, Rupert Roopnaraine, and Omawale for arson. Their appeal had been rejected. Although trial by jury was denied, a panel of international observers arrived to pressure for a just verdict. Opening presentations took place in early June, then the trial was adjourned until August. Among those in attendance was Sam Silkin, British member of Parliament and attorney-general in the last Labour government. After listening to the outline of the prosecution's case, Silkin concluded that "Rodney had played no part in the events which led to the trial."[14]

Then, on the evening of Friday, 13 June, Walter Rodney was killed in bizarre circumstances by a small, but highly sophisticated, antipersonnel bomb. Burnham's cronies promptly charged Rodney with bungling an attempt to blow up the Georgetown Jail--not very likely given the small size of the bomb. The vast majority of Guyanese and most impartial observers were convinced Rodney was murdered by the PNC. According to Donald Rodney, riding in the car with his brother when the bomb exploded, the two men had been engaged in purchasing a "walkie-talkie" from one Gregory Smith. It was their understanding that Smith, an electronics specialist and former sergeant in the Guyana Defense Force, had become disenchanted with the Burnham government. On the evening of Rodney's death, the two brothers picked up what they believed was a radio device from Smith, which they were told to test in several sections of Georgetown. As they carried out Smith's instructions, the bomb exploded. It killed Walter Rodney and injured his brother.

Apparently, Smith was still a member of the Guyana Defense Force. He remains the key witness to the events leading to Rodney's death. On the day following Rodney's demise, Smith was helicoptered to the interior. Three days later he was flown out of the country to an unknown destination. Though Burnham called upon two British experts to aid in the investigation, it seems inconceivable that Smith could have disappeared so rapidly without assistance from highly placed people. The available evidence points to a planned assassination of Walter

Rodney, though it is impossible to know just how far into the corridors of power the conspiracy reached. It is
likely that some underlings, hearing the "Comrade Leader"
curse his enemies, decided to take action on their own.
One is reminded of Henry II and Thomas Becket.

When the death became public knowledge on 14 June,
Forbes Burnham could not have been surprised by the outrage that swept across Guyana. He must have been disturbed, however, by the indignant statements issued by
heads of state he had regarded close friends. His carefully cultivated image as a socialist leader of the non-
aligned world was shattered, for criticism poured in
from Jamaica, Grenada, and Cuba. Grenada's Maurice
Bishop, whose seizure of power in March 1979 had been
greeted enthusiastically by Burnham, referred

> to the recent history of stepped-up violence against po-
> litical opposition in Guyana. . . . If the best of our
> Caribbean sons can be cut down in such a manner, this can
> usher in a new sinister phase of Mafia and CIA-type ap-
> proach to politics by removing violently the progressive
> leadership of the entire Caribbean. Only imperialism and
> reaction can benefit from this murder.
>
> (Catholic Standard 22 June 1980: 1)

Jamaica's Michael Manley thundered: "Dr. Rodney's assassination has robbed the Third World of one of its most
fertile and active minds. It was a wanton and brutal
action and an assault against humanity." Fidel Castro
joined the torrent of criticism when the Cuban Communist
party formally expressed its "regret over the barbaric
murder of Dr. Rodney" and its "total repudiation and
condemnation of this abominable crime." Cuban officials
were present at the funeral.[15]

A memorial service for Walter Rodney was conducted
in the Roman Catholic Cathedral on 21 June, and a massive funeral procession drawing more than 25,000 Guyanese of all races and creeds was held on 23 June. Eulo-
gizing his friend at Merriman's Mall in the middle of
Georgetown, Dr. Rupert Roopnaraine concluded: "You cannot participate in the murder of a good and just man--
before, during, or after the act--without bearing for
all time the stain of disgrace and degeneracy." Standing together with Rodney's wife and three children, many
mourners recalled Rodney's last words to the WPA four
days before his death: "We are determined to work for a
government of national unity and reconstruction; for the
inter-racial unity of all working people." Writing in
The Guardian on 16 June, Sam Silkin reflected:

> That Rodney abhorred violence but believed it necessary
> to be prepared for it was demonstrated by a question
> which he put to me: "At what stage is a people justified
> in taking up arms against its oppressive government?"
> And he plainly agreed with my reply that it could be

justified only when all democratic and peaceful means had been exhausted, with no sign that the oppressors were likely to be influenced.

Demands for an international inquiry into Rodney's death were rejected by the government. The managing editor of Guyana national newspapers, Mohamed Hamaludin, deserted Burnham's ship at the end of June to work for Caribbean Life and Times in Miami, Florida. The government's purge of school teachers continued; Roman Catholic groups were especially outraged at the attempt to oust Sister Hazel Campayne as headmistress of St. Rose's High School. Radio Demerara closed down at the end of June--it had already been taken over by the government. The government-run Guyana Broadcasting Service now had a complete monopoly of the airwaves.

Hoping to focus public attention on the failure of the regime to act when its opponents were murdered, the opposition planned commemorative activities on the first anniversary of the death of Father Bernard Darke. A year had passed, but the preliminary inquiry into the cause of death had never taken place. Bishops Benedict Singh and Randolph George participated in the memorial service. Despite the outrage which had swept the country after Rodney's death, the PNC retained its solid base of about 20 percent of the population. Most important, it controlled Georgetown and the guns of the GDF and the police. PNC thugs were not bothered by verbal abuse; in mid-September they even broke up a meeting of "Women Against Terror." Presided over by Mrs. Sheila George, wife of Guyana's Anglican bishop, the group had assembled in St. Andrew's Church. The two hundred people present were suddenly terrorized by about thirty screaming women who shouted their love for the prime minister.[16]

Tired of criticism from the four militant trade unions and determined to regulate the TUC in the future, the PNC rearranged the 27th Annual Delegates' Conference of the TUC in the last week of September. A senior minister of the government was scheduled to speak about the need to limit trade union rights in the interest of industrial stability. Additional representation was granted to unions aligned with the PNC, enabling them to dominate the Executive Committee. All resolutions calling for fair elections were then rejected. Instead, proposals praising the government and urging greater productivity were passed. The CCWU, NAACIE, GAWU, and UGSA denounced the results. They pointed out that seven small unions with 1,449 members were given twenty-two delegates, while NAACIE with 1,458 members had six delegates and the CCWU with 4,179 members was allocated twelve delegates.[17]

The new constitution would soon be implemented, and a disgusted majority prepared for Burnham's accession to

the executive presidency without a national election
taking place. Resembling Charles de Gaulle's Fifth Republic, the executive president would combine the real
powers of both president and prime minister, even though
there would still be a nominal prime minister. It was
almost impossible to remove the executive president,
even if he were guilty of gross misconduct or a viola-
tion of constitutional rights. Dr. Harold Lutchman,
head of the Political Science Department at the University of Guyana and a president of the Guyana Human Rights
Association, concluded the new constitution would insti-
tutionalize a virtual dictatorship.[18]

Forbes Burnham's great day arrived on Monday, 6
October 1980, when the new constitution went into effect
and he was installed as Guyana's first executive president. He was emperor--but for how long? Children were
marched from their classes in the morning to provide an
audience. Many in the crowd chuckled at the foolishness
of it all and remembered the laughter that had swept the
Caribbean when Burnham, who was also minister of defense
and chairman of the Defense Board, had started wearing a
general's uniform.[19]

Now certain that parliamentary elections would finally be held before the end of the year, the PPP, WPA,
and VLD presented proposals for fair elections. The
proposals were similar to those demanded prior to the
1978 referendum. They provided for a new Elections Commission, presided over by a person of acknowledged integrity, not normally a resident of Guyana. The commission would be responsible for preparing the electoral
registers and for allowing sufficient time for all to
check the lists. Overseas and postal voting would be
virtually abolished, and proxy voting would be limited.
Counting would be done at each polling station as soon
as the polls closed. Agents from all parties should be
present at the counting and reporting of votes. Finally,
the proposals stated that the government must allow all
parties equal access to radio and newspapers, and that
restrictions on political meetings must cease.[20]

The government laughed at the proposals. The prime
minister muttered that he had no objection to foreign
observers, but Guyana would conduct its own elections.
In late October the PNC held a large meeting at the 1763
Monument to announce that elections would be held on 15
December. The party mobilized its militants for this
meeting--more than ten thousand were present to hear the
Comrade Leader. The ruling party had wanted a larger
audience, but even free transportation on a Sunday failed
to produce more bodies. Soldiers and members of the National Service were informed they were expected to be
present in civilian attire.[21]

At the meeting, the government simply asserted that
the elections would be fair and then ridiculed the oppo-
sition--no corruption had ever been associated with a

Guyanese election. Ranji Chandisingh, principal of the
Cuffy Ideological Institute and member of the Central
Executive of the PNC, was certain the PNC's "record of
achievements" would guarantee victory in honest elections. Chandisingh, a defector from PPP ranks, forgot
that as editor of Cheddi Jagan's Thunder in 1973 he had
evaluated the July parliamentary elections of that year.

> The rigging of the electoral roll, the padding of the
> lists, the disenfranchisement of genuine voters, the en-
> franchisement of fictitious persons, the resurrection of
> the dead, the giving of ballots to juveniles, etc. are
> some of the means by which the PNC held on to power.[22]

What should the opposition do? What course of action should it take? The opposition desperately required
a unified approach. Boycotting the House-Mouse referendum had been very impressive. Everything pointed to another massive boycott effort, linked to various forms of
civil disobedience. The WPA and VLD did not hesitate;
they would have nothing to do with dishonest elections.
The VLD concluded that "a confrontation with the PNC is
inevitable if they are to be dislodged." At the time of
the July 1978 referendum, the UF agreed to a boycott
only with great reluctance, and it failed to join the
other opposition parties in the Committee in Defense of
Democracy. Only when the clearly fraudulent electoral
registers were prepared did the UF urge its people to
remain home. Now Feilden Singh observed (one wonders
what his brother, Bishop Benedict Singh, thought of this
reasoning) that other countries had ignored the boycott
of July 1978. He argued it would be better to participate, build up the size of the anti-PNC vote, and hope,
that with God's help, there would be an honest election.
Feilden Singh's conclusion was not unexpected and
could be discounted. Cheddi Jagan's decision to participate in the 15 December parliamentary election, however, startled and disgusted the opposition leaders. No
one could doubt the election would be a monument to dishonesty, and the boycott of the referendum had been such
a great success. Why not, once again, try the boycott
weapon? But Cheddi Jagan, pale shell of what he had
once been, put himself and the PPP before the nation,
for he resented the growing popularity of the Working
People's Alliance. Recently, no one thought very often
about a Jagan government in place of Burnham's. Most
discussion on the left centered on the role of Eusi
Kwayana, Moses Bhagwan, Clive Thomas, and the late Walter Rodney. The one way to obtain a bone, even a taint-
ed one, was to participate in the election. Burnham
would dole out a few seats for the PPP, leaving Cheddi
Jagan with the hollow title of official chief of the opposition in Parliament.
It was a pathetic performance. Cheddi Jagan talked

about Lenin, revolutionary tactics, and all forms of
struggle; then, he urged his followers to vote in a
crooked election. What Jagan refused to confront was
the extent to which his participation in a fraudulent
election legitimized both the voting and the establishment of a de facto one-party state. The opposition had
been treated as jesters and clowns during the infrequent
meetings of the present Parliament. Jagan undermined a
marvellous opportunity for a united boycott.[23]

Quickly oiled, the government propaganda machine
began a massive campaign, mobilizing the state-controlled
radio and newspapers along with the party faithful. Government workers were marched to PNC meetings while party
thugs invaded opposition meetings. Excessively inquisi-
tive foreign journalists were harassed. The police, often wearing emblems of the ruling party, did little to
assist the opposition in exercising its constitutional
rights. For example, during a meeting of the VLD broken
up by hooligans on Sunday, 16 November, police remained
inactive as Brindley Benn, Llewelyn John, and Dr. Ganraj
Kumar were forced to beat a hasty retreat.

Writing in the lead editorial of the Catholic Standard on 23 November 1980, Father Andrew Morrison concluded:

> For the most part, only the views of a few select persons
> of one party are allowed to be aired in the media. Even
> worse, the media have descended to distortion and person-
> al abuse.
>
> Bishop George is falsely reported, Bishop Singh is
> vilified and members of opposition parties are mocked and
> ridiculed with little regard for truth and common decency.
>
> At the same time street-corner meetings are attacked
> and every effort is made to drown out what the opposition
> has to say.
>
> The distinct impression is given that there is much
> to hide, that the ruling party has to resort continually
> to "cover up."

On a visit to police headquarters at Brickdam, Father
Morrison noticed that seventeen PNC posters adorned the
walls. When he entered the Criminal Investigation Division office at Eve Leary, the guard at the gate sported
a PNC cap and a Burnham button. The fairness and impartiality of the police was obviously destroyed.

Rickey Singh, editor of Caribbean Contact, noted
that Guyana's new constitution put Burnham "above the
law." He was "immune from prosecution for any offence
whatsoever either in his official or personal capacity."
As executive president he was head of state, supreme executive authority, and commander in chief of the Armed
Forces. In evaluating sixteen years of PNC control,
Singh observed:

Unscrupulously exploiting racial and ideological divisions, the PNC subverted all the institutions of the country and structured the police, army and the other disciplined forces to achieve the objective of their loyalty pledge to Burnham and the PNC. Later, the party was to evolve under a doctrine of "PNC paramountcy" as "the executive arm of the government." With a muzzled press and effective control of the entire electoral machinery, the PNC was eventually ready with a "socialist constitution" with all the trappings to justify what is nothing less than an identification of Executive President Burnham with the State of Guyana--a sort of Latin American "caudillo."

What, Singh continued, had the PNC achieved in sixteen years? It had failed completely with regard to "national unity; increased productivity; efficient management of the economy; respect for civil and political rights; or the promise of 'the small man becoming a real man.'" Everyone recognized, after the violence of 1961-1964, the danger of "confrontation politics" in Guyana. "Yet for all the assurances of the Burnham government, its 'socialist constitution' is perceived by its opponents as an unmistakable invitation to the politics of confrontation. It therefore seems that Guyana's political turmoil will not disappear with the forthcoming general elections."[24]

Forbes Burnham did confront one complicating element. Not expecting much to evolve from it he had agreed to permit independent observers at the election. He really wanted to keep the rigged elections as quiet as possible, but to his dismay he watched the opposition fashion an International Team of Observers. A very prestigious group was assembled. Lord Avebury, secretary of the British Parliamentary Human Rights Group and monitor of Bolivia's 1978 election, was chairman. He was joined by Lord Chitnis, evaluator of the 1979 Zimbabwe Interim Government elections; Denis Daley, chairman of the Jamaican Council for Human Rights; Peta-Ann Baker, also of the Jamaican Council for Human Rights; Dr. Ramesh Deosaran, professor of sociology at the University of the West Indies in Trinidad and representative of the Caribbean Conference of Churches; Heather Johnston, president of the Canadian Council of Churches; Mel King, a member of the Massachusetts State Legislature; Father William Newell of the Woodstock Theological Center in Washington, D.C., and Vatican observer to the Organization of American States; Reverend Carl Major of the Anglican church in Canada; Lennox Hinds of the International Association of Democratic Lawyers in the USA; and Frances Hollis, a United States lawyer who represented the Washington Office on Latin America.[25]

For once, Burnham had been just a little too cute, and international observers were present in Guyana to observe the voting. The prime minister and his henchmen, having no shame left to lose, did not hesitate. They decided to be brazen and make life as unpleasant as possible for the foreign visitors. The Ministry of Information refused special facilities for the observers. Burnham welcomed them in passing, but reminded everyone that "no one is running these elections but the Government of Guyana."

The PNC infiltrated and intimidated opposition meetings until polling day, 15 December. Then, because so many blacks stayed at home in Georgetown and throughout the country, the PNC transported its dedicated disciples from polling place to polling place. Along the Corentyne coast on the sugar estates, the supporters of Dr. Jagan, following his foolish advice, attempted to vote; but they discovered it was even more hopeless than in 1973. Some names had been eradicated from the electoral lists, other individuals were informed they had already voted. PPP and UF poll watchers were often chased from the scene when vote counting began, and the army collected some ballot boxes over the objections of UF and PPP representatives. Hours often elapsed between the disappearance of these ballot boxes and their reappearance for the formal act of counting the votes. It was a disgusting charade requiring fifteen hours of frantic activity by the PNC to doctor the results satisfactorily.

But the international observers had been courageously active throughout the day. Lord Avebury, harassed and twice arrested, toured the polling stations. While taking a picture near the Houston voting center, the police stopped his car and directed him to Eve Leary Police Station, where he was detained for ninety minutes without explanation. He was not permitted to speak or move, and film was removed from his camera. Released, he resumed his observations, but was again stopped by the police. His notes were seized, thrown in a ditch, and once again he was carted off to Eve Leary Police Station. The government later retorted that the police were protecting Lord Avebury from an angry mob; however, Lord Avebury denied this assertion. Another member of the observer team, Denis Daley, was also detained by the police.[26]

The observer team concluded unanimously that the election had been "rigged massively and flagrantly."[27] Georgetown, Linden, and New Amsterdam were characterized by a low turnout, Avebury estimating that only about 15 percent of Georgetown's voters participated. There had been more voting activity in the PPP strongholds on the Corentyne and in the rural communities, but these votes had not been counted fairly. Lord Avebury noted that the Guyana Elections Commission was a "toothless poodle of the PNC." The election had not been "a free and fair test of the opinion of the people" but rather a "clumsily

managed and blatant fraud designed to perpetuate the
rule of President Forbes Burnham." After noting numerous examples of fraud, Lord Avebury further observed:

> The military presence in certain areas was intimidating.
> The boxes were collected by military personnel who pre-
> vented accredited officials of the opposition, sometimes
> by force or the threat of force, from accompanying or fol-
> lowing the boxes. Militant personnel refused accredited
> representatives of opposition parties access to the count
> at gunpoint in some cases.[28]

Fifteen hours after the polls closed, the PNC finally completed cooking the results and announced that
82 percent of the electorate had participated. The PNC
awarded itself 312,988 votes, or 78 percent of the poll,
and took forty-one of the fifty-three Assembly seats.
The PPP was given 78,414 votes, 19 percent of the vote,
and ten seats as a small bone. The UF was assigned
11,612 votes or 3 percent of the poll and two seats.
Twelve more members of the new National Assembly were to
be selected by the new units of local government which
had also been chosen at the general election. These
were the first local government elections in ten years.
Out of the 205 local council seats, the PNC grabbed 169
and assigned thirty-five to the PPP and one to the UF.
The entire election was all a massive bit of make-believe
which demonstrated unbelievable contempt for the people
of Guyana. At a press conference in London on 19 December, Lord Chitnis noted that the PNC electoral lists included 47,000 Guyanese citizens resident in the United
Kingdom. Only about 1 percent of this number had been
sent voting papers, yet the Burnham government claimed
that 35,000 overseas ballots had been cast in the United
Kingdom. The party very kindly assigned itself 34,000
of these votes.[29]

Hoping to demonstrate a change for the better,
Burnham reshuffled his government, though many old faces
retained office. Ptolemy Reid, still prime minister,
and Hamilton Green at Public Welfare remained the two
most powerful figures in the PNC after the executive
president. In a 1981 New Year message, Burnham acknowledged that sugar production in 1980 had been deficient
by 13 percent and that rice and bauxite were 20 percent
short of target. Burnham believed that the election,
however, signalled an "end" to the "political battle";
all must now cooperate in "righting and streamlining the
economy." He extended an "olive branch to all true Guyanese for us to work together."[30]

Neither the Guyanese nor much of the Caribbean saw
an "end" to the "political battle" after such fraudulent
elections. The Nation, a major newspaper in Barbados,
called Guyana's election an "ugly display of political
rape" and a "massive electoral fraud." It was ashamed

that "a governing party has found it necessary to go to such extremes to retain power." Some argued that Guyana should be expelled from CARICOM. Others compared these events with the recent honest elections in Jamaica. There had been much excitement and some violence, but Michael Manley's People's National party graciously acknowledged defeat at the hands of Edward Seaga's Jamaica Labor party. Manley accepted the people's verdict and resigned from office. Several moderate Caribbean governments, Barbados and Antigua in particular, which had demanded elections from Maurice Bishop's revolutionary regime in Grenada, were strangely silent over events in Guyana.

London's conservative Daily Telegraph regretted Burnham's "increasing authoritarianism behind the democratic facade." Jamaica's Weekly Gleaner concluded that the PNC had been "carefully subverting democracy over the years." The Jamaican Council for Human Rights called upon the entire Caribbean "to isolate the government and party of Forbes Burnham in every Regional and International Forum, and to support the efforts of the Guyanese people to regain those rights which they cherish and which have been so wantonly abused." The Economist of London discussed the "dubious methods" used by Burnham in the election.[31]

On 18 January 1981, Forbes Burnham was formally inaugurated, once again, as Guyana's executive president. The faithful were bussed to the National Park from all over the country. Most watched the cultural show but then drifted away before Burnham spoke. Police tried, unsuccessfully, to stop the deserters. Fortunately, Burnham had an attentive group of uniformed young men from the House of Israel. Burnham announced some economic aid from Trinidad. He also noted Guyana's failure to comply with IMF demands for 5 percent economic growth in 1980. Unmentioned was the fact that some objective economists had concluded that Guyana, in real terms, had experienced an 8 percent negative growth for the previous year.[32]

The opposition groups did obtain comfort from an unexpected source in February. As required by United States law, the State Department delivered its annual report to Congress on "Human Rights Practices" throughout the world in 1980. The report contained some devastating comments in its eight pages on Guyana. It stated that there was "a blurring of the distinction between the ruling party and the government." It was difficult for the opposition parties to function since the PNC had "access to unaudited public funds" and made "full use of the advantages of incumbency." The State Department concluded that "available information indicates that the government was implicated in the June 13 death of WPA activist Walter Rodney and in the subsequent removal of key witnesses from the country."

> The general Guyanese human rights environment has deteri-
> orated in recent years. A worsening economic situation
> has contributed to this process, primarily by fostering
> discontent to which the government sometimes responded
> with repressive measures. The government also has react-
> ed strongly at times to perceived threats from an opposi-
> tion which increasingly despairs of ever taking power le-
> gally.[33]

While Burnham was angered by the report, he could
be consoled by the inauguration of President Ronald
Reagan, much less interested in human rights than his
predecessor. Burnham had cleverly used Jimmy Carter's
criticism in proving that he was not in the pocket of
the United States, even if it had helped bring him to
power.

Then, suddenly, there was a new crisis for the government; but, one which, if skillfully handled, might be
used to force a greater degree of national cohesion.
The one issue uniting all Guyanese regarded Venezuela's
claim to the Essequibo region. The twelve-year agreement to maintain the status quo in the area was to ex-
pire in 1982. It would be automatically renewed unless
denounced by either signatory prior to the end of 1981.
Of course, Guyana had always been concerned over the
failure of the Venezuelan Congress to formally ratify
the 1970 Port of Spain protocol.

Venezuela had adopted a more belligerent posture
during the previous six months. Maps again appeared
showing Essequibo as a part of Venezuela. On 2 April,
Forbes Burnham journeyed to Caracas for a one-day visit
with the Social Christian president of Venezuela, Luis
Herrera Campins. It had been made clear by the Venezuelans that an "urgent" matter would be discussed.
Burnham was rudely informed that Venezuela would not re-
new the treaty. Instead, the Venezuelans intended to
resume their claim to the entire Essequibo area and to
further insist that Guyana not undertake its hydroelectric project on the Upper Mazaruni River since it was in
the disputed zone.[34]

Burnham was aghast at the swing in Venezuelan policy, but he shrewdly set out to exploit it for his own
purposes. All Guyanese were called upon to support
their government against the wicked Venezuelans. The
PPP, WPA, indeed the entire Guyanese nation, thundered
their outrage at the Venezuelan action. The opposition,
however, clearly stated that Burnham could not expect to
lead a united country, since he was in power only because of electoral fraud. They further argued that it
had been an error on Burnham's part to sign the Geneva
Agreements of 1966, which had been negotiated with Great
Britain and Venezuela just prior to independence. And
why, the opposition complained, was Parliament not called
more frequently to discuss these grave matters? No

serious debates ever occurred; the PNC-controlled Parliament simply ratified Burnham's decisions.[35]
The leadership of the PNC knew it was unlikely
Venezuelan tanks would roar across the border. Not only
were there no roads, but Venezuela would surely never
destroy its reputation as a leader of the third world by
invading a small neighbor. Possibly, the Venezuelans
were trying to drive a wedge between Guyana and Brazil.
Relations had improved between the conservative generals
in Rio and the Burnham government. Talks had taken
place over development of the Amazon region and the construction of roads through Guyana to the Caribbean Sea.
Venezuela has never smiled upon Brazilian pretensions in
the northern part of South America.
The government suffered another blow in May when
the off-again, on-again trial of Drs. Roopnaraine and
Omawale was brought to an end. The outcome also demonstrated there were still some independent judges in Guyana who could not be beaten into line by the PNC. There
were numerous contradictions in the evidence against the
accused. Under cross-examination, Detective Sergeant
Eustace Lam admitted lying when he stated no one had ordered him to arrest Rupert Roopnaraine on 11 July 1979.
He acknowledged a telephone call from a voice he recognized; the voice ordered him to seize Roopnaraine. Evidence offered by the security guards who had been bound
and gagged by the arsonists was so contradictory that
Magistrate Fung-Kee-Fung agreed with the defense that
"the prosecution had failed to establish any ingredient
of the charge; and that if there is any evidence, it is
so unreliable as to be discredited." The case was dismissed and the defendants released, but the government
had not finished with Roopnaraine and Omawale. It
promptly ordered them not to travel abroad. Once again,
however, an independent judge, Prem Persaud, ruled that
Police Commissioner Lloyd Barker acted unconstitutional-
ly in refusing Omawale and Roopnaraine permission to
leave the country.[36]
Harassment of the opposition continued throughout
1981. Homes were searched for incriminating evidence,
travel abroad was made difficult, newsprint was denied,
and meetings were impeded. Academics at the University
of Guyana who challenged the government were warned that
their jobs might soon be gone.[37] Independent trade unions
such as the CCWU and NAACIE were denounced in the government press when they demanded better conditions for
Guyana's working class.
The economy continued to deteriorate. An emergency
budget in June devalued the Guyanese dollar by 18 percent, cut subsidies and public expenditures, and increased taxes. The budget was another blow to the Guyanese standard of living. Twelve percent of the budget
would go to the army and the police, but nothing was
available for public housing. Most of the budget pro-

posals were aimed at pleasing the International Monetary Fund. Desperately in need of loans, Burnham knew there would be no funds without cuts in spending.[38]

The International Monetary Fund agreed to an additional loan of $40 million, but the United States, a supporter of Guyana's requests at the International Monetary Fund and the World Bank, suddenly vetoed a low-interest agricultural loan for $20 million from the Inter-American Development Bank. The State Department argued that Guyana's plans for employing the loan were too vague and would not really help the rice farmer. Burnham grumbled, sent some pickets to the United States embassy, and then capitulated. Needing the money, he agreed to raise the price paid to rice farmers by a minimum of 10 percent. The United States then withdrew its veto.[39]

Continually denied permission by the police to hold peaceful demonstrations, the WPA organized a march in Georgetown on Thursday, 17 September 1981. A group of less than one hundred began to march behind banners calling for a reasonable living wage, support for Guyana's territorial integrity, and opposition to the South African regime. Police quickly intervened, arrested the leaders, and began to club those who would not disperse. Eusi Kwayana's wife was badly mauled when she came to the assistance of some youths being manhandled by police officers. Police Commissioner Barker made no apologies and no concessions. He had refused a permit for the march and had used only reasonable force to bring it to an end.[40]

Once again, the government had made clear to the opposition that it had the guns and that it would use them to retain power. The opposition faced the unpalatable fact that both honest elections and peaceful demonstrations were unacceptable to the PNC regime. The government still accepted some criticism in the press, an occasional harsh word in the Legislative Assembly, and a few independent judges, but it would permit no organized opposition that threatened its own existence. Was revolutionary violence destined to be the only available alternative? The WPA drew back from this conclusion--more civil disobedience was required. The Guyanese people would never support "armed struggle" until "all peaceful means have been used and set aside." It concluded: "That is why at chosen moments the citizens, together or apart, must disobey the State. This is called civil disobedience. It is the highest form of non-cooperation with evil." An unarmed people could participate effectively in this type of campaign.[41] Writing in the Catholic Standard, Mike James agreed and called for "the full exploration of all non-violent means of resistance to injustice." The battle of 17 September had not been without its glory: "For the first time in a long time, Guyanese stood fearlessly last Thursday and did not run from the raised batons and pointed guns."[42]

Up to the present time, public services have continued to decay, electricity shortages have become a
regular irritant, and the sewer lines of Georgetown have
started to burst. The sewage system, over fifty years
old, is in danger of complete collapse. Supplies of
pure water have become inadequate, there are numerous
defective septic tanks and pit latrines, and the mos-
quito control program is at a standstill. Nothing, however, aggravates the government more than the small box
on the front of each issue of the Catholic Standard
which lists the names of skilled people fleeing the
country.[43]

The government demonstrated its scorn for the opposition and its overweening confidence when it brought
Donald Rodney to trial for illegal possession of an explosive device. Refusing to search for Sergeant Gregory
Smith or any others involved in Walter Rodney's death,
and rejecting demands for the release of a forensic report prepared by two British experts on the explosion,
the Burnhamites smirked as a leading, pro-PNC magistrate,
Norma Jackman, sentenced Donald Rodney to eighteen months
in prison.

Speaking in a crowded courtroom on 24 February 1982,
Donald Rodney concluded it was ludicrous to assert that
he "knew that the object was a lethal explosive device,
took it from someone I hardly knew, handed it to my
brother, and sat next to him while it exploded." Patri-
cia Rodney, Walter's widow, denounced Magistrate Jackman's decision and observed "that the real assassin of
my husband sits in power in Georgetown, masquerading as
a friend of the poor and of the forces of liberation in
Africa." As Donald Rodney had predicted, the government
did not fail to reward its friends. Both Magistrate
Norma Jackman and the principal detective bringing evidence against Donald Rodney were promptly promoted to
higher positions.[44]

About forty Guyanese opponents of the regime continue to face a variety of charges from treason to caus-
ing "public terror." There is a growing concern over
their safety while in prison due to charges of police
brutality and torture. The United States State Department Report on Human Rights Practices for 1981 concluded
that the "Guyanese constitution prohibits torture, but
there have been credible reports that prisoners have
been beaten with rubber truncheons, kicked, and burned
with cigarettes during detention." Concern was also expressed over "an apparent increase in police use of lethal force in 1981."[45] The State Department, in effect,
corroborated a detailed report prepared by the Guyana
Human Rights Association for the period from January
1980 until June 1981, which included the names of twenty-
two people killed by the police. Proper inquests have
never been held to determine the validity of the police

contention that the dead men had either attacked the police or had been trying to escape.[46]
    One happy note, however, was the decision in the
long-delayed case of Dr. Makepeace Richmond, leader of
the Liberator party, against the Guyana National Newspapers Ltd., publisher of The Chronicle. The government
newspaper had refused to publish a political advertise-
ment paid for by the Liberator party at the time of the
1978 referendum. Dr. Richmond persisted in his case
through numerous postponements. His case was finally
heard before Justice Aubrey Bishop in April 1982. The
justice found that Dr. Richmond's constitutional right
of free expression had been violated. Alas, Justice
Bishop awarded Dr. Richmond only the token sum of G$100
as damages. A writer in the Catholic Standard observed:

> One can well see The Chronicle continuing to deny freedom
> of expression and to discriminate knowing that, if the
> matter were taken to court, the damages would only be
> G$100. One can see the police denying the right of citi-
> zens to travel and being prepared to pay a mere G$100 of
> the taxpayers' money in damages. The courts need to in-
> culcate in the regime more respect for the law.[47]

    Delivering his New Year message to the nation at
the start of 1982, the executive president acknowledged
that production of bauxite, sugar, and rice had failed
to reach their targets in 1981. After seventeen years
of power, Burnham still insisted that a better life for
all Guyanese would be found in the not too-distant future.[48] Just a few months before, however, the United
States Department of State had concluded that the
achievements of its Guyana protege were less than spectacular.

> The $560 annual per capita gross national product of Guy-
> ana ranks the country among the poorest of Latin America
> and the Caribbean. More than 50% of the Guyanese people
> live in conditions of poverty with extremely low incomes
> and high unemployment.[49]

    By March the economy had almost staggered to a halt.
A secret memorandum, prepared for PNC activists, informed them the nation was bankrupt. They were ordered
to blanket the countryside, appeal to the patriotism of
the Guyanese people, and assign all blame to the enemies
of Forbes Burnham. The people must tighten their belts.
Unable to meet its foreign exchange obligations and to
service the national debt, the government saw no alternative but to discharge more public sector employees and
to further limit imports.[50]
    Even the docile TUC complained when it was announced
that six thousand government workers would join the unemployed. The April budget turned out to be "tax-free"

for there was nothing left to tax. The balance of pay-
ment deficit of G$558 million was the worst in Guyana's
history; foreign exchange reserves had fallen to minus
G$500 million. A national debt of G$500 million in 1972
had now soared to G$4 billion. Seventy-five percent of
current revenue was required to service the debt.[51]

The collapse of domestic agriculture along with
massive cuts in food imports led to serious food shortages and long lines at local shops. Responding to this
grave crisis, the Guyana Council of Churches convened a
meeting on 7 April 1982. All political parties, trade
unions, religious bodies, business groups, service clubs,
and other national organizations were invited. The response, with one notable exception, was remarkable.
About 80 percent of the nation was prepared to unite at
a moment of disaster; however, the PNC failed to attend
and deprecated the proposals and resolutions that were
passed.

After full and free discussion, it was agreed that
the Guyana Council of Churches should assume responsibility for obtaining and distributing emergency supplies
of food from overseas agencies. An Unemployment Council
would be established to assist those who lost their jobs.
But--and this was the heart of the matter--it was clearly and precisely stated that the present economic crisis
was a consequence of the PNC's unconstitutional and corrupt control of the Guyanese people. "There is a need
for a broad-based democratic government; no single party
can effectively govern Guyana at this stage."[52]

For a moment, Burnham thought a foreign event might
increase his support at home. The Argentine invasion of
the Falkland Islands in early April made all Guyanese
wonder if Venezuela might assault the Essequibo region.
Appeals for national unity in the face of foreign aggression were again urged by PNC militants. Then, suddenly, rumors roared through Georgetown that Burnham's
health and nerves had collapsed, that he was preparing
to resign and flee the country.[53]

The executive president buried this speculation
during a May Day speech in which he also tried to con-
jure away the food shortages. He went on to add, however, that the Guyanese would have to choose between
flour and new electrical generating equipment. Lengthy
electricity outages to service old equipment had become
common throughout the country. On the following day,
Burnham reorganized his cabinet and personally assumed
the extra portfolios of consumer protection and internal
trade. Of considerable significance was the shift of
Vice President Hamilton Green from Labour and Public
Welfare to Agriculture. Since 80 percent of the economy
is state-owned, Green wielded considerable power as minister of labour and public welfare, and he remains next
in line if Burnham were to be hit by the proverbial
truck. But now that the people are hungry, local farming

in disarray, and no funds available to import food, domestic agriculture has become absolutely decisive if the
regime is to survive. Food must be produced at home or
the nation will starve.[54]

While continuing to affirm its commitment to socialism, the PNC prepared a secret document for IMF and
World Bank officials in May indicating that in return
for the renegotiation of its foreign loans to ease the
immediate crisis, Guyana would concede a larger role for
foreign and local private investment. Representatives
from the World Bank and the IMF were in Guyana in July
to investigate. There apparently also was a tentative
agreement about bringing in foreign managers for some of
the nationalized industries, especially bauxite. This
concession would be humiliating for Forbes Burnham. The
exchange shortage was so bad, however, that twenty-five
Brazilian buses and twelve thousand cartons of Canadian
powdered milk remained at the docks until money could be
found to pay for them. Four local insurance companies
were coerced into depositing about $1.5 million of their
overseas funds into the Bank of Guyana.[55]

Local enthusiasts of Burnham's brand of socialism
were surprised by the capitalist parade through Georgetown in 1982. By October, the government had retained
the British commercial banking firm of Morgan Grenfell
to prepare a "Debt Restructuring and Resource Mobilization" scheme. Assistance was also to be provided by the
United Nations Development Program and the Overseas Development Administration of the British government.
Three other commercial banking firms--Kuhn Loeb Lehman
Brothers, Lazard Freres, and S. G. Warburg--agreed to
"examine the financial and organizational structure of
the Guyana State Corporation and advise on alternative
models to ensure greater effectiveness in its management
functions."[56]

Fearful that the Soviet Union might try to advance
the cause of its ally, Cheddi Jagan, Burnham has been
wary of embracing the Russians. Earlier in the year,
one Soviet diplomat, George Kouzenetsov, lamented rejection of a proposal to provide "unlimited credit to Guyana for Soviet goods at reasonable interest rates with
substantial grace periods."[57] Attempts to negotiate a
bauxite treaty that would have guaranteed sales to the
Soviet Union were also unsuccessful. An enthusiastic
team of Yugoslav economic experts arrived during the
summer to apply their more pragmatic version of communism to Guyana's problems. They were, however, ushered
rather rudely from the country when they recommended reducing the bureaucracy and a more rational approach to
economic planning.[58]

The education, health, and housing of the Guyanese
people continue to deteriorate. Schools are overcrowded,
independent teachers are fired, and the government con-
centrates on indoctrination rather than education. Test

scores of Guyanese students on Caribbean-wide examinations are among the worst in the region.[59] There are far too few physicians and a desperate shortage of hospital beds. Writing to the minister of health about Georgetown's Public Hospital in October, a group of concerned doctors concluded: "The shortage of basic drugs, medical supplies, surgical dressings, and antiseptics make meaningful health care difficult, if not impossible." Dilapidated buildings are home for most working class Guyanese. Plans for the construction of seventy thousand housing units in the 1970s went unfulfilled; only six thousand were completed. Housing starts are now at a standstill.[60]

Food shortages have intensified fears of malnutrition and hunger. The collapse of domestic production and the curtailment of foreign imports have created a black market of enormous proportions; government officials appear to be implicated in smuggling and illegal currency operations. Many items can only be found on the black market where prices are double and triple the officially regulated price. A chronic shortage of milk has been particularly troublesome, especially when so much of the population is composed of babies and children. Flour, cheese, cooking oil, split peas, salt, garlic, chicken, eggs, onions, and potatoes are also difficult to find and, when available, the word spreads and massive lines quickly form.[61]

Divisions within the opposition to Burnham were again highlighted at the meeting of the Trades Union Council (TUC) in September 1982. The sad state of the economy created a real chance that the Burnham-dominated unions might finally lose the presidency of the TUC. In previous years, Jagan's sugar worker's union had supported Gordon Todd of the CCWU. Todd, a political moderate with friends in the United States trade union movement, dislikes unions controlled by political parties. This view strikes at both the PNC and the PPP. Now, Jagan refused to endorse Todd, and the Burnhamites retained the presidency with Todd elected as one of the vice presidents. Rumors again began circulating in Georgetown that Jagan and Burnham might be engaged in secret talks to resolve the crisis to their own advantage.[62]

Despite constant harassment, opposition newssheets have continued to appear. Angered by the criticism, the government has retaliated with a number of libel suits designed to bankrupt the editors. Four suits have been filed against Father Morrison of the Catholic Standard, one cites Brian Rodway of Open Word, and another is directed at Eusi Kwayana's Dayclean. The executive president was outraged when the Catholic Standard published a reader's letter stating that Burnham's signing of the 1966 Geneva Agreement with Venezuela was either "a blunder" or "treason." Vice President Desmond Hoyte brought

two actions against Father Morrison, whom he has referred
to as a "congenital liar" and a "cassocked obscenity."
The entire Caribbean press rushed to the defense of the
beleaguered journalists. A Committee in Defense of the
Catholic Standard was quickly established with Bishops
Benedict Singh and Randolph George among the organizers.[63]
An earlier libel case against the Catholic Standard,
filed by Hamilton Green over the reporting of events of
August 1979, was finally heard in court in January 1983.
Justice George Pompey decided in favor of Green and
awarded damages of G$20,000 to Green. Father Morrison
was able to report a short time later that the fine was
paid by public subscription. The four outstanding libel
suits hang like a heavy sword over Guyana's partially
free press.[64]

Attempts to obtain a proper investigation into
Jonestown and the death of Walter Rodney still remain
unsuccessful. Pressure on both the Guyanese and the
British governments failed to pry loose Dr. Frank Skuse's
forensic report on the bomb explosion which killed the
historian and political activist.[65] But in early June
1982, three years after the event, the accused assassin
of Father Bernard Darke, Bilal Ato, a House of Israel
member, was finally brought to trial. Most of Ato's associates were released within forty-eight hours of the
murder, after paying small fines. After numerous postponements, Ato was finally permitted to plead guilty to
manslaughter. Justice George Pompey sentenced him to
eight years in prison. It is generally believed Ato is
treated with great consideration by his jailers.[66]

In September 1982, the Guyana Human Rights Association issued its report for the period between July 1981
and August 1982. It noted the "total collapse" of Guyana's economy and a massive increase in the suffering of
the people. "The social and public services have deteriorated rapidly, the health and educational systems
have been harshly affected by the economic collapse."
This crisis had produced "an acute shortage of food and
drugs, rocketing prices, widespread unemployment, shut-
down of businesses and a continuing high rate of migration." The "root cause" of Guyana's crisis was "the
rigid party control of all facets of life in Guyana."
This control was being tightened by a frightened government rather than reduced.

The more serious violations of political and civil rights
are, for the most part, directly related to the control
of the State by a minority government. It is the exten-
sive control of jobs in the State sector, backed by a
disproportionately large military organisation which makes
that control possible. There is, therefore, little pros-
pect of an improvement in human rights observance until
some measure of democratic participation in government becomes possible.[67]

The United States Department of State provided powerful support for Burnham's opponents when it released
the Country Reports on Human Rights Practices for 1982.[68]
It noted that Burnham and the PNC "have imposed a racially oriented, minority government on the nation . . .
through such non-democratic means as electoral fraud,
access to unaudited public funds, harassment of the opposition, and interference with the judiciary." Party
paramountcy has turned the government into "an appendage
of the party, and the party employs the apparatus and
power of the state to advance its aims."

> The belief that the state security forces have become the
> private protectors of the ruling party has done more to
> undermine political activism than any other single factor.
> Disenchantment, fear, despair, and apathy characterize the
> attitudes of the majority of Guyanese toward politics.
> The East Indian majority often complains of having no
> stake in the political life of the nation. However, these
> attitudes have not manifested themselves in subversive ac-
> tivities against the government.

The report accepted evidence that the WPA had been
"engaged in para-military training, illegal gun importation, and other such illicit activities." But the WPA
seemed to have lost momentum with the death of Walter
Rodney, and "the remaining opposition groups, mostly
moderate in nature, have been unsuccessful in generating
mass support." One hopeful sign was that "overt antagonism between Afro-Guyanese and Indo-Guyanese has decreased since the vicious race riots of the early six-
ties," even though "the two principal political parties
. . . continue to exploit racial differences for political gain."
The report could not maintain that there had been a
"major deterioration in the human rights climate" over
the past year. There were even a few positive developments amidst all that was negative. Unfortunately,
though, "the human rights prognosis is not favorable as
the Government is becoming less and less accountable to
the electorate, the constitution, the courts and other
checks and balances associated with democratic traditions."

> The human rights environment has significantly deterio-
> rated over the years from the traditions once respected
> in Guyana prior to independence and from what is current-
> ly observed in most of the English-speaking Caribbean.
> It has become increasingly clear, moreover, that tradi-
> tional conceptions of human rights--the integrity of the
> person and civil and political liberties--are being sub-
> ordinated to the Government's efforts to remain in power.

Burnham had been hoping throughout the first half

of 1982 that he might be able to hush his critics by
hosting the first meeting of the heads of state of
CARICOM since 1975. Desperately needing to enhance his
diminished image, Burnham sought a repeat of the successful assemblage of the Non-Aligned States in Georgetown in 1972. The hostility of the late Eric Williams
of Trinidad toward what he felt was the incompetence of
his fellow Caribbean leaders had made a summit session
impossible for many years. Williams's death in 1981 removed the only stumbling block to a formal conclave of
the CARICOM chieftains. For a moment Burnham thought he
had won, but then Trinidad's George Chambers, Jamaica's
Edward Seaga, and Barbados's Tom Adams--all democratically elected--had second thoughts.[69]

Adams, in particular, had become very critical of
Maurice Bishop's failure to hold elections in Grenada
after the March revolution of 1979. The United States
was also deeply disturbed over Bishop's drift to the
left and his close ties with both Fidel Castro and the
Sandinistas in Nicaragua. It would be difficult to urge
free elections on Bishop while meeting in Guyana, where
fraudulent elections had been the order of the day for
the past fifteen years. Guyana was rejected, and Jamaica became the host country.

The first CARICOM summit in seven years convened at
Ocho Rios in Jamaica in November 1982. Burnham arrived
in princely style. His forty-member delegation was the
largest among the twelve states represented. Eugenia
Charles of Dominica, the only female head of government,
was content with two advisers. The moderate leaders
were so happy that a meeting was in session after so
many years that they set out to defuse the controversy
over the Bishop regime in Grenada. Eventually agreement
was hammered out with most controversial issues deferred
until the tenth anniversary meeting scheduled for Trinidad in 1983.[70]

As brazen as ever, Burnham indicated his firm support for human rights and free elections. He brushed
off lengthy statements by the leading newspapers of Jamaica (Gleaner), Trinidad and Tobago (Guardian and Express), and Barbados (Nation and Advocate-News) critical
of Guyana and Grenada for denying political freedom, human rights, and a free press.[71]

Burnham had been hoping for the full support of the
CARICOM states in the boundary dispute with Venezuela;
but, not wishing to completely alienate oil-rich Venezuela, the CARICOM leaders simply "urged both Guyana and
Venezuela to continue their pursuit of a peaceful settlement of the controversy in accordance with the Geneva
Agreement of 1966 so as to arrive at a final decision as
promptly as possible." This statement was in sharp contrast to the strong statement issued in defense of the
territorial integrity of newly independent Belize which
confronted a hostile Guatemala.[72] A divided Guyanese

people finds rallying behind Burnham on this issue increasingly difficult, even though there is unanimity in
rejecting the Venezuelan claim. The Venezuelans continue to fish in troubled waters, for they have nothing to
lose.

The protracted negotiations with the IMF and the
World Bank continued through the end of 1982 and into
1983. The 1979, 1980, and 1981 agreements with the IMF
were terminated due to the failure of the Guyanese government to adhere to the requirements of the IMF.[73] The
IMF could not be pleased as it looked at Guyana's performance for 1982. The bauxite industry was, according
to GUYMINE Chairman Dunstan Barrow, in a "precarious position." Only 65,000 tons of alumina had been exported
in 1982, compared to 165,000 the previous year. Calcined bauxite production was down from 513,000 tons in
1981 to 361,000 tons in 1982. Both metal grade and
chemical grade bauxite production had decreased. It was
expected that losses in the bauxite industry would be
greater than the G$96 million deficit of the previous
year. Rice production was up 15,000 tons over 1981, but
was still 32,000 tons below target. Sugar production
was close to the target of 300,000 tons, but the industry continued to operate at a loss and expected to do so
for another two years.[74]

There was little to celebrate on Forbes Burnham's
sixtieth birthday in February 1983, commemorated along
with the thirteenth anniversary of the establishment of
the Cooperative Republic. The faithful marched forth to
applaud the Comrade Leader,[75] but the noise of the festivities could not drown forever the harsh reality of Desmond Hoyte's budget. The vice president for economic
planning and finance conceded Guyana's "poor performance
in 1982" and acknowledged the failure to export sufficient quantities of bauxite, sugar, and rice.[76] He attempted to put a fine gloss on a dreary picture, but a
hungry, underemployed, suffering people could not be de-
ceived.

The government knew that only the IMF and the World
Bank could provide the funds it required to pay its foreign obligations and to refinance a number of loans.
Still, Burnham hesitated; the demands of the capitalist
bankers would be severe. A team from the IMF/World Bank
arrived in Georgetown in April.[77] After two weeks, negotiations came to an end and rumors rapidly circulated
that the IMF had insisted upon its orthodox remedies for
sick economies: devaluating the currency, cutting the
number of government workers to aid in balancing the
budget, and reducing government subsidies. These requirements would further decrease the Guyanese standard
of living. The first reaction, no doubt carefully calculated, on the part of Burnham and the PNC was to reject the terms as much too harsh. Speaking at a May Day
rally, Burnham called the terms unacceptable, but also

indicated that "we will continue to have discussions because we believe in dialogue and we hope to make our
point." It was clear to even Burnham's most severe
critics that the government had little alternative but
to accept the terms of the IMF and the World Bank.[78]

Sensing his isolation, Burnham seems, once again,
to be reaching out to Jagan in order to split the opposition. Emphasizing that the PNC has considered itself
a Marxist-Leninist party since 1974, the PNC has wondered why Jagan, also a Marxist-Leninist, finds himself
cooperating with bourgeois moderates hostile to socialism. Both the PPP and the PNC, fearful of the WPA, have
tried to turn the latter body into a right-leaning organization. This characterization is clearly inaccurate
if the policies and tactics of the WPA are carefully investigated; but, the WPA has refused to become embroiled
in rigid ideological definitions. It has argued that a
national crisis must be met with a national response.

> At this time of widespread hunger and suffering and with
> the increased insecurity among sugar, bauxite and other
> workers, all of the resources of all Guyanese against
> starvation and dictatorship are required for the struggle
> to survive. No party or organization opposed to the suf-
> fering can, in this period, afford the luxury of an ide-
> ological war against other anti-PNC forces.[79]

Shortly after rejecting the latest IMF terms, the
executive president reorganized the tasks of his five
vice presidents. Once again, Hamilton Green's authority
was enlarged. He had been responsible for agriculture
and public welfare; now Green was named vice president
for production and made responsible for agriculture,
fisheries, forestry, mines, manufacturing, and construction. An analyst in the Catholic Standard concluded
that Green had emerged "notably more powerful than any
of his Vice-Presidential associates." Apparently,
Green's "accumulation of all the productive ministries"
might be a sign "to the IMF that Burnham is prepared to
take a tough line with the unions or anyone else who
might use the impending austerities to stir up industrial unrest." Green had to confront an immediate crisis. On 6 May, one thousand bauxite workers in Linden
refused to work due to food shortages. They agreed to
strike one day each week until there was sufficient food
in the city.[80]

Refusing to be intimidated by the weekly stoppages,
the government responded with fury at the end of May by
cutting the work week to three days. The Guyana Mine
Workers Union and the Guyana Bauxite Supervisors Union
promptly struck the entire bauxite industry. By mid-
June, more than 95 percent of the bauxite workers at
Linden, Kwakwani, Everton, and Ituini were on strike.
In Linden—once a Burnham stronghold—only about three

hundred of four thousand workers refused to answer the strike call. Units of the Guyana Defense Force were sent to intimidate the strikers.[81]

Other unions offered support; even the cautious leadership of the TUC agreed that the government must permit the importation of "an adequate supply of basic food items, including wheaten flour." Government attempts to break the unity of the strikers were unsuccessful and by mid-July a compromise had been negotiated. The five-day work week was restored but the unions agreed to halt the weekly one-day stoppages. Union leaders stressed their right to resume this form of industrial action if it should become necessary. The unions were to be represented on a commission that would investigate the condition of the bauxite industry, and both management and union leaders agreed to improve food distribution in the bauxite towns. Although the Catholic Standard and Caribbean Contact seemed overly euphoric when writing of Burnham "backing down" and the bauxite workers "winning out," it is certainly true that the solidarity of the mostly black bauxite workers was most impressive and must have given the government cause for concern.[82]

Food shortages continued throughout the summer of 1983. A black market rapidly increased as smugglers brought in food from Brazil and Surinam. Prices on the parallel market soared. The police often winked at the black market merchants but, at other times, stepped in with ferocity. Government action remained arbitrary and inconsistent. The crisis deepened during the summer as the first rice crop of the year totalled only 60,000 tons rather than the expected 92,000 tons. When the government placed a ban on the importation of wheat, wheat flour, and powdered milk, it had urged the Guyanese to substitute rice and rice flour. Rice flour was disliked by the people for its taste, and health authorities argued it lacked the nutritional value of wheat flour and could be especially harmful to children. Now there would be neither wheat nor adequate supplies of rice.

There was little for Burnham to be happy about when the PNC held its fifth biennial Congress in August. Unwilling to accept responsibility for Guyana's sorry condition, Burnham assailed the United States for sabotaging his attempts to obtain needed funds from the Inter-American Development Bank. The party faithful roared its approval for the Comrade Leader.[83] But when the once loyal TUC met for its thirtieth annual Delegates Conference in late September, representatives from the PNC used parliamentary tactics to stymie criticism of the government. Nothing was accomplished as the meeting collapsed in disorder. It was obvious, however, that unions representing 52,000 of the 77,000 workers allied to the TUC were hostile to the government's handling of

the economy. The CCWU, GAWU, NAACIE, and the University
Guyana Staff Association were now joined by some former
PNC stalwarts, the two bauxite unions, the National
Union of Public Service Employees, and a section of the
Transport Workers Union. If this alliance became per-
manent it could herald the beginning of the end for the
Burnham dictatorship. The government still controlled
the daily activities of the TUC by its domination of the
Executive Committee of the TUC. Small unions, loyal to
the PNC, were given representation on the Executive Committee out of all proportion to their total membership.[84]
     Then, suddenly, Guyanese eyes turned from their
agony to the Grenada tragedy. Maurice Bishop and his
New Jewel Movement had achieved much since they seized
power from the inept Sir Eric Gairy in March 1979. But
the United States and moderate procapitalist leaders in
the Caribbean had been unhappy with Bishop's socialist
policies, his friendship with Fidel Castro, and his
failure to hold elections. Looking for a pretext to invade and flaunt United States power in a region where it
had suffered several reverses, the Reagan administration
sighed with relief as Grenada's revolutionary front began to devour itself. The death of Maurice Bishop during a power struggle with the more rigidly Marxist Bernard Coard provided a perfect reason to invade. Tom
Adams of Barbados and Edward Seaga of Jamaica had long
been in Washington's pocket and were delighted to join
the small, eastern Caribbean islands in supporting a
United States assault on Grenada. Although encountering
more opposition than expected, Grenada was quickly
brought under control by the United States troops.
     The British government objected to the United States
invasion, as did George Chambers, successor to Eric
Williams in Trinidad. Forbes Burnham did not hesitate.
With the major exception of the United States support
which had helped bring him to power in 1964, he had always been an opponent of imperialism and a supporter of
nonintervention in the internal affairs of other states.
This commitment was central to Guyana's membership in
the non-aligned movement. Burnham promptly denounced
the United States invasion of Grenada. He had also to
consider what the United States might do to Guyana itself if he continued his leftist course. There had been
contradictory reports about United States attempts to
remove the military regime in Surinam towards the end of
1982. For once, Burnham found himself basking in a moment of national unity. The PPP and the WPA echoed
Burnham's outrage over the Grenada invasion.[85]
     The very fact that the PNC, the PPP, and the WPA
could enthusiastically censure the United States for oc-
cupying Grenada caused immense theoretical and practical
difficulties for all three organizations. Some Burnhamites wondered if this might not be the moment to bring
the PPP into some form of coalition government. But the

PNC militants and racists feared the loss of their posts
in the civil service and the security organizations if
the East Indians demanded equal access to jobs. The police had recently been implicated in new acts of violence in East Indian villages.[86]

Cheddi Jagan remains resentful that the PNC and the
WPA, along with his PPP, claim to be genuine Marxist-
Leninist parties. This term has been so abused it is
almost meaningless. Jagan has been especially unhappy
that the WPA leaders have apparently become a more acceptable alternative to Burnham than the PPP. His preference seemingly is for a Burnham-Jagan alliance exclud-
ing the WPA. Jagan believes the WPA has become more
conservative since Walter Rodney's death, when it began
to cooperate with middle class, church, and professional
groups. He is particularly annoyed by the willingness
of the WPA to collaborate with the Vanguard for Liberation and Democracy.[87] The WPA advocates a broad coalition to replace Burnham, but insists the discredited PNC
must be excluded.

The Guyana Council of Churches has been sympathetic
toward WPA policies aimed at building racial harmony and
moving away from the rigid attitudes associated with the
PPP and the PNC. But it worries, along with other moderates, about the implications of the WPA calling itself
Marxist-Leninist. By early 1984, the WPA had become an
associate member of the Socialist International. The
membership of this organization, which also includes the
British Labour party, the French Socialist party, and
the Social Democratic party of West Germany, seems to
support the view that the WPA is committed to free elections and political pluralism rather than to Soviet despotism and one-party domination. Responding to a commentary in the Catholic Standard, Eusi Kwayana and Rupert Roopnaraine, co-chairpersons of the WPA, retorted
that the membership of the WPA was not "debating Leninism as against social democracy," but rather "the type
of party most suited to meet the needs of the struggle
against dictatorship."[88] They affirmed the commitment of
the WPA to "political pluralism, tolerance of internal
dissent, free pluralist elections, press freedom, and
open party debate." It would not be "correct to judge
all who today define themselves as Leninist by the standards which the Soviets say were applied by Stalin,"
just as it would be improper "to judge all who today define themselves as Roman Catholics by methods used by
the church for conversion centuries ago." Labels could
be "misleading." They concluded: "The WPA believed that
the immediate needs of Guyana are for democracy, survival, and reconstruction. Our position is the same as in
1979. When the people are free, they will choose for
themselves their path for the future."[89]

During 1983, Forbes Burnham and a large entourage
had flown off in splendor to meetings of CARICOM and the

Commonwealth prime ministers while the Guyanese people struggled with food shortages and unemployment. By the end of the year, medical facilities at the Georgetown Hospital had collapsed. The water supply in the capital was permanently brown and smelly. Shortages of teachers and books placed Guyanese students at the lowest educational level among the Caribbean countries. The government seemed to be preparing itself for further cuts in social programs and the public services when it devalued the currency by 25 percent in January 1984, and introduced a budget designed to win IMF approval. There was no other alternative but to go humbly to the lords of capitalism. Reflecting upon the budget and the plight of the Guyanese people, Terrence K. Millington remembered George Lamming's 1981 remark that the Guyanese are living "in a dangerous place at a dangerous time." Millington concluded:

> Rather than the economic collapse itself, the unwillingness of the government to accept any responsibility for it (it blames the weather, the world economy and the workers), or even acknowledge that it exists constitutes the more serious problem. Survival in power is the only creed the party adheres to, and it appears prepared to destroy the country rather than abandon power.[90]

The Burnham government was again embarrassed when the United States Department of State presented its report on human rights practices throughout the world in 1983. It concluded that, "since independence, the political scene has been marked by fraudulent elections, wholesale emigration, frustration of the educated and politically aware middle class, and repression of the political opposition." Guyanese security services employed "wire taps, mail interception, and physical surveillance . . . to monitor and intimidate political opponents of the government." Arbitrary restraints were imposed on press freedom and on the right to assemble peaceably. There had been "a serious decline in discipline and standards in the Guyana police force." Strict loyalty to the PNC was required for advancement in the judiciary, the security forces, and the public service. The most important decisions were made by President Burnham himself whose survival was ultimately "based on the security forces. . . . The Burnham government has ruled Guyana for nearly twenty years, using the form of parliamentary democracy, but not the substance."[91]

What to do? How to do it? These questions remain for a troubled people in an unhappy land. How does one remove an illegal government which refuses to conduct fair elections? All decent and sane human beings must hesitate at the thought of violence; injuries and deaths are surely to be avoided if at all possible.[92] But how else is Forbes Burnham to be ejected? A general strike

might succeed; more trade unions than ever before, most
traditionally loyal to the PNC, have become hostile to
the government's failed policies. But Joseph Pollydore,
general secretary of the TUC, constantly draws back from
a direct attack. Writing in a <u>Catholic Standard</u> editorial on 21 September 1980, Father Andrew Morrison concluded that despite a government assault on trade union
rights, including the right to strike, the leadership of
the TUC had "constantly failed to take a firm stand.
Instead, it has in each case, entered into dialogue. . . .
The warning of the Polish workers needs to be taken to
heart. When leaders fail to be militant in representing
their interests, the workers will find other means of
asserting their rights."

In March 1984, the government may finally have committed the act of desperation and folly that will bring
together all Guyanese working people in defense of trade
union freedom. Seeram Teemal, a member of NAACIE, went
to court to claim a pay increase promised by the Guyana
Sugar Corporation (GUYSUCO) in 1978, the same year
Forbes Burnham had called for a wage freeze as part of
his austerity program. GUYSUCO informed Teemal he would
not receive his raise because of Burnham's directive.

By the end of 1983, after lengthy litigation, the
courts held in favor of Teemal and concluded that wages,
like property, were protected under Guyana's 1980 constitution. GUYSUCO could not unilaterally abrogate its
agreement with Teemal. Expecting a flood of court cases
that could destroy its austerity program and ruin negotiations with the IMF, the government responded three
months later by rushing draconian legislation through
Parliament. The new law amended the constitution so
that wages would no longer have the safety accorded
property. It also restricted collective bargaining and
further limited the right to strike. The Executive Committee of the Trades Union Congress was designated the
sole bargaining agent for all public sector employees.
Since the undemocratically elected Executive Committee
is dominated by PNC enthusiasts, negotiations between
the Executive Committee and the government will really
amount to the government negotiating with itself. The
new legislation makes it almost impossible for the public sector employees to strike, and also impedes the
freedom of nonpublic sector workers to withdraw their
services. If the nonpublic sector employees were to
strike without exhausting all grievance procedures, the
government could intervene, seize union assets, and jail
union officials.[93]

The militant unions, joined by a few of the moderate unions, immediately protested. Joseph Pollydore,
the decent, well-intentioned, general secretary of the
TUC, was unable to convince the PNC majority on the Executive Committee that the new trade union legislation
should be discussed. Many believe Burnham wanted the

new legislation so that, when he finally capitulates to
the IMF, he will be able to state that Guyana's trade
unions have been tamed and the capitalist world need not
worry about demands for pay increases.

Shortly after Walter Rodney's death, Mike James,
assistant editor of the Catholic Standard (20 July 1980),
observed that "the choice for many will be either to be
willing to shed their blood for justice in Guyana or to
wash the martyr's blood from their hands, by participation in the work of the assassins or by silent connivance. There is no middle ground." And, in a letter to
the Catholic Standard (29 June 1980), Sister Mary Noel
Menezes, member of the History Department at the University of Guyana, noted: "Those who speak out against injustice pay a high price in blood." She quoted Martin
Luther King: "The quality, not the longevity of one's
life, is what is important. If you are cut down in a
movement that is designed to save the soul of a nation,
then no other death can be more redemptive."

Forbes Burnham and the PNC would be crushed in free
and fair elections. A frightened man with a bad heart,
he is only kept in power by the black-dominated Guyana
Defense Force and police though, even there, one hears
new rumors of discontent. The one thing that might yet
redeem Burnham in the eyes of the nation he has so
cruelly betrayed, would be to step aside so that honest
elections could be held and some form of broad coalition
established to fulfill his failed pledges to "feed,
clothe, and house" the nation. Ironically, Burnham's
oppressive tactics and inability to create a Guyanese
nation are having a beneficial consequence in one crucial area--they are forcing blacks and East Indians to
cooperate once again.[34] As they oppose the Burnham dictatorship, the people of Guyana seem to be rediscovering
their essential unity and humanity. One hopes that
Burnham will depart peacefully; there can be no national
reconciliation so long as he remains. When Burnham lies
awake at night he would do well to recall the admonition
that the sins we commit two by two, we must pay for one
by one, and to remember also the frightened hulk, once
the "Emperor Jones," who screamed out in agony just
prior to being shot: "Mercy, Oh Lawd! Mercy! Mercy on
dis po' sinner."

NOTES

1. Catholic Standard, 20 January 1980, p. 1.
2. This concluding chapter is based upon a careful reading of
the Catholic Standard, Caribbean Contact, Caribbean Monthly Bulletin
(published by the Institute of Caribbean Studies at the University
of Puerto Rico), Latin America Regional Reports: Caribbean (published

214

by Latin American Newsletters Ltd., London), and the polemical literature published by Guyana's political parties and pressure groups.

. *Caribbean Contact*, June 1980, p. 1.

. See the January 1980 and February 1980 issues of the *Catholic Standard*.

. *Caribbean Monthly Bulletin*, March/April 1980, pp. 1-7. This bulletin includes Jeremy Taylor's "Letter from Georgetown" which appeared in *Express*, 2 March 1980. See the evaluation of the constitution in the article by Mike James, *Catholic Standard*, 3 February 1980, p. 4.

. *Catholic Standard*, 10 February 1980, p. 4.

. *Catholic Standard*, 16 March 1980, pp. 1-7.

. For the Surinam coup, see Edward Dew, "The Year of the Sergeants," *Caribbean Review*, 9 (Spring 1980), pp. 5-7, 46-47; and Gary Brana-Shute, "Politicians in Uniform: Suriname's Bedeviled Revolution," *Caribbean Review*, 10 (Spring 1981), pp. 24-27, 49-50. A discussion of the recent violent lurch to the left can be found in Edward Dew, "Suriname Tar Baby," *Caribbean Review*, 12 (Winter 1983), pp. 4-7, 34.

. *Catholic Standard*, 23 March 1980, p. 3.

10. Clive Thomas, "Inside Burnham's Cooperative Republic," *Caribbean Contact*, February 1980, p. 5. Thomas is head of the Department of Economics at the University of Guyana and a leader of the Working People's Alliance.

11. Guy Standing and Richard Szal, *Poverty and Basic Needs: Evidence from Guyana and the Philippines* (Geneva, Switzerland, 1979), pp. 78-79.

12. See *Catholic Standard*, 27 April 1980, p. 3; and *Caribbean Contact*, May 1980, p. 7.

13. *Caribbean Contact*, June 1980, pp. 8-9; and *Caribbean Monthly Bulletin*, May 1980, pp. 32-33. There is a good discussion of the hydroelectric project and of the Amerindian tribes that will be uprooted in *Caribbean Contact*, December 1980, p. 7.

14. *Catholic Standard*, 29 June 1980, p. 8.

15. In order to follow the reaction to Walter Rodney's death, see especially the *Catholic Standard* of 22 June 1980, 29 June 1980, 6 July 1980, 13 July 1980, and 20 July 1980; *Caribbean Contact*, July 1980, August 1980, and September 1980; and *Caribbean Monthly Bulletin*, June/July 1980 and August 1980. The manuscript of Walter Rodney's most recent book was already in the hands of The Johns Hopkins University Press at the time of his death. It appeared under the title, *A History of the Guyanese Working People, 1881-1905*, in 1981 and was awarded the prestigious Albert J. Beveridge award in 1982 by the American Historical Association for the best book published in English on the history of the United States, Canada, or Latin America during the previous year. For an assessment of Rodney's life see Edward A. Alpers and Pierre-Michel Fontaine, eds., *Walter Rodney: Revolutionary and Scholar* (Los Angeles, 1982).

16. *Caribbean Monthly Bulletin*, September/October 1980, p. 36.

17. *Catholic Standard*, 5 October 1980, pp. 1, 7; 12 October 1980, p. 5; and *Caribbean Monthly Bulletin*, September/October 1980, p. 37.

18. *Catholic Standard*, 12 October 1980, pp. 1-2; and *Caribbean Monthly Bulletin*, November/December 1980, pp. 41-46.

19. Caribbean Contact, December 1975, p. 7.
20. Catholic Standard, 9 November 1980, pp. 1, 6.
21. Caribbean Contact, November 1980, pp. 7, 10.
22. This account of the election of 15 December 1980 is based primarily upon the Catholic Standard, Caribbean Contact, Caribbean Monthly Bulletin, and Something to Remember: The Report of the International Team of Observers at the Elections in Guyana, December 1980 (London, 1980).
23. See the editorial by Father Andrew Morrison, Catholic Standard, 9 November 1980, p. 4.
24. Caribbean Contact, November 1980, pp. 7, 10.
25. Something to Remember, p. 3.
26. Ibid., Appendix I, pp. 30-32.
27. Ibid., Conclusion, p. 28.
28. Caribbean Contact, January 1981, pp. 1, 16. There is a summary of the Avebury team's report in Caribbean Review, 10 (Spring 1981), pp. 8-11, 44.
29. Catholic Standard, 21 December 1980, pp. 7-11; and Caribbean Monthly Bulletin, January/February 1981, pp. 1-9. The response of Guyana's minister of home affairs to the Avebury team's report can be read in Appendix VIII, pp. 45-60 of Something to Remember.
30. Latin America Regional Reports: Caribbean, 16 January 1981, pp. 6-7.
31. See Caribbean Contact, February 1981, pp. 8-9; and Catholic Standard, 11 January 1981, p. 5.
32. Latin America Regional Reports: Caribbean, 20 February 1981, pp. 4-5; Catholic Standard, 25 January 1981, pp. 1, 8; and Caribbean Contact, March 1981, p. 7.
33. Department of State, Country Report on Human Rights Practices (Washington, D.C., 1981), pp. 450-58.
34. Latin America Regional Reports: Caribbean, 8 May 1981, pp. 1-2; Caribbean Contact, April 1981, p. 16; May 1981, p. 5; and June 1981, pp. 10-12; and Catholic Standard, 26 April 1981, p. 4; and 3 May 1981, p. 1.
35. Caribbean Monthly Bulletin, May 1981, pp. 30-35.
36. See the Catholic Standard for April, May, and June of 1981; and Caribbean Contact, July 1981, pp. 1, 7.
37. Caribbean Contact, April 1981, p. 8; and the Catholic Standard, 15 March 1981, pp. 1, 7. See Paul Nehru Tennassee, Guyana: A Nation in Ruins (Toronto, 1982). Tennassee, a native-born Guyanese, had been teaching in Canada. He became a researcher in the Institute of Development Studies at the University of Guyana in January 1982 but was fired by the Council of the University, a Burnham-controlled group, two months later.
38. Latin America Regional Reports: Caribbean, 17 July 1981, pp. 3, 4. For an excellent evaluation of Burnham's opportunistic, ideological shifts, see Percy C. Hintzen and Ralph R. Premdas, "Race, Ideology, and Power in Guyana," The Journal of Commonwealth and Comparative Politics, 21 (July 1983), pp. 175-94.
39. Caribbean Monthly Bulletin, August 1981, pp. 39-41; and September 1981, pp. 26-29.
40. Caribbean Contact, October 1981, p. 5. See the two interesting articles by WPA activist, Eusi Kwayana, in Caribbean Contact, November 1981, pp. 17-18; and December 1981, pp. 8, 14.

216

41. Latin America Regional Reports: Caribbean, 25 September 1981, pp. 4-5; and 30 October 1981, pp. 3-4.
42. Catholic Standard, 27 September 1981, p. 4.
43. See Clive Thomas, "Collapse of Guyana's Economy," Caribbean Contact, January 1982, pp. 5, 7.
44. Caribbean Contact, April 1982, pp. 7, 10; and Caribbean Monthly Bulletin, March 1982, p. 12.
45. Catholic Standard, 21 February 1982, pp. 1, 4; and 28 February 1982, p. 4.
46. Guyana Human Rights Association, Human Rights Report, January 1980-June 1981 (Georgetown, Guyana, 1981).
47. Catholic Standard, 25 April 1982, pp. 1, 4; and 2 May 1982, p. 2.
48. Caribbean Contact, February 1982, p. 16; and Caribbean Monthly Bulletin, January 1982, pp. 6-8.
49. Catholic Standard, 25 October 1981, p. 1.
50. Caribbean Contact, May 1982, p. 5.
51. Caribbean Monthly Bulletin, April 1982, pp. 27-31; and Catholic Standard, 28 March 1982, pp. 1-3; 4 April 1982, p. 4; and 11 April 1982, pp. 1-2.
52. Catholic Standard, 18 April 1982, pp. 1-4.
53. See Rickey Singh's editorial, "Why Not Go in Peace, Mr. Burnham," Caribbean Contact, July 1982, pp. 1, 3.
54. Latin America Regional Reports, 7 May 1982, pp. 1-2; and Caribbean Monthly Bulletin, May/June 1982, pp. 64-67.
55. Latin America Regional Reports: Caribbean, 11 June 1982, pp. 5-6; and 20 August 1982, pp. 4-5; and Catholic Standard, 13 June 1982, p. 1; 20 June 1982, pp. 1, 3; and 25 July 1982, pp. 1, 4.
56. Catholic Standard, 26 September 1982, pp. 1, 4; and 3 October 1982, pp. 1, 4.
57. Caribbean Monthly Bulletin, April 1982, pp. 30-31.
58. Catholic Standard, 18 July 1982, p. 1; and 15 August 1982, p. 1.
59. For an excellent discussion of Guyana's schools, see M. K. Bacchus, Education for Development or Underdevelopment: Guyana's Educational System and its Implication for the Third World (Waterloo, Canada, 1980). See also Ahamad Baksh, "Formal Education and the Guyanese Social Structure," Transition, 2 (1979), pp. 113-30.
60. Catholic Standard, 24 October 1982, pp. 1-2.
61. Caribbean Contact, November 1982, p. 6.
62. Catholic Standard, 10 October 1982, p. 2; and 17 October 1982, pp. 2-3.
63. Catholic Standard, 5 September 1982, p. 1; and 3 October 1982, p. 1; and Latin America Regional Reports: Caribbean, 1 October 1982, p. 4; and 5 November 1982, pp. 6-7 (this article is titled "Catholic Church Under Siege").
64. Catholic Standard, 16 January 1983, pp. 1, 4; 23 January 1983, pp. 1, 4; and 6 March 1983, p. 1.
65. Catholic Standard, 2 May 1982, pp. 1, 4.
66. Caribbean Contact, August 1982, p. 5; December 1982, p. 6; Catholic Standard, 13 June 1982, p. 1.
67. Guyana Human Rights Association, Human Rights Report, July 1981-August 1982 (Georgetown, Guyana, 1982). See also Caribbean Contact, October 1982, p. 5.

68. U.S. Department of State, <u>Country Reports on Human Rights Practices for 1982</u> (Washington, D.C., 1983), pp. 532-43.

69. <u>Catholic Standard</u>, 6 June 1982, pp. 1, 3.

70. <u>Latin America Regional Reports</u>, 10 December 1982, pp. 1-2.

71. <u>Caribbean Contact</u>, December 1982, pp. 1, 2, 14, 16; and January 1983, p. 6.

72. <u>Catholic Standard</u>, 26 November 1982, pp. 1, 2.

73. <u>Latin America Regional Reports</u>, 10 December 1982, p. 3.

74. <u>Latin America Regional Reports</u>, 21 January 1983, p. 4. For a discussion of the bauxite industry, see <u>Caribbean Contact</u>, September 1982, pp. 13-14.

75. See the sharp criticism of the PNC in the two articles by black lawyer and former deputy mayor of Georgetown Cleveland Hamilton in <u>Caribbean Contact</u>, February 1983, pp. 7, 10; and April 1983, pp. 5, 10.

76. <u>Caribbean Contact</u>, March 1983, p. 7; and <u>Catholic Standard</u>, 27 February 1983, pp. 1, 4.

77. <u>Catholic Standard</u>, 24 April 1983, p. 1; 1 May 1983, pp. 1, 4; and 8 May 1983, pp. 1, 3.

78. <u>Latin America Regional Reports</u>, 25 February 1983, pp. 7-8; and 31 March 1983, p. 2. See also <u>Caribbean Contact</u>, May 1983, p. 1.

79. <u>Caribbean Contact</u>, March 1983, p. 7; and <u>Catholic Standard</u>, 27 February 1983, p. 4. See also the two articles about Walter Rodney by James Petras and Trevor A. Campbell in <u>Latin American Perspectives</u>, 8 (Winter 1981), pp. 47-63. This issue of <u>Latin American Perspectives</u> also contains a reprint of Rodney's 1979 pamphlet, "People's Power, No Dictator" (pp. 64-78), where the author concluded that Burnham must be replaced by "a government of national unity."

80. <u>Latin America Regional Reports: Caribbean</u>, 13 May 1983, pp. 3-4; and <u>Catholic Standard</u>, 15 May 1983, pp. 1, 4.

81. See the June 1983 issues of the <u>Catholic Standard</u>. See also <u>Caribbean Contact</u>, July 1983, p. 5; and <u>Latin America Regional Reports: Caribbean</u>, 17 June 1983, p. 3.

82. <u>Catholic Standard</u>, 24 July 1983, p. 4; and <u>Caribbean Contact</u>, August 1983, p. 16.

83. <u>Latin America Regional Reports: Caribbean</u>, 26 August 1983, p. 1; and <u>Caribbean Contact</u>, September 1983, p. 7.

84. <u>Caribbean Contact</u>, November 1983, p. 6. See also the <u>Catholic Standard</u> of 9 October 1983, and 16 October 1983.

85. For some excellent articles on the Grenada crisis see the Fall 1983 issue of <u>Caribbean Review</u>. See also <u>Caribbean Contact</u>, December 1983, p. 3. Sadly, the Guyanese journalist Rickey Singh, whose rugged independence led him to leave Guyana when press freedom was restricted, has been a victim of the Grenada invasion he vigorously opposed. Singh has been editor of <u>Caribbean Contact</u> since 1974. His first editorial home, Trinidad, was lost when Eric Williams deprived him of a work permit due to Singh's criticism of the Trinidad government. Rickey Singh then moved to Barbados where Tom Adams, critic of the lack of press freedom in Bishop's Grenada, has now withdrawn Singh's work permit and caused him to give up the editorship of <u>Caribbean Contact</u>.

86. <u>Caribbean Contact</u>, October 1983, pp. 5-6.

87. See the summary of an interview with Cheddi Jagan in <u>Latin</u>

218

America Regional Reports: Caribbean, 23 July 1983, pp. 7-8.

88. Catholic Standard, 12 February 1984, p. 1; and 19 February 1984, p. 4.

89. Middle class leaders were not entirely satisfied with the WPA statement and demanded further specifics. See the article by David De Caires in the Catholic Standard of 26 February 1984.

90. Caribbean Contact, January/February 1984, p. 17; and March 1984, p. 12. See also Latin America Regional Reports: Caribbean, 20 January 1984, p. 7.

91. Catholic Standard, 19 February 1984, p. 1; and Latin America Regional Reports: Caribbean, 24 February 1984, p. 5.

92. See the fascinating chapter "Violence and Counter-Violence" in Patrick O'Farrell's England and Ireland Since 1800 (Oxford, 1975), pp. 155-80. In a provocative footnote (p. 175) O'Farrell acknowledges "that violence has accumulated a mythological veneer which gives it a false heroic appeal and sham dignity." While agreeing that this myth should be destroyed, he argues that the "real problem" is to remove the causes of violent activity if that is possible. "While the immorality of individual violent acts may be clear, the question of the immorality of violence as part of the historical process might be another matter." O'Farrell concludes with a quotation from the Jesuit, Jean Danielou: "Men are often more squeamish than God and more easily scandalized. They take exception to violence, although violence is one of the ways in which life bursts forth."

93. Catholic Standard, 18 March 1984, p. 1; 25 March 1984, p. 1; and Caribbean Contact, April 1984, p. 1.

94. See R. S. Milne's excellent comparative study, Politics in Ethnically Bipolar States: Guyana, Malaysia, Fiji (Vancouver, Canada, 1981). See also Milne's "Politics, Ethnicity and Class in Guyana and Malaysia," Social and Economic Studies, 25 (March 1977), pp. 18-37. He concludes his article with the comment (p. 31): "Nevertheless, Guyana is of unusual interest because its ethnic cleavages are maybe less intractable than elsewhere."

Abbreviations

AFSCME	American Federation of State, County, and Municipal Employees
ASCRIA	African Society for Cultural Relations with Independent Africa
BGEIA	British Guiana East Indian Association
BGLU	British Guiana Labour Union
CARICOM	Caribbean Common Market
CARIFTA	Caribbean Free Trade Association
CCC	Concerned Citizens' Committee
CDD	Committee in Defense of Democracy
CCWU	Clerical and Commercial Workers Union
CIA	Central Intelligence Agency
CNS	Council of National Safety
DEMBA	Demerara Bauxite Company
GAWU	Guyana Agricultural Workers Union
GCC	Guyana Council of Churches
GDF	Guyana Defense Force
GIWU	Guyana Industrial Workers Union
GNS	Guyana National Service
GUYBAU	Guyana Bauxite Company
GUYMINE	Guyana Mining Corporation
GUYSUCO	Guyana Sugar Corporation
ICFTU	International Confederation of Free Trade Unions
IPRA	Indian Political Revolutionary Associates
LCP	League of Coloured People
LP	Liberator Party

MPCA	Man-Power Citizens Association
NAACIE	National Association of Agricultural, Commercial, and Industrial Employees
NDP	National Democratic Party
NLF	National Labour Front
PAC	Political Affairs Committee
PDM	People's Democratic Movement
PNC	People's National Congress
PPP	People's Progressive Party
PSI	Public Services International
SPA	Sugar Producers Association
TUC	Trades Union Council
UDP	United Democratic Party
UF	United Force
UGSA	University of Guyana Staff Association
VLD	Vanguard for Liberation and Democracy (an alliance of PDM, LP, and WPVP still in existence in 1984
WFTU	World Federation of Trade Unions
WPA	Working People's Alliance
WPVP	Working People's Vanguard Party

Critical Bibliography

The best introduction to Guyana is Raymond T. Smith, British Guiana (London: Oxford University Press, 1962). An excellent shorter assessment can be found in the Institute of Race Relations' paperback by Peter Newman, British Guiana: Problems of Cohesion in an Immigrant Society (London: Oxford University Press, 1964). There is much information of interest in Roy Arthur Glasgow, Guyana: Race and Politics among Africans and East Indians (The Hague: Martinus Nijhoff, 1970); and Harold A. Lutchman, From Colonialism to Co-operative Republic: Aspects of Political Development in Guyana (Rio Piedras, Puerto Rico: Institute of Caribbean Studies, 1974). Many useful facts can be found in the volume by William Mitchell et al., Handbook for Guyana (Washington, D.C.: Government Printing Office, 1969), prepared under the auspices of the Foreign Areas Studies of the American University in Washington, D.C. An up-to-date assessment with many valuable quotations is Robert H. Manley, Guyana Emergent: The Post-Independence Struggle for Nondependent Development (Cambridge, Mass.: Schenkman Publishing Co., 1979). A vast literature exists on cultural pluralism and its significance. For an introduction to the problem see Michael G. Smith, The Plural Society in the British West Indies (Berkeley: University of California Press, 1965). Smith's theoretical concepts about the divisive characteristics of culturally plural societies are applied in Leo A. Despres, Cultural Pluralism and Nationalist Politics in British Guiana (Chicago: Rand McNally, 1967). For the opposite view which stresses the essential unity of the Guyanese people despite their ethnic and cultural differences, see the previously mentioned volume by Raymond T. Smith along with his numerous articles. Also of interest is Cynthia H. Enloe, Ethnic Conflict and Political Development (Boston: Little, Brown, and Co., 1973). Life on the plantations after the abolition of slavery is evaluated in Alan H. Adamson, Sugar Without Slaves: The Political Economy of British Guiana, 1838-1904 (New Haven: Yale University Press, 1972). See also Jay R. Mandle, The Plantation Economy: Population and Economic Change in Guyana, 1838-1960 (Philadelphia: Temple University Press, 1973).

Sociologists and anthropologists have found Guyana a fertile field for study. See Raymond T. Smith, The Negro Family in British Guiana: Family Structure and Social Status in the Villages (London: Routledge and Kegan Paul, 1956); Chandra Jayawardena, Conflict and Solidarity in a Guianese Plantation (London: Athlone Press, 1963); Mohammed A. Rauf, Indian Village in Guyana: A Study of Cultural Change and Ethnic Identity (Leiden: E. J. Brill, 1974); and Marilyn Silverman, Rich People and Rice (Leiden: E. J. Brill, 1980).

For Cheddi Jagan, see the revised paperback edition of his The West on Trial: The Fight for Guyana's Freedom (East Berlin: Seven Seas, 1972). Forbes Burnham's speeches have been compiled by C. A. Nascimento and R. A. Burrowes, eds., A Destiny to Mould: Selected Discourses by the Prime Minister of Guyana (London: Longman, 1970).

For an eyewitness account of the violence of the 1960s, see Peter Simms, Trouble in Guyana (London: Allen and Unwin, 1966). On the involvement of the Central Intelligence Agency and the AFL-CIO in destroying the Jagan regime between 1962 and 1964, see Colin V. F. Henfrey, "Foreign Influence in Guyana: The Struggle for Independence," in Emmanuel De Kadt, ed., Patterns of Foreign Influence in the Caribbean (London: Oxford University Press, 1972); Ronald Radosh, American Labor and United States Foreign Policy (New York: Random House, 1969); Serafino Romualdi, Presidents and Peons: Recollections of a Labor Ambassador in Latin America (New York: Funk and Wagnalls, 1967); Philip Agee, Inside the Company: CIA Diary (Harmondsworth: Penguin Books, 1975); and the Insight Team Report in London's Sunday Times of 16 and 23 April 1967.

The 1968 elections are explored in a dispassionate way in J. E. Greene, Race versus Politics in Guyana: Political Cleavages and Political Mobilisation in the 1968 General Election (Kingston, Jamaica: University of the West Indies, 1974). But there is no substitute for the two Granada television programs for the "World in Action" series, "The Trail of the Vanishing Voters," and "The Making of a Prime Minister."

For a summary of East Indian achievements, see Dwarka Nath, A History of Indians in Guyana (London: Published by the Author, 2nd revised edition, 1970). See also Nath's three volumes, A History of Guyana (London: Published by the Author, 1974-1976). A good summary of working class organization can be found in Ashton Chase, A History of Trade Unionism in Guyana (Georgetown, Guyana: New Guyana Co., 1964).

There are a variety of articles in Brian Irving,
ed., Guyana: A Composite Monograph (Hato Rey, Puerto
Rico: Inter-American University Press, 1972). The role
of the United Nations has been explored in Basil A.
Ince, Decolonization and Conflict in the United Nations:
Guyana's Struggle for Independence (Cambridge, Mass.:
Schenkman Publishing Co., 1974). For the current state
of radio communication, see Ron Sanders, Broadcasting in
Guyana (London: Routledge and Kegan Paul, 1978). The
police force is analyzed in George K. Danns, Domination
and Power in Guyana: A Study of the Police in a Third
World Context (New Brunswick, New Jersey: Transaction
Books, 1982).

Guyana's economy is analyzed in Wilfred L. David,
The Economic Development of Guyana, 1953-1964 (London:
Oxford University Press, 1969); Kempe R. Hope, Develop-
ment Policy in Guyana: Planning, Finance, and Adminis-
tration (Boulder:Westview Press, 1979); and Guy Standing
and Richard Szal, Poverty and Basic Needs: Evidence from
Guyana and the Philippines (Geneva: International Labour
Office, 1979).

There is a fine section on Guyana in V. S. Naipaul,
The Middle Passage (Harmondsworth: Penguin Books, 1962).
Much interesting information can be found in the strong-
ly pro-British books of Michael Swan, British Guiana:
The Land of Six Peoples (London: HMSO, 1957); and The
Marches of El Dorado (Boston: Beacon Press, 1958).

For a commentary on the moment Guyana became a Cooperative Republic, see Andrew Salkey, Georgetown Journal (London: New Beacon Books, 1972). There are signi-
ficant references to Guyana's bauxite in Robert Chodos,
The Caribbean Connection (Toronto: James Lorimer, 1977).
A fine assessment can be found in Ralph R. Premdas, "Guy-
ana: Socialist Reconstruction or Political Opportunism?"
Journal of Interamerican Studies and World Affairs, 20,
No. 2 (May 1978), pp. 133-64. There is a stimulating
analysis of "transplanted Fabian labourism, Jaganite
Marxism-Leninism, and Burnhamite co-operation" in Paul
Singh, Guyana: Socialism in a Plural Society (London:
Fabian Research Series 307, 1972). The East Indians of
Guyana and Trinidad is a perceptive short report pre-
pared by Malcolm Cross in 1972 under the auspices of
London's Minority Rights Group.

The student of Guyanese affairs will certainly wish
to consult the reports by a number of constitutional
commissions and conferences which were established to
move Guyana toward independence. Among the most important were Sir Eubule J. Waddington's Constitutional Commission Report of 1951 (Colonial Office No. 280, 1951);
the British government's attempt to justify the suspension of the constitution in 1953 (Command 8980, 1953);
Sir James Robertson's Constitutional Commission Report
of 1954 (Command 9274, 1954); the Report of the Constitutional Conference of 1960 (Command 998, 1960); the

224

Report of the Commission of Inquiry into Disturbances in
British Guiana in February 1962 (Colonial Office No. 354,
1962); the Report of the British Guiana Independence
Conference of 1962 (Command 1870, 1962); the Report of
the British Guiana Constitutional Conference of 1963
(Command 2203, 1963); and the Report of the British
Guiana Independence Conference of 1965 (Command 2849,
1965).

There is a mass of fascinating material in the five-
part submission the Burnham-D'Aguiar coalition government presented to the Commission of Inquiry, selected by
the International Commission of Jurists to investigate
racial imbalance in British Guiana and to make proposals
as to what could be done to rectify any inequities. The
information submitted by the government of British Guiana
was published along with the Report of the Commission of
Inquiry (Geneva: International Commission of Jurists,
1965).

The finest introduction to the history of the Caribbean region is Gordon K. Lewis, The Growth of the
Modern West Indies (New York: Monthly Review Press,
1968). Indispensable for keeping up with current events
are Caribbean Contact, a monthly newspaper published in
Barbados by the Caribbean Conference of Churches; and
the Latin America Regional Reports: Caribbean which is
published at five-week intervals by Latin American Newsletters Ltd. in London. For an honest, up-to-date commentary on events, the Catholic Standard, edited in
Georgetown by Father Andrew Morrison, is required reading.

An interesting comparative study is R. S. Milne,
Politics in Ethnically Bipolar States; Guyana, Malaysia,
Fiji (Vancouver: University of British Columbia Press,
1981). Amidst a mass of sensationalism written about
the Jonestown catastrophe, three commentaries stand out:
Shiva Naipaul, Journey to Nowhere: A New World Tragedy
(New York: Simon and Schuster, 1980); James Reston, Jr.,
Our Father Who Art in Hell (New York: The New York Times
Book Co., 1981); and the excellent analytical essay by
Gordon K. Lewis, "Gather with the Saints at the River":
The Jonestown Guyana Holocaust of 1978 (Rio Piedras,
Puerto Rico: Institute of Caribbean Studies, 1979).

Select Bibliography[*]

BOOKS

Alpers, Edward A. and Pierre-Michel Fontaine, eds. Walter Rodney: Revolutionary and Scholar. Los Angeles: Center for Afro-American Studies, 1982.

Axline, W. Andrew. Caribbean Integration: The Politics of Regionalism. London: Frances Pinter, 1979.

Bacchus, M. K. Education for Development and Underdevelopment: Guyana's Educational System and its Implications for the Third World. Waterloo, Canada: Wilfred Laurier University Press, 1980.

Blake, Byron. The Development from a Free Trade Association to a Common Market: CARICOM and its Effects on the Guyana Economy: Opportunities and Challenges. Georgetown, Guyana: Caribbean Community Secretariat, 1976.

Burnham, L. F. S. The Case of Pedro Beria. Georgetown, Guyana: Government publication, 1968.

_____. It Is a Matter of Survival. Georgetown, Guyana: Government publication, 1968.

_____. To Own Guyana. Georgetown, Guyana: PNC publication, 1971.

_____. Address on the Occasion of the Opening of the Conference of Non-Aligned Countries. Georgetown, Guyana: Ministry of Foreign Affairs, 1972.

_____. Our World of the Caribbean. Georgetown, Guyana: Government publication, 1972.

_____. Perform Now Comrades: The National Revolution in Guyana. Georgetown, Guyana: Ministry of Information, 1972.

_____. Declaration of Sophia. Georgetown, Guyana: PNC publication, 1974.

Chase, Ashton. 133 Days Towards Freedom in Guyana. Georgetown, Guyana: Published by the Author, 1954.

Clementi, Sir Cecil. A Constitutional History of British

[*]Publications included in the Critical Bibliography are not listed here.

226

Guiana. London: Macmillan, 1937.

Cohen, Warren I. Dean Rusk. Totowa, New Jersey: Cooper
Square Publishers, 1980.

D'Aguiar, Peter. Chaos in Guiana. Georgetown, British
Guiana: UF publication, 1963.

Daly, Vere T. A Short History of the Guyanese People.
London: Macmillan, 1975.

Davis, David B. The Problem of Slavery in Western Culture. Ithaca: Cornell University Press, 1966.
_____. The Problem of Slavery in the Age of Revolu-
tion. Ithaca: Cornell University Press, 1975.

Dew, Edward. The Difficult Flowering of Surinam: Ethnicity and Politics in a Plural Society. The Hague:
Martinus Nijhoff, 1979.

Grant, Cedric. Company Towns in the Caribbean: A Preliminary Analysis of Christianburg-Wismar-Mackenzie.
Georgetown, Guyana: Ministry of Information, 1970.

Hirsch, Fred. An Analysis of our AFL-CIO Role in Latin
America or Under the Covers with the CIA. San Jose,
California: Published by the Author, 1974.

Horowitz, Michael M., ed. Peoples and Cultures of the
Caribbean. Garden City, New York: Natural History
Press, 1971.

Jagan, Cheddi. The Caribbean Revolution: Tasks and Perspectives. Georgetown, Guyana: PPP publication, 1972.

Jagan, Janet. Army Intervention in the 1973 Elections in
Guyana. Georgetown, Guyana: PPP publication, 1973.
_____. An Examination of National Service. George-
town, Guyana: PPP publication, 1977.

Kilduff, Marshall and Ron Javers. Suicide Cult. New York:
Bantam Books, 1978.

King, K. F. S. Land and People in Guyana. Oxford: Commonwealth Forestry Institute, 1968.

Knowles, William H. Trade Union Development and Industrial Relations in the British West Indies. Berkeley: University of California Press, 1959.

Krause, Charles. Guyana Massacre. New York: Berkley Publishing Co., 1978.

LaFeber, Walter. America, Russia, and the Cold War 1945-
1980. New York: John Wiley, 1980.

La Guerre, John, ed. Calcutta to Caroni: The East Indians of Trinidad. London: Longman, 1974.

Lewis, S. and T. G. Mathews, eds. Caribbean Integration.
Rio Piedras, Puerto Rico: Institute of Caribbean
Studies, 1967.

Macmillan, Harold. At the End of the Day, 1961-1963. New
York: Harper and Row, 1973.

Mars, Perry. Structural Inequalities and Political Vio-
lence in a Multi-Racial State: The Guyana Example.
Georgetown, Guyana: Dept. of Political Science,
University of Guyana, 1973.

McIntyre, Alister. The Role of the Economic Process in
Regional Development: The Caribbean Experience.
Georgetown, Guyana: Caribbean Community Secretariat,

1976.

Menezes, Mary Noel. British Policy Towards the Amerindians in British Guiana, 1803-1873. London: Oxford
University Press, 1977.

Mitrasing, F. E. M. The Border-Conflict Between Surinam
and Guiana. Paramaribo, Surinam: Kersten and Co.,
1975.

O'Farrell, Patrick. England and Ireland Since 1800. London: Oxford University Press, 1975.

Reno, Philip. The Ordeal of British Guiana. New York:
Monthly Review Press, 1964.

Ridgwell, W. M. The Forgotten Tribes of Guyana. London:
Tom Stacey, 1972.

Rodney, Walter. The Groundings with my Brothers. London:
Bogle-L'Ouverture Publications, 1969.

_____. A History of the Upper Guinea Coast, 1545-
1800. London: Oxford University Press, 1970.

_____. How Europe Underdeveloped Africa. London:
Bogle-L'Ouverture Publications, 1972.

_____. A History of the Guyanese Working People,
1881-1905. Baltimore: Johns Hopkins University
Press, 1981.

Rodway, James. History of British Guiana from 1668. 3
vols. Georgetown, British Guiana: J. Thomson, 1891-
1894.

Ryan, Selwyn D. Race and Nationalism in Trinidad and Tobago: A Study of Decolonization in a Multiracial
Society. Toronto: University of Toronto Press, 1972.

Schlesinger, Arthur M., Jr. A Thousand Days: John F.
Kennedy in the White House. Boston: Houghton Miffin,
1965.

Searwar, L., ed. Co-operative Republic: Guyana 1970.
Georgetown, Guyana: Ministry of Information, 1970.

Singh, Paul G. Landmarks in Working-Class Revolt in Guyana: Enmore, 1948. Georgetown, Guyana: GAWU publication, 1973.

Tennassee, Paul Nehru. Guyana: A Nation in Ruins: The
Puerto Rican Model Failed. Toronto: Guyanese Research and Representation Services, 1982.

Vatuk, Ved Prakash. British Guiana. New York: Monthly
Review Press, 1963.

Walton, Richard J. Cold War and Counterrevolution. New
York: Viking Press, 1972.

Waugh, Evelyn. Ninety-Two Days. London: Duckworth, 1934.

Welch, Claude E., Jr., ed. Civilian Control of the Military. Albany: State University of New York Press,
1976.

Williams, Eric. Inward Hunger: The Education of a Prime
Minister. London: Andre Deutsch, 1969.

228

ARTICLES

Avebury, Lord and the British Parliamentary Human Rights
     Group. "Guyana's 1980 Elections: The Politics of
     Fraud." Caribbean Review, 10 (Spring 1981), pp. 8-
     11, 44.
Baksh, Ahamad. "Formal Education and the Guyanese Social
     Structure." Transition, 2 (1979), pp. 113-30.
Bradley, C. Paul. "The Party System in British Guiana
     and the General Election of 1961." Caribbean Stud-
     ies, 1 (1961), pp. 1-26.
Brana-Shute, Gary. "Politicians in Uniform: Suriname's
     Bedeviled Revolution." Caribbean Review, 10 (Spring
     1981), pp. 24-27, 49-50.
Brewer, Samuel Pope. "Bitterness in Guiana's Sugar Bowl."
     New York Times Magazine, 1 November 1953, pp. 1-6.
Campbell, Sir Jock. "The Development and Organization of
     Bookers." Paper delivered in November 1959 to a
     seminar at the London School of Economics on Prob-
     lems in Industrial Administration.
Campbell, Trevor A. "The Making of an Organic Intellec-
     tual: Walter Rodney (1942-1980)." Latin American
     Perspectives, 8 (Winter 1981), pp. 49-63.
Collins, B(ertram). A. N. "The Civil Service of British
     Guiana in the General Strike of 1963." Caribbean
     Quarterly, 10 (June 1964), pp. 3-13.
_____. "Acceding to Independence: Some Constitu-
     tional Problems of a Poly-ethnic Society (British
     Guiana)." Civilisations, 15 (1965), pp. 376-96.
_____, "The End of a Colony-II." The Political
     Quarterly, 36 (Oct.-Dec. 1965), pp. 406-16.
_____. "'Consultative democracy' in British Guiana."
     Parliamentary Affairs, 19 (Winter 1965-1966), pp.
     103-12.
_____. "Racial Imbalance in Public Services and Se-
     curity Forces." Race, 3 (1966), pp. 235-53.
Danns, George K. "Mobilization and Development: An Ex-
     periment in Nation-Building." Transition, 1 (1978),
     pp. 23-44.
Despres, Leo. "The Implications of Nationalist Politics
     in British Guiana for the Development of Cultural
     Theory." American Anthropology, 6 (October 1964),
     pp. 1052-72.
Dew, Edward. "The Year of the Sergeants." Caribbean Re-
     view, 9 (Spring 1980), pp. 5-7, 46-47.
_____. "Suriname Tar Baby." Caribbean Review, 12
     (Winter 1983), pp. 4-7, 34.
Farley, Rawle. "Kaldor's Budget in Retrospect: Reason
     and Unreason in a Developing Area, Reflections on
     the 1962 Budget in British Guiana." Inter-American
     Economic Affairs, 16 (Winter 1962), pp. 25-63.
Greene, J. E. "The Politics of Economic Planning in Guy-
     ana." Social and Economic Studies, 23 (June 1974),
     pp. 186-203.

Halperin, Ernst. "Racism and Communism in British Guiana." Journal of Inter-American Studies, 7 (January 1965), pp. 95-134.

Hendrickson, Embert. "New Directions for Republican Guyana." The World Today, 27 (January 1971), pp. 33-39.

Hinden, Rita. "The Case of British Guiana." Encounter, 2 (January 1954), pp. 18-22.

Hintzen, Percy C. and Ralph R. Premdas. "Guyana: Coercion and Control in Political Change." Journal of Interamerican Studies and World Affairs, 24 (August 1982), pp. 337-54.

_____. "Race, Ideology, and Power in Guyana." The Journal of Commonwealth and Comparative Politics, 21 (July 1983), pp. 175-94.

Hope, Kempe R. and Wilfred L. David. "Planning for Development in Guyana: The Experience from 1945 to 1973." Inter-American Economic Affairs, 27 (Spring 1974), pp. 27-46.

Hubbard, H. J. M. "Guyana--Another U.S. Satellite?" New World Review, 34 (August-September 1966), pp. 35-40.

Hughes, Colin A. "The British Guiana General Elections, 1953." Parliamentary Affairs, 7 (Spring 1954), pp. 213-20.

Insight Team. Sunday Times, 16 April 1967, pp. 1, 3; and 23 April 1967, p. 3.

Jayawardena, Chandra. "Religious Belief and Social Change: Aspects of the Development of Hinduism in British Guiana." Comparative Studies in Society and History, 8 (1966), pp. 211-40.

Jessop, David A. "Can Guyana Remain Non-Aligned." West Indies Chronicle, 93 (April/May 1978), p. 4.

Kramer, Jane. "Letter from Guyana." The New Yorker, 16 September 1974, pp. 100-28.

La Guerre, John. "The Moyne Commission and the West Indian Intelligentsia, 1938-39." Journal of Commonwealth Political Studies, 9 (July 1971), pp. 134-57.

Lutchman, Harold A. "Constitutional Developments in Guyana During the Second World War." Occasional Paper Number One, Department of Political Science, University of Guyana, Georgetown, Guyana, 1972.

Mahant, E. E. "The Strange Fate of a Liberal Democracy; Political Opposition and Civil Liberties in Guyana." The Round Table, No. 265 (January 1977), pp. 77-89.

McKitterick, T. E. M. "The End of a Colony: British Guiana 1962." The Political Quarterly, 33 (January-March 1962), pp. 30-40.

Meisler, Stanley. "Meddling in Latin America: The Dubious Role of the AFL-CIO." The Nation, 10 February 1964, pp. 133-38.

Milne, R. S. "Guyana's Co-operative Republic." Parliamentary Affairs, 28 (Autumn 1975), pp. 352-67.

_____. "Politics, Ethnicity and Class in Guyana and Malaysia." Social and Economic Studies, 26 (March 1977), pp. 18-37.

230

New Commonwealth and World Development, No. 2 (1971).
    This issue contains several articles about Guyana's
    economy.
Newman, Peter. "Racial Tension in British Guiana." Race,
    3 (May 1962), pp. 31-62.
Petras, James. "A Death in Guyana Has Meaning for Third
    World." Latin American Perspectives, 8 (Winter 1981)
    pp. 47-48.
Premdas, Ralph R. "Elections and Political Campaigns in
    a Racially Bifurcated State: Guyana." Journal of
    Interamerican Studies and World Affairs, 14 (August
    1972), pp. 271-96.
_____. "The Rise of the First Mass-Based Multi-
    Racial Party in Guyana." Caribbean Quarterly, 20
    (1974), pp. 6-20.
_____. "Guyana: Communal Conflict, Socialism, and
    Political Reconciliation." Inter-American Economic
    Affairs, 30 (Spring 1977), pp. 63-83.
_____. "Guyana: Socialist Reconstruction or Politi-
    cal Opportunism?" Journal of Interamerican Studies,
    20 (May 1978), pp. 133-64.
Prince, Ethlyn A. "The Development of Public Enterprise
    in Guyana." Social and Economic Studies, 23 (June
    1974), pp. 204-15.
Rodney, Walter. "People's Power, No Dictator." Latin
    American Perspectives, 8 (Winter 1981), pp. 64-78.
Sackey, Jim. "The Migration of High Level Personnel from
    Guyana: Towards an Alternative Analysis." Transi-
    tion, 1 (1978), pp. 45-58.
Sires, Ronald. "British Guiana: Suspension of the Con-
    stitution." Western Political Quarterly, 7 (Decem-
    ber 1954), pp. 554-69.
Smith, Raymond T. "British Guiana's Prospects." New So-
    ciety, 1 August 1963, pp. 6-8.
_____. "Race and Political Conflict in Guyana."
    Race, 12 (1971), pp. 415-27.
Spinner, Thomas J., Jr. "Belize, Guatemala, and the Brit-
    ish Empire." Revista/Review Interamericana, 6 (Sum-
    mer 1976), pp. 282-90.
_____. "Nationalism, Socialism, and Cultural Plur-
    alism in Guyana." Queen's Quarterly, 84 (Winter
    1977), pp. 582-92.
_____. "The Emperor Burnham Has Lost His Clothes."
    Caribbean Review, 9 (Fall 1980), pp. 4-8.
_____. "Guyana Update: Political, Economic, Moral
    Bankruptcy." Caribbean Review, 11 (Fall 1982), pp.
    9-11, 30-32.
"Stockholders' Meeting of Banks DIH Ltd. in Guyana, A."
    Reprint of two articles appearing in the Brewers
    Digest of June and July 1973.
Tomasek, Robert D. "British Guiana: A Case Study of
    British Colonial Policy." Political Science Quar-
    terly, 74 (September 1959), pp. 393-411.
Verrier, Anthony. "Guyana and Cyprus: Techniques of

Peace-Keeping." Journal of the Royal United Service
Institution, 111 (November 1966), pp. 298-306.
Wallace, Elizabeth. "British Guiana: Causes of the Pre-
sent Discontents." International Journal, 19 (Au-
tumn 1964), pp. 513-44.
Waters, Donald J. "Jungle Politics: Guyana, The Peoples
Temple, and The Affairs of State." Caribbean Review,
9 (Spring 1980), pp. 8-13.

OTHER PUBLICATIONS

Government Documents:

Colonial Report, British Guiana, 1953. London, 1955.

Debates of the British Guiana House of Assembly.

Debates of the British Guiana State Council.

Debates of the Legislative Council of British Guiana.

Guyana: Parliamentary Debates.

Great Britain: Hansard's Parliamentary Debates.

Report of a Commission of Inquiry into the Sugar Indus-
try of British Guiana. Colonial Office No. 249,
1949.
Report by the Commonwealth Team of Observers on the
Election in December 1964. Colonial Office No. 359,
1965.
Report on the National Assembly General Election of 1968.
Georgetown, Guyana, 1969. Prepared by the Chief
Election Officer, Reginald C. Butler, in accordance
with regulation 74 of the Election Regulations,
1964.
Report of the West India Royal Commission 1938-39. The
Moyne Commission. Command 6607, 1945.
United States Department of State. Country Reports on
Human Rights Practices for 1980. Washington, D.C.,
1981.
_____. Country Reports on Human Rights Practices
for 1981. Washington, D.C., 1982.
_____. Country Reports on Human Rights Practices
for 1982. Washington, D.C., 1983.

Magazines:

United Kingdom: The Economist; The New Statesman

United States: Caribbean Monthly Bulletin

Newspapers:

Guyana: The Daily Argosy; The Daily Chronicle; The Clarion;

232

The Guyana Graphic; The Sunday Graphic
United Kingdom: The Guardian; The Sunday Times; The
    Times
United States: The Christian Science Monitor; The New
    York Times; The Washington Post

Miscellaneous:

Guyana Human Rights Commission. Human Rights Report,
    January 1980-June 1981. Georgetown, Guyana, 1981.
    _____. Human Rights Report, July 1981-August 1982.
    Georgetown, Guyana, 1982.
Highways to Happiness. 1964 Election Manifesto of the
    United Force.
NBC Television, Meet the Press: Interview with Cheddi
    Jagan on 15 October 1961.
Party Constitution and Meeting Companion and A Supple-
    ment to the Declaration of Sophia. People's Nation-
    al Congress publications about the important Sophia
    Special Congress of December 1974.
Public Record Office, Kew Gardens, United Kingdom, C.O.
    111/787/60542, British Guiana Correspondence.
    There are some interesting letters written by Janet
    Jagan to various administrative officials complain-
    ing about the quality of low-cost housing in the
    colony.
Something to Remember: The Report of the International
    Team of Observers at the Elections in Guyana, De-
    cember 1980. Chairman, Lord Avebury. The British
    Parliamentary Human Rights Group. London, 1980.
This Is Guyana. People's Progressive Party publication,
    1976.

Index

207-208; and effectiveness in
toppling the government, 211-
212; general, 95-98, 101-102;
sugar, 27, 41, 105, 109, 162-
164
Suez Canal, 67-68
Sugar, 2, 5-9, 26-28; estate
consolidation, 9-10; nationalization of the, industry,
149; and politics, 11, 148;
prices of, 10, 11, 159, 160,
183, 184; production of, 70,
159, 176, 193, 199, 206;
strikes, 27, 41, 105, 109,
162-164
Sugar Producers Association,
23, 41, 43, 105
Sunday Chronicle, The, 129(n7)
Sunday Graphic, The, 129(n7),
152(n39); on Guyana in 1972,
141-142; on the 1973 elections, 146
Surinam, 183, 209

Taylor, Humphrey: on the 1968
election, 125, 128
Teekah, Vincent: murder of,
175-176
Teemal, Seeram: and GUYSUCO,
212
Tello, Rupert, 56, 73, 78, 124
Thomas, Clive, 157, 170, 214
(n10)
Thunder, 30, 57, 80
Todd, Gordon, 171, 173, 175,
202
Trades Union Council (TUC),
23, 101, 116, 202; and the
budget crisis of 1962, 94,
95-98; and the ICFTU, 40-41;
and ORIT, 91-92; pro-Burnham
representation in the, 171,
187, 202, 208-209; and
strikes, 139, 163, 208
Trade unions: development of,
11, 23, 26, 40; legislation
against, 212-213
Trinidad, 70, 160, 194; and
race, 11, 107

Undesirable Publications Act,
31, 39
Unemployment and unemployment: during the first De-

pression, 11; in the 1960s,
70, 74, 137; in the 1970s,
141, 155, 160; in the 1980s,
184, 185, 199, 211
Unions of Government Employees
(FUGE), 95
United Democratic party (UDP),
70-71, 75; and the 1957
election, 72, 73
United Force (UF), the, 78,
124, 158, 166; and the 1961
elections, 78, 79, 81; and
the 1962 budget crisis, 95,
96, 98; and the 1964 elections, 114; and the 1968
elections, 125, 127; and
the 1973 elections, 145;
and the 1980 elections, 189,
193
United Nations, 74; Special
Committee on Colonialism,
89-90, 103
United States: and the British
Guiana-Venezuela boundary
dispute, 13-14; and Burnham,
140, 148, 149, 159, 195,
197; economic aid from the,
82, 84-85, 117, 121, 183;
and fear of communism, 108,
110, 113, 144; and interven-
tionism, xii, 52-53, 74,
85, 109-110, 209; invasion
of Grenada by the, 209; and
Jagan, 82-85
United States State Department:
on the Guyanese economy, 199;
reports on human rights of
the, 194-195, 198, 204, 211
University of Guyana: and national service, 157, 158;
delayed opening of, 174, 181
University of Guyana Staff Association (UGSA), 163-164,
165, 171, 187

Vanguard for Liberation and
Democracy (VLD), 174, 188,
189, 190, 210
Venezuela, 124-125; and the
boundary dispute with Guyana, 13-14, 134, 135, 195-
196, 200, 205-206; and the
hydroelectric project, 184;
and the Rupununi uprising,